SUPPRESSED BOOKS

Suppressed Books

A HISTORY OF THE CONCEPTION
OF LITERARY OBSCENITY

BY ALEC CRAIG

FOREWORD BY *Morris L. Ernst*

THE WORLD PUBLISHING COMPANY

CLEVELAND AND NEW YORK

Published by The World Publishing Company
2231 West 110 Street, Cleveland 2, Ohio

Library of Congress Catalog Card Number: 63-14785

FIRST EDITION

This book was published in Great Britain under the title
The Banned Books of England and Other Countries.

HC763

CONTENTS

CONTENTS

FOREWORD

THE CONCEPT of censorship is a sophisticated one and, of course, applies rather exclusively to those few cultures where literacy has taken hold. When man chipped on stone tablets, those few who could read were naturally undisturbed by their own corruption. Even today I have never met a human being who felt he could be corrupted by any concept—blasphemous, seditious, or obscene. The censorious are worried only about the souls of others than themselves.

Man's original fear, in terms of control of the market place of thought, as distinguished from tribal folkways, was no doubt directed exclusively at what we now call blasphemy. But as the power of the clerics declined and a new instrument of man called the State was created, blasphemy tended to evaporate and the fear of seditious utterances arose as a peril to the power of the Crown. In more recent days, as the world became somewhat literate and people could communicate with each other sufficiently to elect their own rulers, democracy was born and the crime of sedition was temporarily reduced. But since man seemingly must always be afraid of something, a new terror, known as obscenity, was created with peculiar speed and wide impact. In those continents where millions have as yet not risen to the point of enjoying a written language and where the literate are few in number, the concept of obscenity has not even been created.

In this volume one can learn the absurdity of man's fears with respect to sexual titillation in print or picture. After touching on the early bookish history of man in various parts of the globe, with examples of censorship—such as the suppression in China of writings of Confucius—the author carries us along through the

7

great battles in England around the middle of the nineteenth century, when literacy became so prevalent that the superior people became intent upon censoring the reading of the newly literate.

This volume is concerned not only with our Anglo-Saxon culture in England, but also with the parallels carried on on this side of the Atlantic. For anyone concerned with censorship in the United States, this volume raises endless queries—natural queries—since through a historical coincidence the psychotic rampages of Anthony Comstock coincided with new legislation in England which was trying to define the contours of the obscene. And toward the end of this inquiry into the mad fears of the obscene, we can discern the intriguing nuances in attempted definitions of the "lewd," "indecent," "lascivious," "obscene," and "prurient" in England as well as in our own republic. In England under recent legislation, as interpreted in the Lady Chatterly case, we are impressed with the British approach, namely, that the literary quality of a writing may be used as one attribute to justify sexual material which might fall under any one of the above synonyms—and hence be deemed capable of corrupting either part or all of the human race.

In our republic, I suggest that we are going toward a more scientific approach in our endeavor to find the obscene or even the pornographic. When we read about the present status of the law and about prosecutions in England, we can all be mindful of the fact that at long last we are gaining knowledge from scientific laboratories. For about a century, critics, juries, and judges have based their approaches on the thesis that "It's all right for us men but we must save the women," and only recently with somewhat of a shock have we learned from many scientific studies and polls that women are not interested in the obscene. Moreover, science has recently pronounced that the censorious have attacked the wrong material in the market place—assuming, of course, that any material is provably corrupting. We now know that if there be any influence at all on children, it flows not from fiction, which has been the subject of most of the assaults, but from nonfiction and, more particularly, from the daily press which is brought into the home to be read by children as the Truth and understood to be Life itself.

Since we in the United States are now approaching a pivotal

junction in this legal-intellectual maze, this volume, if widely read not only by lawyers and judges but by all folk, can be an effective instrument to tidy up the law of censorship. It might even educate us to a more adult approach to the mystery of life. Man will and should always have a great interest in the beginning and the end of everything: of birth and death. Birth connotes sex and death is not remote from sadism. I suggest that whenever man tries to suppress an interest in the beginning, an undue accent is laid on the end. Some day science may prove a causal relationship between reading and behavior, but Alec Craig's volume negates even a clue in that direction. Hence his volume must worry and disturb all readers in our culture, particularly those who feel that much of our television and daily press perverts the dignity of the people of our republic by laying undue emphasis on the tawdry treatment of birth (sex) and death (sadism).

For a quarter of a century I have been in debt to Alec Craig. I am happy to have been asked to write a foreword about this expanded story of the banning of books—and more particularly the suppressions because of so-called literary obscenity. Despite the flattering words that the author has written about my meager efforts in this ever-exciting battle against the Frightened, it seems clear to me that all readers who are interested in liberty of the market place of thought may conclude, as I do, that this documented history of attacks on literature in England and the United States tells a more persuasive story even than the great exhortation of Milton's *Areopagitica*. Any person concerned with law and the obscene will proceed with embarrassment and peril if unacquainted with Alec Craig's great catalogue of man's attempted suppressions of material sexual.

MORRIS L. ERNST

New York City, 1963

PREFACE

THE SUBJECT of this book is the conception of literary obscenity as found in law and practice and its cultural and social effects. My primary concern is the restraint which the conception exercises on serious literature and consequently on intellectual freedom and artistic creation. In surveying this subject I have devoted the greatest space to England because that is the country which first developed a law of libel to fill the vacuum created by the abolition of direct censorship by Church or State authorities. So much of past history (including material from my *The Banned Books of England* and *Above all Liberties*) is given as is necessary to a proper understanding of the present position, and important information not readily accessible elsewhere is given in some detail. The purview of the book is extended to include America, France, and other parts of the world where the freedom of the press has traditionally been held in esteem and is relied upon as an instrument of intellectual and social well-being.

The bibliography is intended to stand on its own as a fairly complete preliminary guide to the subject. The treatment of individuals in the body of the book will be found to be supported by the items given in Part VII of the bibliography. The notes are mainly confined to authorities outside the scope of the bibliography and to references to specific statements and quotations.

I thankfully acknowledge the help I have received from the officials of the British Museum throughout the quarter of a century during which I have used the library for the investigations into this subject. My gratitude is also due to Dr. E. J. Dingwall, Mr. George Legman, Dr. Maurice Parmelee, and Mr. W. H. W. Sabine for supplying me with information and answering my queries; and to Mr. R. S. W. Pollard for legal guidance.

ALEC CRAIG

AND INDEED we see it ever falleth out that the forbidden writing is thought to be certain sparks of a truth that fly up in the faces of those that seek to choke it, and tread it out, whereas a book authorized is thought to be but *temporis voces*, the language of the time.

BACON: *An Advertisement touching the Controversies of the Church of England*

Give me the liberty to know, to utter, and to argue freely according to conscience, above all liberties.

MILTON: *Areopagitica*

We have now recognized the necessity to the mental well-being of mankind (on which all their other well-being depends) of freedom of opinion, and freedom of the expression of opinion, on four distinct grounds; which we will now briefly recapitulate.

First, if any opinion is compelled to silence, that opinion may, for aught we can certain know, be true. To deny this is to assume our own infallibility.

Secondly, though the silenced opinion be an error, it may, and very commonly does, contain a portion of truth; and since the general or prevailing opinion on any subject is rarely or never the whole truth, it is only by the collision of adverse opinions that the remainder of the truth has any chance of being supplied.

Thirdly, even if the received opinion be not only true, but the whole truth; unless it is suffered to be, and actually is, vigorously and earnestly contested, it will, by most of those who receive it, be held in the manner of a prejudice with little comprehension or feeling of its rational grounds. And not only this, but, fourthly, the meaning of the doctrine itself will be in danger of being lost, or enfeebled, and deprived of its vital effect on the character and conduct; the dogma becoming a mere formal profession, inefficacious for good, but cumbering the ground, and preventing the growth of any real and heartfelt conviction, from reason or personal experience.

JOHN STUART MILL: *On Liberty*

Toleration or liberty have no sense or use except as toleration of opinions that are considered damnable, and liberty to do what seems wrong.

BERNARD SHAW: Preface to *The Showing-up of Blanco Posnet*

No argument for the suppression of "obscene" literature has ever been offered which, by unavoidable implication, will not justify, and which has not already justified every other limitation that has ever been put upon mental freedom.

THEODORE SCHROEDER: *"Obscene" Literature and Constitutional Law*

Our civilization cannot afford to let the censor-moron loose.

D. H. LAWRENCE: Letter to Morris Ernst

We were right, yes, we were right
To smash the false idealities of the last age,
The humbug, the soft cruelty, the mawkishness,
The heavy tyrannical sentimentality,
The inability to face facts, especially new facts;
All of which linger on so damnably among us.

* * *

I think we were right to go groping in all forbidden places,
Uncovering horrors politely forgotten
And facing them too, . . .

RICHARD ALDINGTON: *The Eaten Heart*

The censor shall dream of knickers, a nasty beast.

W. H. AUDEN: *The Orators*

What concerns me is the harm you are doing to yourselves. I mean by perpetuating this talk of guilt and punishment, of banning and proscribing, of whitewashing and black-balling, of closing your eyes when convenient, of making scapegoats when there is no other way out. I ask you pointblank—does the pursuance of your limited role enable you to get the most out of life?

HENRY MILLER: *Defense of the Freedom to Read*

SUPPRESSED BOOKS

The Control of Books

IN PRIMITIVE SOCIETIES man's expression of his thoughts and feelings is essentially communal. The song, the dance, and the design and decoration of shrines and graves are all integrated into the religious cult of the tribe. Even with the coming of writing, this totalitarianism is preserved, and it can continue concurrently with a complex civilization as in ancient Egypt. The first fissure to appear in the homogeneity is generally a division of function, and even a conflict of interest, between the priestly and the warrior castes. We are familiar with the situation in the Old Testament in the struggle between Samuel and Saul, which was carried on by the Hebrew prophets on one side and the kings of Israel and Judah on the other. Even so, there is no freedom for individual expression. The only question is the proper dividing line between sacred and civil control. Individual expression first emerged in ancient Greece where a high degree of freedom was attained, particularly in philosophical speculation. But this freedom was enjoyed under the shadow of the old authoritarianism and tribal prejudice, as the trial and death of Socrates so outstandingly illustrates.

It is writing rather than speech that attracts authoritative attention and social pressures because it is so much more enduring and effective; and books have been subject to control of some sort wherever they have been an important medium of communication. In ancient China the Emperor Chi Huang Ti ordered the destruction of the *Analects* of Confucius. In the classical world the multiplication of manuscript books reached a high degree of efficiency, and the *Ars Amatoria* was a contributory cause of the banishment of Ovid from Rome by Augustus. When the Empire became Christianized much of the literary heritage of pagan times was lost to posterity either through deliberate destruction or neglect.

During the Middle Ages in Europe, the production of manuscripts was largely carried on by monks and confined to biblical and devotional works. Any infraction of the Church's control of thought and belief was dealt with as a matter of course by the ecclesiastical authorities. Originally they relied on admonition and excommunication but gradually fines, imprisonment, and the stake were added to the sanctions. With the revival of learning, books of theological speculation which did not meet with the approval of authority began to appear. Quite early, in 1120, Peter Abelard's *Introductio ad Theologium* was deemed to be heretical and condemned to be burned by the Synod of Soissons. As the Reformation approached, the number of suspect and unorthodox books increased, and the translations of the Scriptures into the vernacular which appeared were especially offensive to authority. The power of princes and of the great nobles sometimes gave protection to humbler men. For instance, it was the protection of John of Gaunt that enabled Wycliffe, who produced the first English Bible, to die a natural death at Lutterworth in 1384, leaving the Church to wreak a futile vengeance on his remains. Freedom, however, was uncertain and exceptional; and intellectual speculation and the dissemination of knowledge were dangerous pursuits.

When printing was invented in the fifteenth century the Church, apprehending the threat to her domination over thought and belief, endeavored to intensify her control over books, and in 1557 the Inquisition under Pope Paul IV drew up the first *Index Librorum Prohibitorum*. This *Index* should not be confused with the *Index Librorum Expurgatorius*, a projected catalogue, never published, of works allowed to be read after the deletion or amendment of specified passages. The *Index Librorum Prohibitorum* has been revised from time to time and now[1] lists some four thousand books forbidden throughout the world and in every translation. No layman may read or possess any of them without special permission granted only for single books and in urgent cases. The latest edition of the *Index*, published in the Vatican City in 1948, contains some astonishing items: Gibbon's *Decline and Fall of the Roman Empire*, J. S. Mill's *Principles of Political Economy*, Pascal's *Pensées*, Samuel Richardson's *Pamela*, all the works of David Hume and Voltaire, and all the novels of Balzac, Dumas *père et fils*, Anatole France, Stendhal, and Zola. It is understood that the present Pope, John XXIII, contemplates instigating a revision of this remarkable list.

In countries affected by the Reformation, it was not long before the *Index* ceased to have any legal force; but it continues to bind the consciences of Roman Catholics, and its influence, in conjunction with the control exercised over authorship, on freedom of thought cannot be ignored. As regards authorship, no Roman Catholic, priest or layman, may publish without prior permission any book on theology, ecclesiastical history, canon law, ethics, or other religious or moral subject. The effect of this regulation was brought home to the late Alfred Noyes, a convert to the Roman Church, over his book on Voltaire in 1938. Denounced to the Holy Office by an anonymous informer, the book was withdrawn by the publishers, and the author then made his peace by writing an explanatory preface for the new edition,[2] making affirmations of historical and religious opinions agreeable to the censors.

Until comparatively recent times the Roman Church's control of books was almost exclusively concerned with the suppression of heresy and maintaining the prestige of the clergy. Political order and good morals were considered as a natural consequence of correct doctrine. The attitude of authority is illustrated by the fact that although Boccaccio's *Decameron* was at one time on the *Index*, an edition in which all the gallantries were retained but the clerical sinners and erring nuns were metamorphosed into lay folk was allowed under the auspices of the Council of Trent in 1573. In the following pages, however, we note more than one instance where Roman Catholic authors have had to toe the line over their treatment of sexual matters.

In countries where the Reformation took hold, the control of books was taken over by the Renaissance princes and the Reformed Churches. Henry VIII of England entrusted the matter to the new Court of Star Chamber. Elizabeth, in 1559, confirmed a charter giving the Stationers' Company a monopoly of printing in return for which they undertook to search out all undesirable and illegal books. At the same time the Queen issued a decree providing that no book was to be printed unless first licensed by royal authority or by the Archbishops of Canterbury and York or other specified censors. There was a saving clause which exempted the classics and other works which had previously been commonly used in universities and schools.

The Tudor censorship was mainly concerned with political matters, which of course included religious issues. But the moralists of the time had their voice, too, and they were especially perturbed with the flood of translation from Italian, one of the features of the Renaissance in England. There is a familiar ring to modern ears about Robert Ascham's denunciation in his *Schoolmaster* (1570):

It is a pity that those which have authority and charge, to allow and disallow books to be printed, be no more circumspect herein, than they are. Ten sermons at Paul's cross do not so much good for moving men to true doctrine, as one of those books do harm, with inticing men to ill living. . . . They open, not fond and common ways to vice, but such subtle, cunning, new and diverse shifts, to carry young wills to vanity and young wits to mischief, to teach old bawds new school points, as the simple head of an Englishman is not able to invent, nor never was heard of in England before.

Ascham had particularly in mind Painter's *Palace of Pleasure*, that treasury of story which Shakespeare and his contemporary dramatists rifled for their plots; but he was too wily to advertise the book by naming it. The controversial device of defaming an opponent's work without specifying it sufficiently to enable the reader to form an independent judgment by referring to it is not uncommon among moralistic writers today. Ascham, however, specifically denounced the *Morte d'Arthur*, as basing its appeal to the reader solely "in open mans slaughter, and bold bawdrye."

Under the Stuarts the censorship grew more severe and the existing powers of the bishops did not satisfy English prelate William Laud. In 1637 he obtained from the Star Chamber a decree dealing with books imported from abroad. It provided that no packages of books could be imported for sale without a catalogue being first submitted to the Archbishop of Canterbury or the Bishop of London, who, by their agents, were to superintend the unloading of the books.

In 1640 the Long Parliament abolished the detested Court of Star Chamber and printing enjoyed a brief period of liberty. This freedom was, unhappily, of short duration and Parliament reintroduced licensing in 1643 in spite of the protest made by Milton in his *Areopagitica*, which exposed for all time the anomalies, absurdities, and tyrannies inherent in literary censorship. The Commonwealth censors, like their predecessors, were preoccupied with political and religious controversy, but Henry Vaughan in his *Silex Scintillans* (1655) voiced the concern of those who worried about moral corruption:

Divers persons of eminent piety and learning (I meddle not with the *seditious* and *schismatical*) have, long before my time, taken notice of this *malady*: for the complaint against *vitious verse*, even by peaceful and obedient *spirits*, is of some antiquity in this Kingdom. And yet, as if the evil consequences attending this inveterate *error* were but a small thing, there is sprung very lately another prosperous *device* to assist it in the subversion of *souls*. Those that want the *genius* of *verse* fall to *translating*; and the people are, every *term*, plentifully furnished with various Foreign vanities; so that the most lascivious compositions of France and Italy are here *naturalized* and made *English*; and this, as it is sadly observed, with so much favour and success, that nothing *takes* (as they rightly phrase it) like a *Romance*.

Censorship was continued after the Restoration by the Licensing Act of 1662 which was aimed at "heretical, seditious, schismatical, or offensive books or pamphlets." There was little interference on purely moral grounds and the censors did not think it worth their while to concern themselves with chapbooks and similar light literature, some of which was very coarse.

The seventeenth century produced some of the most exquisite poetry in the English language, as well as the last music that was wholly English in character. Today, madrigal societies sing prudently selected examples and emasculated versions of songs which were then heard up and down the country: while the books of

"Drolleries" serve to remind us of a time when England was "merry." The contrast in taste was illustrated in 1959 at a Festival Hall concert when the audience was restricted to men, and some of the singers were masked, because seventeenth-century songs were sung in integral versions.[3]

The statute of 1662 was allowed to expire in 1695, and nothing like it has been put into force since except in wartime. Books and journals were no longer censored in the true sense of that word, that is, subjected to control before publication. The liberty of the press has become part of the English heritage. This liberty was briefly defined by Lord Mansfield in R. v. *Dean of St. Asaph* in 1784: "The liberty of the Press consists in printing without previous license subject to the consequences of the law."

The law whose consequences may follow publication is the law of libel. A "libel" is by derivation a "little book," but in legal terminology it includes any volume, journal, paper, picture, or other representation. The libel may be defamatory, seditious, blasphemous, or obscene in character. Defamatory and seditious libel are fairly familiar to the newspaper-reading public. The most notorious cases of blasphemous libel were the prosecutions in 1822 and 1841 in respect of Shelley's *Queen Mab*.[4] Thereafter the law against blasphemy began to fall into desuetude, but as late as 1922 a humble man named John William Gott was given nine months' hard labor for publishing pamphlets in which Christ's entry into Jerusalem was described as a circus act. It may still crop up in out-of-the-way places as the following case during the last war shows:

On a charge of having published a blasphemous libel, W——, forty-seven, proprietor of the ——Hotel, Jersey, described as a free-lance photographer, was at Jersey Assizes yesterday sentenced to a month's imprisonment.

Mr. Clifford Orange, Chief Aliens Officer, stated that when W—— called at his office at St. Helier to obtain an exit permit his passport contained two photographs, one of which showed W—— lying on the beach wearing bathing drawers, and with arms outstretched. Sketched in were a cross and other marks, making the picture what Mr. Orange described as a representation of Christ crucified.[5]

It was obscene libel that was the most serious branch of the law so far as nonpolitical literature was concerned. When we speak of a "banned book" we generally mean one that has been condemned by the courts as obscene, or has been treated by some authority, library, or other institution as if it were. From the point of view of creative writing, speculative thought, scientific investigation, and educational and social welfare, the law relating to literary obscenity is of considerable importance as it is the purpose of this present study to demonstrate.

Obscene libel was a last and late comer to the category of libels. The ecclesiastical courts continued to exercise some power over morals after the Reformation, and there was much learned argument in the famous case of Sir Charles Sedley as to whether Sir Charles and his companions should not have been tried before an ecclesiastical court instead of before the Lord Chief Justice.

Sir Charles Sedley was one of the boon companions of Charles II and a member of the young Circle of Wits, which the Earl of Rochester later joined. Besides their activities as courtiers, these young men haunted the taverns of London. There they functioned as the perhaps degenerate heirs of the tradition of Shakespeare, Ben Jonson, and the revelers of the Mermaid Tavern. They were, however, instrumental in handing on that tradition, through Addison and Steele, to Johnson and Goldsmith. The taverns in the neighborhood of Charing Cross were accustomed to witness the most unseemly scenes enacted by these young Restoration blades, but on one occasion all limits were exceeded and the hand of justice fell.

Anthony à Wood tells the story in these words:

In the month of June 1663 this our author, Sir Ch. Sedley, Charles Lord Buckhurst (afterwards Earl of Middlesex), Sir Tho. Ogle, etc., were at a cook's house at the sign of the Cock in Bow Street near Covent Garden, within the liberty of Westm. and being inflam'd with strong liquors, they went into the balcony belonging to that house, and putting down their breeches they excrementiz'd in the street: which being done, Sedley stripped himself naked, and with eloquence preached blasphemy to the people; whereupon a riot being raised, the people became very clamorous, and would have forced the door next to the street open: but being hindered, the preacher and his company were pelted into their room, and the windows belonging thereunto were broken. This frolick thing being soon spread abroad, especially by the fanatical party who aggravated it to the utmost, by making it the most scandalous thing in nature, and nothing more reproachful to religion than that; the said company were summoned to the court of justice in Westminster Hall, where being indicted of a riot before Sir Rob. Hyde, lord chief justice of the common pleas, were all fined, and Sir Charles being fined 500l, he made answer that he thought he was the first man that paid for shitting.[6]

The law report gives a slightly different account of the offense:

He was fined 2,000 mark, committed without bail for a week and bound to his good behaviour for a year, on his confession of information against him for shewing himself naked in a balcony and throwing down bottles (pist in) *vie et armis* among the people in Covent Garden *contra pacem* to the scandal of the government.[7]

Sedley, for all his wild ways, was a respectable poet. His only daughter, Katherine, became the mistress of the Duke of York. When the Duke ascended the throne he created her Countess of Dorchester. These circumstances "greatly shocked" the dissolute Sir Charles and put some strain on his loyalty. After the abdication he supported the accession of William and Mary. When someone found this attitude strange in an old courtier of Charles II, Sedley answered, "Well, I am even in point of civility with King James. For as he made my daughter a Countess, so I have helped to make his daughter a Queen."

Katherine's influence on her royal lover was good. She worked hard for the Protestant cause, and if anything could have saved James from his fate it would have been her strong understanding good nature and acute sense of humor. When James was no longer King she married a worthy knight to whom she bore two sons. When sending them off to school she is reported to have said: "If anybody call either of you the son of a whore, you must bear it; for you are so: but if they call you bastards, fight till you die; for you are an honest man's sons."

The power of the ecclesiastical courts was gradually eroded by custom and legislation, although it was not until 1876 that the desuetude of their jurisdiction over the laity was judicially recognized in *Phillimore v. Machin*. Today their activities are confined to cases of clerical discipline. In the early eighteenth century they seem to have been impotent to deal with indecent writing and there had not so far been developed any doctrine which firmly established the legality of prosecutions before the civil courts. This is quite clear from the remarks of Mr. Justice Powell in 1708 when discussing a common law indictment[8] against a man named Read for printing a book entitled *The Fifteen Plagues of a Maidenhead*:

This is for printing bawdy stuff, that reflects on no person, and a libel must be against some particular person or persons, or against the Government. It is stuff not fit to be mentioned publicly. If there is no remedy in the Spiritual court, it does not follow there must be a remedy here. There is no law to punish it: I wish there were: but we cannot make law. It indeed tends to the corruption of good manners, but that is not sufficient for us to punish. As to the case of Sir Charles Sedley, there was something more in that case than showing his naked body in the balcony.

And the judge pointed out that the gravamen of Sedley's offense was his assault on the people in the street below. We thus reach a stage where the law books present a clean slate so far as any sanctions against literary obscenity are concerned.

II

Edmund Curll

IT IS CLEAR from Read's case that at the beginning of the eighteenth century a bawdy book could be published in England
with impunity. The development of the law of obscene libel had
not begun. The first stage was connected with the activities of an
interesting rascal named Edmund Curll who is chiefly remembered
today as a figure in Pope's *Dunciad*.

Curll was a remarkable man in a remarkable setting. A compari-
son between the Grub Street of the Augustan age of English
literature and the publishing world of today should provide encouragement to those lugubrious philosophers who assure us that
nothing can improve and that human nature is incorrigible. In the
first part of the eighteenth century paid authorship, let alone publishing, was scarcely considered an occupation proper to a gentleman. The law of copyright was in its infancy, and that of
defamatory libel, a puny forerunner of its present self. Piracy, spuri-
ous title pages, sharp practice, lying, and even fraud were the order
of the day. In this literary jungle, Curll was conspicuous as a beast
of prey who always knew a trick a little shadier than the tricks of his
rivals; whose daring and impudence were regarded with astonishment and, likely enough, with envy; whose bawdiness upset the
susceptibilities of a coarse age; and whose treatment of his hack
authors outraged the by no means exacting standards of his time.
On the other hand, he had taste, ability, and a genuine enthusiasm

for literature and scholarship; and was treated quite seriously by many reputable men of letters.

This dual character resulted in a lively and troublous existence. Born in 1675 Curll came to London in 1705. As early as 1708 he was involved in bitter controversies with rivals over his *Charitable Surgeon,* a quack treatise on venereal disease recommending remedies which, curiously enough, could always be bought in Curll's shop. A little later he entered with gusto into current religious controversy and lent his own pen to champion the superior merits of the Church of England against all comers.

Things became serious when his unauthorized publication of some poems opened his long quarrel with the great Alexander Pope. Incredible as it may sound, Pope won one bout of this conflict by administering an emetic to Curll in the guise of a friendly bottle of wine at the Swan Tavern in Fleet Street. Pope then wrote a lampoon mocking at Curll's suffering when he returned to the bosom of his family. This was followed by another similar pamphlet, and finally, at a later date, Pope produced: *A Strange but True Relation how Mr. Edmund Curll out of an Extraordinary Desire of Lucre, went into Change Alley and was converted from the Christian religion by Certain Eminent Jews; and how he was circumcized, and initiated into their Mysteries.* Curll did not take all this lying down, but retorted with squibs which made up in venom for what they lacked in genius.

The quarrel with Pope began in 1715, the year of the first Jacobite rising. Curll was to get into further trouble for publishing a cheap edition of the proceedings in the House of Lords against the Earl of Winton, the only one of the impeached peers who did not plead guilty and throw himself on the mercy of George I. The Lords regarded this as a breach of privilege and Curll was reprimanded on his knees by the Lord Chancellor after three weeks' loss of liberty. Curll must have regarded this affair as particularly unfortunate as he had taken the precaution of describing his print as "translated from the French" and of issuing it under the imprint of a woman bookseller who happened to be ill at the time.

A few years later he was again on his knees in the House of Lords. Curll could give points even to modern publishers and authors in the alacrity with which he would produce a biography of a deceased person of eminence. When the first Duke of Buckingham died, sure enough, Curll was first in the field with an announcement of Works, Life, and Last Will and Testament of the late peer, all of course unauthorized. The Lords took umbrage, and Curll was again reprimanded, although this time he escaped imprisonment.

The House of Lords was not the only institution in Westminster offended by (and able to revenge itself on) the ambitious Mr. Curll. In 1716 the captain of Westminster School pronounced a funeral oration in Latin over the body of the famous Dr. Robert South. Curll thought it worth while to print this effusion with an English translation. Perhaps he thought it would prepare the ground for the inevitable "Life." Anyway it was not to be expected that in such a case a man like Curll would worry about authorization, but he was probably flattered to receive a letter of thanks and a polite invitation to visit the school. He complied with the invitation, and a contemporary plate illustrates the subsequent proceedings in three stages. First we see him vigorously tossed in a blanket by the scholars, next he is stretched along a table, untrussed and receiving a schoolboy birching, finally he is shown kneeling and begging pardon in Dean's Yard.

The following year Curll attracted the attention of the future author of *Robinson Crusoe*. In an anonymous article in the *Weekly Journal*, Defoe denounced Curll and all his works with a wealth of moral indignation which forestalls the efforts of certain modern journalists in a similar vein. He coined the word "Curlicism" to denote the iniquities he trounced and wanted to know why Curll's "abominable Catalogue" was not suppressed "in a Country where Religion is talk'd of (little more, God knows)." But the authorities were less easily drawn than they have been in some modern instances. It was not in Curll's nature to suffer in silence. Willingly adopting his opponent's neologism he replied with a pamphlet *Curlicism Displayed* which, under cover of defending his activities, was really an impudent advertisement of his less reputable publications. His printing of Lord Essex's divorce case in a volume of his "best-seller" series, *Cases of Impotency and Divorce*, is complained of. But who drew up the original report? No less a person than Dr. George Abbot, then Archbishop of Canterbury, and presumably he

did it in the public interest. What more desirable then than that
the public should have the opportunity of perusing the spicier
passages as printed in detail by Curll? Again, take the objection to
a translation of Meibomius's *De usu Flagrorum in re Medica et
Venerea* by the late Dr. George Sewell of Hampstead (one of
Curll's hacks): how could a layman, like Defoe, judge a purely
medical treatise? One can hear eunuchs singing at the opera: what,
then, is reprehensible about a book dealing with them? And so
on. . . .

Defoe was silenced, and Curlicism flourished. Curll soon took
service as a political spy under Sir Robert Walpole. The job was
perhaps lucrative and certainly congenial; and Curll no doubt had
an eye to possible protection from the bluff, hearty, and broad-
minded Whig minister. This hope did not stand him in any great
stead, however, in the major disaster which overtook him in 1725.

The previous autumn Curll had published a singularly scandalous book. It was a translation of a French pseudonymous publication of the previous century by the Abbé Barrin called *Venus dans
le Cloutre, ou la religieuse en chemise*. Somebody made a serious
complaint to the authorities and Curll got wind of coming trouble.
He hastily printed *The Humble Representation of Edmund Curll,
Bookseller and Stationer of London, Concerning Five Books, complained of to the Secretary of State*. A good move, no doubt! But
the trouble was that the *Representation* was not really humble at
all, but a defense and exposition of his works hardly less saucy than
his reply to Defoe. The blow fell in March. Curll was arrested on
account of two of the books objected to: *Venus in the Cloister or
the Nun in her Smock* and the Meibomius previously referred to.
He did not obtain bail till July, and in November he stood his trial
before the King's Bench[1] at Westminster Hall. It appears that
everybody (except Curll) speedily agreed that he was *homo iniquus
et sceleratus*. But was that a punishable offense? His counsel moved
in arrest of judgment on the ground that it was not a libel and, if
punishable at all, was a matter for the spiritual courts. The Lord
Chief Justice seemed clear that a matter in writing could not be the
concern of the spiritual courts. There was considerable argument
among the judges. Curll in his lowly position may have followed
enough of it to hope that he would fall neatly between two stools.

Read's case gave the bench a lot of trouble. The Attorney-General insisted that to corrupt the morals of the King's subjects was an offense at common law. The King's peace could be broken without *vi et armis.* If you destroyed morality, he argued, you destroyed the peace of government. At last the Lord Chief Justice decided that the case was of such great consequence that it must stand over for fuller argument. Curll left the Court on bail—a guilty but unsentenced man.

He went off in a huff. If he could not publish what books he chose, he would publish none. Prudence also counseled a graceful retreat. Accordingly a solemn apology and announcement of his retirement appeared in the newspapers. He would never offend again. The Old Adam was, however, hard of dying. It was only reasonable that he should finish off two books "now in the Press" before he went, and he could not resist the temptation to announce them in his valedictory statement. One of the two happened to be *The Case of Seduction translated from the French by Mr. Rogers being the late Proceedings at Paris against the Rev. Abbé des Rues.* . . .

Soon after this ill-advised announcement Curll was rearrested, his shop raided, and nine books and pamphlets seized. In his prison Curll turned reformer and wrote a pamphlet called *The Prisoner's Advocate* exposing abuses with which his position made him only too well acquainted.

It was July 1726 before (apparently thanks to Walpole) he was on bail again. Counsel managed to get his case postponed till the following year, but even prison could not keep him out of mischief. Before his release he had become involved in publishing some political memoirs of a "seditious and scandalous" character. Jacobite tendencies were even more serious in the eyes of his judges than bawdry.

In Curll's favor it was argued that *The Nun in her Smock* had been published as long ago as 1683 by Henry Rhodes, a noted bookseller on Fleet Street. But Rhodes had had no powerful enemies, or political black marks. All Curll's twists and turns could not save him from coming up for judgment on February 13, 1739. We hear no more of the legal argument or his initial offenses. He is fined twice: once for the moral offenses and once for the political offense, and, in addition to the latter, ordered to stand in the pillory for one hour. It is interesting to note the precise terms of the sentence, for it has been repeatedly stated (and by good authorities) that Curll stood in the pillory for publishing obscene books, but this is not true. He wore "the wooden ruff," as it was called, for a political misdemeanor.

The pillory was no joke. Even an hour of it could be an unpleasant experience. By law the populace could throw anything but stones, and when so inclined, they made the most of their opportunities for displaying their disapproval of the culprit. Not long before Curll's turn some unfortunates whose offenses upset the professional susceptibilities of the ladies of Drury Lane were lucky to escape from the pillory with their lives. It was only the previous May that an elderly man had stood in the pillory right in front of Curll's shop. In spite of all the efforts of the victim's friends, and in spite of the fact that he "had got Armour under his Cloathes, and an Iron Cap under his Hat," he had to be taken down after half an hour to prevent his being murdered. And Curll's windows had been broken! Naturally he took his own precautions for his forthcoming appearance. A broadsheet was prepared for the mob, who were flatteringly addressed as "Gentlemen." Their reverence for the late Queen Anne was played on, and it was cunningly suggested that the "Gentleman who now appears before you" had been guilty of nothing except excessive zeal for the good memory of the departed monarch. Thrust into the hands of the crowd who assembled at Charing Cross on February 23, 1728, this ingenious document had the desired effect. One man decided to exercise his constitutional privilege and threw an egg. He was nearly lynched. The wily Curll left the pillory unscathed.

After these troubles he found himself in low water for a time, but Pope's attack in the *Dunciad* came as a whiff of oxygen to his flagging fortune. He counterattacked with spirit and became a sort of leader of those "dunces" who were not prepared to take their chastisement lying down. This pamphleteering helped to reline Curll's pockets. The long, long quarrel with Pope no sooner died down than it took on fresh life—and Curll always exploited it to his profit. Then, of course, copies of *The Case of Seduction* could always be trotted out when a clergyman got into hot water. In one of his better moods we find him collaborating with some learned Fellows at Oxford University over the issues of a series of volumes on English antiquities.

Our subject does not require us to follow this incorrigible, but game, rogue to his grave in 1747. Our interest in Curll is chiefly concerned with the fact that in 1727, nineteen years after Read's case, his prosecution authoritatively established the publication of an obscene libel as a misdemeanor at common law. A misdemeanor is an offense less grave than a felony, and is tried on indictment normally with a jury. No Act of Parliament had been passed. The law was judge-made law. The change in those nineteen years is a good illustration of that chameleonlike property of English law of which we shall see more later on and which has been exemplified in more than one branch in recent times.

The case illustrates two aspects of the moral censorship of literature that are worthy of note. One is the connection between that censorship and politics, a connection which has been much more important in France than in England. The other is the fact that "obscenity" or "pornography" are by no means clear-cut terms indicating something of indubitable moral worthlessness. In English law courts it is customary to speak of a vendor of pornography as necessarily a man of low type (for some reason he is generally "foreign") and his wares as totally repulsive. But Curll's case already shows that things are not so simple as that. Curll was undoubtedly a rascal: but there were sides to his character which won him the respectful attention of earnest and scholarly men. He undoubtedly selected many of his wares for no other reason than for their appeal to salacious tastes. But the two books for which he was convicted were by no means ephemeral trash. Meibomius's treatise has its place in the history of medicine; and *The Nun* started her career as a Protestant tract on the religious controversies of France. Thus we see, even at this early stage, that the web the law was weaving promised many a tangle and many a contradiction.

III

From George III to Victoria

AFTER BEING ESTABLISHED by Curll's case little was heard of the common law against literary obscenity, and for a long time it was a sort of poor relation in the libel family. The reputable literature of the time was often very broad, and pornographic works circulated freely. The classic example of the latter type of writing is John Cleland's *Memoirs of a Woman of Pleasure*, a novel commonly known by the name of its heroine Fanny Hill and published a year or so before 1750. Cleland was a Scotsman born in 1709 and had served as consul at Smyrna and with the East India Company at Bombay. The *Memoirs of a Woman of Pleasure* was his first novel and when arraigned before the Privy Council for writing it he pleaded poverty as an excuse. Such was the mildness of the prevailing attitude that the case was settled by the President of the Council, the Earl of Graville, who was a relation of Cleland, granting him a pension of £100 a year on condition that he did not repeat the offense.

The book deals with the familiar theme of the young country girl who came to London, and is composed of a series of episodes describing the many amorous adventures that followed. At first it is eminently readable and not without literary merit. The account of Fanny's sexual experiences with her lover at Chelsea are to my mind superior, at least from an instructional point of view, to the famous incidents between Mellors and the heroine of *Lady Chat-*

terley's Lover which moved Bernard Shaw to say that the book should be given to every young woman about to be married.

But the difficulties of his task soon began to weigh on the author. By the pen of Fanny he confesses:

> I imagined, indeed, that you would have been cloyed and tired with the uniformity of adventures and expressions, inseparable from a subject of this sort, whose bottom or groundwork being in the nature of things eternally one and the same, whatever variety of forms and modes the situations are susceptible of, there is no escaping a repetition of near the same images, the same figures, the same expressions, with this further inconvenience, added to the disgust it creates, that the words JOYS, ARDOURS, TRANSPORTS, ECSTASIES, and the rest of those pathetic terms so congenial to, so received in the PRACTICE OF PLEASURE, flatten and lose much of their due spirit and energy by the frequency they indispensably recur with, in a narrative of which that PRACTICE professedly composes the whole basis.

As the book proceeds the author attempts to combat the inevitable tedium of his genre by introducing brothel scenes including descriptions of erotic flagellation. It will be remembered that Snarl in Shadwell's *Virtuoso* (1676) had a partiality for this eccentricity that he attributed to his attendance at Westminster School—the same academy which educated Cleland.

Cleland sold the copyright of his book for £20 and Ralph Griffiths, the publisher, is reputed to have made £10,000 from the enormous sales. In spite of all attempts at suppression it has continued to be an underground best-seller to this day and has been translated into quite a few foreign languages. A subsequent novel from Cleland's pen, *The Memoirs of a Coxcomb*, is an altogether less lurid affair. He lived down the scandal of his first book and was responsible for many political and philological publications before he died in London at the age of 82.

When the law of obscenity was invoked in the eighteenth century it was generally in the role of a hanger-on to its more substantial cousins, seditious and blasphemous libel. It was undoubtedly the fact that the radical agitations of John Wilkes were distasteful to George III and his Government that caused Lord Sandwich to read to the House of Lords in 1763 from *An Essay on Woman*, a clever but indecent parody of Pope's *Essay on Man*, attributed to Wilkes. Lord Lyttelton demanded that the reading should cease but other noble lords cried, "Go on!" In the end the House resolved that the poem was "a most scandalous, obscene and impious libel" but members were more shocked by the blasphemy than by the obscenity. The author's arrest was ordered, but he escaped to the Continent instead of answering the charge and was outlawed.

Before the end of the eighteenth century an astonishing change had come over English literature. From being as outspoken as any other it had become so strait-laced as to be a historical curiosity. Andrew Lang tells us:

English literature had been at least as free spoken as any other from the time of Chaucer to the death of Smollett. Then, in twenty years at most, English literature became the most pudibund, the most respectful of the young person's blush, that the world has ever known.[1]

The change is well illustrated by an anecdote related by Sir Walter Scott in one of his letters:

A grand-aunt of my own, Mrs. Keith Ravelstone, who was a person of some condition, being a daughter of Sir John Swinton— lived with unabated vigour of intellect to a very advanced age. She was very fond of reading, and enjoyed it to the last of her long life. One day she asked me, when we happened to be alone together, whether I had ever seen Mrs. Behn's novels?—I confessed the charge.—Whether I could get her a sight of them?—I said, with some hesitation, I believed I could; but that I did not think she would like either the manners, or the language, which approached too near that of Charles II's time to be quite proper reading. "Nevertheless," said the good old lady, "I remember them being so much admired and being so much interested in them myself, that I wish to look at them again." To hear was to obey. So I sent Mrs. Aphra Behn, curiously sealed up, with "private and confidential" on the packet, to my gay old grand-aunt. The next time I saw her afterwards, she gave me back Aphra, properly wrapped up, with nearly these words: "Take back your bonny Mrs. Behn; and, if you will take my advice, put her in the fire, for I found it impossible to get through the very first novel. But is it not," she said, "a very odd thing that I, an old woman of eighty and upwards, sitting alone, feel myself ashamed to read a book which, sixty years ago, I have heard read aloud for the amusement of large circles, consisting of the finest and most creditable society in London."[2]

Even Shakespeare was reprimanded for coarseness and an expurgated edition of his works which added the verb "to bowdlerize" to the English language was published by Thomas Bowdler in 1818.

This change in literary taste was a facet of social changes. In the first half of the eighteenth century the English masses were illiterate and were governed by an educated and often highly cultivated aristocracy. An oppressed populace and especially a populace oppressed by a sexually licentious governing class (as were the gentry of the eighteenth century) is a good breeding ground for puritanism. The difference of attitude to sexual matters between Richardson, Goldsmith, and Johnson on the one hand, and Fielding, Sterne, and Gibbon on the other, is illuminating. To Richardson the height of virtue is exemplified by a servant girl who retains her virginity in spite of her master's advances until he marries her. Gibbon asks: "Shall I blush to translate what a bishop was not ashamed to write?" It is the difference in attitude between the social classes from which they sprang.

Methodism was the religious expression of this puritanical tendency. Although it made some aristocratic recruits like the Countess of Huntington, it spread most readily among the lower classes. Its adherents were committed to a very restricted view of life. Many of them whom the Industrial Revolution raised to varying degrees of wealth and power carried the cultural marks of their origin with them. Reinforced by the Evangelical Movement they constituted a middle-class influence which spread over England like a damp and suffocating blanket. As the country became richer they made it uglier. If the people were to have more leisure as time went on, they saw to it that dullness rather than gaiety should prevail. These forces were reinforced by the agnostic Utilitarians between whom and the religious puritans there was little to choose so far as moral views were concerned. Voluntary societies were formed to make this body of opinion effective. In 1787 George III issued a proclamation against vice and Wilberforce formed the Proclamation Society to enforce the royal injunctions. Like its successors up to the present day this society included the suppression of obscene publications among its activities. A more formidable Society for the Suppression of Vice which eventually absorbed the Proclamation Society was formed in 1802 and it was very energetic in instituting prosecutions against pornography.

English law usually moves very tardily in the wake of changes in public opinion and taste. In the early nineteenth century the cultural changes which had been accumulating during the previous fifty years finally began to make their impact on the law.

It wasn't long before the judges decided[3] that it was no defense to the common law charge of obscene publication that the matter complained of was a fair and accurate report of judicial proceedings and the Law of Libel Amendment Act, 1888, exempted obscenity and blasphemy from the privilege it conferred on newspaper reporting of court cases and public meetings. The Act, however, provided a safeguard by requiring the consent of a judge in chambers to any prosecution of a newspaper for criminal libel.

The state of the law is typical of the medieval gloom which has surrounded the development of the law of obscenity and often makes it difficult for the ordinary citizen to know what the courts have commended as obscene and to judge the justice and wisdom of the condemnation. He must accept the findings of the bench or the jury in the dark. Even if he attends the court the passages complained of are often not read out but copies of the book are handed around to witnesses and jury. The book is sometimes roundly condemned in intemperate language from the bench; and when one knows the work, or can get access to a copy afterward, one is often amazed that so much moral indignation can be caused by so little impropriety. It may be argued that to allow publication in any form of passages alleged to be obscene would to some extent perpetuate an evil which the law is attempting to stop. But this applies to defamatory and seditious libel, and the advantages of open and comprehensible justice is thought to be an overriding consideration in those cases.

As not infrequently happens in the process of English lawmaking, statutory provisions enacted by Parliament to deal with obscenity were later in time than the common law developed by the judges, and they did not follow any clear or scientific line. A start was made with section 4 of the Vagrancy Act of 1824 which made it a summary offense, that is, one triable by the magistrates, to exhibit obscene prints or other indecent matter in public places, and an amending Act of 1838 brought exhibition in shop windows within the purview of the law. Special provisions penalizing the sale of obscene books and other matter were incorporated in the Metropolitan Police Act, 1839, and the Town Police Clauses Act, 1847.

At this stage, the law was never invoked against anything that by any stretch of imagination could be called serious literature, and the morals of the well-to-do were not interfered with. Sydney Smith dubbed the Society for the Suppression of Vice a society for suppressing the vices of persons whose incomes do not exceed £500 a year.[4] With the accession of Queen Victoria, however, the open licentiousness which had characterized the Regency finally disappeared from the upper ranks of society. It was prevailing taste and public opinion that set up the standards governing reputable literature with regard to which Thackeray summed up the situation in 1850. Voices had been heard during the serialization of *The History of Pendennis* that passages in the novel were immodest, and when it appeared in volume form he wrote in the preface:

Since the author of *Tom Jones* was buried, no writer of fiction among us has been permitted to depict to his utmost power a MAN. We must drape him, and give him a certain conventional simper. Society will not tolerate the Natural in our Art. Many ladies have remonstrated and subscribers left me, because, in the course of the story, I described a young man resisting and affected by temptation. My object was to say, that he had the passions to feel, and the manliness and generosity to overcome them. You will not hear—it is best to know it—what moves in the real world, what passes in society, in the clubs, colleges, news'-rooms—what is the life and talk of your sons. A little more frankness than is customary has been attempted in this story; with no bad desire on the writer's part, it is hoped, and with no ill consequence to any reader.

The stage is now set for the appearance of two figures who made the most important contributions to the law of literary obscenity and turned it from being a minor and rather ineffective branch of the law into a powerful, if arbitrary and illogical, weapon against, not only pornography, but serious literature embodying novel or unorthodox tendencies in sexual matters.

Campbell and Cockburn

THE SUPERFICIAL RESPECTABILITY and coercive propriety of Queen Victoria's reign, with its necessary concomitant of repression and inhibition, naturally produced an underworld of prostitution and allied vices. This side of the Victorian scene is admirably depicted by Michael Sadleir in his novels *Fanny by Gaslight* and *Forlorn Sunset*. The latter specifically deals with the thriving pornographic book trade whose principal center in London was Holywell Street, one of the maze of thoroughfares demolished when the new Aldwych buildings were erected at the beginning of this century. The trade dealt with a wide range of wares from highly priced books designed for bibliophiles to cheap trash intended to extract money from the pockets of callow youths. Pornographic periodicals appeared from time to time and publications catering for flagellomaniacs provided the distinctively English flavor of this subliterature. The dealers found a ready market among the undergraduates of Oxford and Cambridge, and many a revered paterfamilias had a secret shelf in his library and one or more folders of "special" plates.

All of the wares thus furtively enjoyed were not so bad as others. One great standby of nineteenth-century youth was the now almost forgotten Paul de Kock. This taste, according to Kock himself,[1] was shared by Pope Gregory XVI; and the novels achieved such a vogue in Italy that when Ferdinand Brunetière came to visit Leo XIII the Pope asked, without any preliminary courtesies, after "the good Paôlo de Koko."[2] Unhappily the gay novelist had been dead for many years. In 1835 Marston and Coy began an edition of Kock in which it was

proposed to give a translation of his best works, carefully weeded from the indelicacy and impiety from which scarcely any French work is entirely exempt.[3]

The introduction went on to say:

A more thorough insight into French manners and customs may be acquired from one of de Kock's novels, than from fifty volumes of travels, and an English father may judge from the portrait of a Frenchwoman (painted by a countryman, recollect) how much he is likely to gain by educating his family abroad.

As we shall see later on, this fear of French literature and manners has continued to influence the English up to the present day.

For all the crusading zeal of the anti-vice societies the law fought a losing battle with early Victorian pornography. Suppression was difficult because of the safeguards to the liberty of the subject which surrounded the administration of the common law and the inadequacy of the penalties for statutory offenses. Further, stocks could not be seized, and even if a shopkeeper were successfully prosecuted and imprisoned, his wife would often continue the business until he was at liberty to resume it.

This state of affairs began to change when a bill to restrict the sale of poisons was considered in the House of Lords contemporaneously with a particularly lurid pornography trial before Lord Campbell, the Lord Chief Justice of England. His lordship turned his mind to "a sale of poison more deadly than prussic acid, strychnine or arsenic" as he described the Holywell Street traffic. This intemperate language is typical of much that is said and written on the subject, and the mischief of the exaggeration has been ably exposed by Theodore Schroeder:

Much of the justification for intolerance derives its authority from false analogies, wrongfully carried over from physical relations into the realm of the psychic. . . .
Ethics is not one of the exact sciences. Probably it never will be. Until we are at least approximately as certain of the existence and

tests of "moral poison," as we are of the physical characteristics and consequences of carbolic acid, it is folly to talk of "moral poison" except as a matter of poetic licence.[4]

Lord Campbell's moral indignation moved him to promote in the House of Lords a bill which introduced a new principle into the law of obscenity. It was aimed not primarily at the publisher but at the books themselves which were to be liable to summary destruction by the magistrates. The bill was strongly opposed in both Houses and only passed on Lord Campbell's assurance that:

The measure was intended to apply exclusively to works written for the single purpose of corrupting the morals of youth and of a nature calculated to shock the common feelings of decency in any well-regulated mind. . . . He was ready to make what was indictable under the present laws a test of obscenity.

The circulation of literary works even though they were certainly of a polluting character, Lord Campbell assured his peers as he held *The Lady of the Camellias* in his hands and regarded it with horror, could be stopped only by the force of public opinion and an improved taste. Substantial amendments were made in the Commons and the bill became law as the Obscene Publications Act, 1857. It provided that a search warrant could be issued on sworn information that obscene publications were kept at the premises concerned for sale or distribution, and that a sale of such a publication had actually been made. Any obscene matter found on search had to be brought into court and the proprietor of the premises called upon to show cause why it should not be destroyed. The provision in regard to an actual sale was generally met by sending a plain-clothes policeman to make a purchase. The police sometimes acted as *agents provocateurs*. In one case, for instance, a constable posing as an army officer pestered a bookseller on six occasions to obtain books which he did not normally stock.[5]

It cannot be too firmly insisted that this Act did not become the basis of the law concerning literary obscenity. It created no new offense, but was a preventive measure which sought to forestall the sale of obscene books by destroying them. As we have seen, Lord Campbell was emphatic that the Act did not alter the existing common law with respect to what was regarded as obscene, and he promised that it would not be used against anything but gross pornography. This promise, however, proved a hollow one, as is often the case with assurances given in Parliament as to the manner in which legislation will be administered.

The reinforced law and increasing prudish public opinion began to have repercussions which were felt by reputable authors writing for the educated public. A classic example is the fear of prosecution in the case of Swinburne's *Poems and Ballads*. In 1866 the first copies of the first series of poems were just out when the poet's "hound of a publisher," as he called him, withdrew the book. He was distracted by terror of the public prosecutor. John Morley had written a hysterical denunciation in the *Saturday Review* and Payne believed that *The Times* was going to demand a prosecution. It seems certain that a crushing review had been written for the newspaper holding both poet and publisher up to the execration of all decent people. Happily for posterity, Swinburne found another and less timorous, if not particularly reputable, publisher in John Hotten, and with characteristic moral courage refused to alter a word of what he had written.[6]

Eleven years after the passing of the 1857 Act the common law was changed, not by Act of Parliament but by a judge, or perhaps it would be truer to say by the authors of legal textbooks. There had been in existence since the early years of the century a Protestant pamphlet which sought to discredit the Roman Catholic Church by quoting standard works on moral theology used by confessors. These works enter into the most intimate details of married life with a profundity of erudition and a wealth of logic that is far from edifying to the untheological mind. It is fortunate, therefore, that they are obtainable only in Latin. The pamphlet in question gave extracts from the original with English translations in parallel columns. In the course of its career it had appeared under various titles, and had even undergone some bowdlerization out of deference, no doubt, to the temper of the time. A certain Henry Scott, a metal broker of Wolverhampton, obtained from time to time supplies of the pamphlet (at the time entitled *The Confessional Unmasked*) from "The Protestant Electoral Union." Out of religious zeal he sold them to all comers at the price he paid for them—one shilling each. In 1867 the justices of Wolverhampton made an order that his stock of 250 copies which had been seized under Lord Campbell's Act should be destroyed. Scott appealed to quarter sessions and the Recorder, a Benjamin Hicklin, found in his favor on the ground that although the pamphlet was obscene and its indiscriminate sale and circulation was calculated to prejudice good morals, his motive in selling it was the innocent one of promoting the objects of the Protestant Electoral Union and exposing the error of the Church of Rome, particularly as regards the confessional. The Roman Catholics did not, of course, take this lying down, and there was an appeal to the Queen's Bench *sub nom. R. v. Hicklin*.[7] The question for decision was: If it be granted that a book is obscene and its publication likely to prejudice good morals, is such publication lawful because the publisher's object was a lawful one? The answer of the court was No. But it is not that decision which makes the case important. In the course of his judgment, Lord Chief Justice Cockburn gave his opinion as to what "obscenity" was. His words were clearly *obiter dictum*, and therefore not binding as law, since the issue of obscenity was not before the court, the Recorder having admitted the obscenity of the pamphlet. Nevertheless, the Cockburn definition was repeated in the textbooks and accepted as the criterion by which allegations of obscenity were judged. Here it is:

The test of obscenity is this, whether the tendency of the matter charged as obscenity is to deprave and corrupt those whose minds are open to such immoral influences and into whose hands a publication of this sort may fall.

Clearly, if consistently applied, this definition would have reduced literature to the level of the nursery. Arbitrarily applied, it proved a fruitful source of injustice to individuals and of damage to science, literature, and society.

The significance of the new interpretation of the law in relation to social reform was made manifest in the celebrated prosecution of Charles Bradlaugh and Annie Besant.[8] In the winter of 1876 a bookseller in Bristol was convicted for selling an edition of Charles

Knowlton's *Fruits of Philosophy: An Essay on the Population Question* to which some questionable illustrations had been added. Charles Knowlton was an American physician of repute, and the pamphlet had been on sale in England for forty years. It explains the physiology of sex in simple language and advises and expounds the use of some rather primitive methods of contraception.

The printing plates of the pamphlet had been acquired by Charles Watts, a business associate of the famous Charles Bradlaugh. Bradlaugh urged Watts to go to Bristol and declare himself the responsible publisher of the work. He did so and was arrested and committed for trial at the Central Criminal Court on January 12, 1877. While the trial was pending Watts changed his mind, withdrew his plea of "Not Guilty" and entered a plea of "Guilty." He was subsequently bound over in £500 and at the trial it was contended that it was unlawful to publish such physiological details. Bradlaugh, who had severed all connection with Watts, determined to take the matter into his own hands. In association with Annie Besant he republished the pamphlet without the illustrations. They were both arrested, marched through the streets to Bridewell, searched, and ultimately released on bail pending trial at the Old Bailey.

Bradlaugh then applied to the Queen's Bench for a writ of *certiorari* for the case to be removed to that court and tried before a judge and special jury. This was granted, Lord Chief Justice Cockburn saying:

> We have looked at the book which is the subject matter of this indictment, and we think it really raises a fair question as to whether it is a scientific production for legitimate purposes.

While the case was pending, books sent out from Bradlaugh's publishing house were seized in the post under the powers of the Post Office in relation to obscene matter. These powers in their present form are embodied in Section 11 of the Post Office Act, 1953, which makes it an offense to send indecent matter through the post even though under cover, and gives the Post Office power to open any postal packet suspected of containing such matter. Notice must be served on the consignee so that if he wishes he may be present at the opening; and any obscene articles may be detained. There is a more general power to open packets under the express warrant of a Secretary of State.

The trial of Charles Bradlaugh and Annie Besant took place on June 18, 1877. One of the witnesses was H. G. Bohn, the founder of the famous library. The jury returned the following verdict:

We are unanimously of opinion that the book in question is calculated to deprave public morals, but at the same time we entirely exonerate the defendants from any corrupt motives in publishing it.

The Lord Chief Justice instructed the jury that this was a verdict of guilty and subsequently sentenced the defendants to six months' imprisonment, a fine of £200 each, and to enter into recognizances for £500 each for two years. The defendants had continued publication after the verdict of the jury. Had they not done so but submitted to the law, the Lord Chief Justice said, the court would have been prepared to discharge them on their own recognizances to be of good behavior. After some argument they were released on bail pending appeal on a writ of error.

An appeal to quash the indictment on the ground that the words relied upon by the prosecution as proving their case ought to have been expressly set out was heard by Lord Justices Bramwell, Brett, and Cotton in February 1878. The appeal was allowed, but the ground of the judgment was, of course, a purely technical one which in no way affected the merits of the case or decided the obscenity issue. The technicality was cleared up later by The Law of Libel Amendment Act, 1888, which provided that in such cases a copy of the book should be deposited with the indictment, together with particulars showing precisely the parts complained of. This provision was embodied in the Indictments Act of 1915.

The defendants were of course released, but the scandal of the trial enabled Annie Besant's husband to deprive her of the society of her daughter for ten years.

In a scurrilous biography of Bradlaugh[9] published ten years after the trial, the author complains that the judge was unduly complaisant to the defendants. He alleges that "Sir Alexander Cockburn in his younger days, and in his older days, had, as far as feminine intrigues were concerned, been anything but a strictly moral man." *The Encyclopaedia Britannica* (11th edition) also refers to his "frivolities." The life of Bradlaugh referred to was written by a fellow Rationalist and it shows that freethinkers are in no way behind theologians in the acrimony of their disputes. Indeed, Bradlaugh's opinions on sexual matters aroused as much hostility among the opponents of religious bodies as among their followers.

The early leaders of rationalist thought such as Godwin, Wollstonecraft, and Shelley recognized that the reasoned attitude to life must be all-embracing in its compass. Bradlaugh was the last popular leader to follow their path; and his activities occasioned a definite split in the ranks. After his time the main body of radicalism and free thought purchased an easy victory in the field of theological and political thought by hauling down its flag in the sexual and ethical field. Henceforward, the radical freethinker, though he might deny the existence of God and proclaim that a beggar was as good as a king, could be relied on to behave exactly like an orthodox churchgoer in his everyday life, or at least to accept the same hypocrisies and concealments.

In a case similar to Bradlaugh's the prosecution succeeded in putting the defendant behind prison bars. The bookshop in High Holborn kept by Edward Truelove, a disciple of Robert Dale Owen, was raided and copies of Owen's *Moral Physiology* and of another pamphlet, *Individual Family and National Poverty*, were seized by representatives of the Society for the Suppression of Vice, who instituted a prosecution. Truelove was tried twice. The first time the jury disagreed. But at the second trial he was found guilty and sentenced to four months' imprisonment as well as a fine of £50. Although nearly seventy years of age, he was imprisoned with common felons and made to pick oakum, and had to sleep on a plank bed.

The Bradlaugh and Besant case gave the eminent jurist, Sir James Stephen, food for thought and apprehension with regard to the course that the law of obscenity was taking under the influence of the Cockburn definition. The first (1877) edition of his *Digest of the Criminal Law* includes the following note to what he has to say about obscene publication:

I confine this article to obscenity because I have found no authority for the proposition that the publication of a work immoral in the wider sense of the word is an offence. A man might with perfect decency of expression, and in complete good faith, maintain doctrines as to marriage, the relation of the sexes, the obligation of truthfulness, the nature and limits of the rights of property, etc., which would be regarded as highly immoral by most people, and yet (I think) commit no crime. Obscenity and immorality in this wide sense are entirely distinct from each other. The language used in reference to some of the cases might throw some doubt on this, but I do not think any instance can be given of the punishment of a decent and *bona fide* expression of opinion commonly regarded as immoral.

Subsequently he added:

I leave this note unaltered, but since it was written the case of R. v. *Bradlaugh* may be considered to have gone some way towards establishing a different principle, and to have invested juries to a certain extent with the powers of *ex post facto* censors of the Press so far as such publications on the relations of the sexes are concerned. I think that juries ought to exercise such a power with the greatest caution when a man writes in good faith on a subject of great interest and open to much difference of opinion, and when no indecency of language is used, except such as is necessary to make the matter treated of intelligible.

Sir James Stephen was wise in his appreciation of the position and justified in his uneasiness. Although juries have from time to time displayed traditional common sense by their verdicts, the administration of the law has put them and the magistrates in possession of power in no way consistent with liberty of thought or liberal culture.

The Bradlaugh and Truelove cases showed that the law as developed by the Cockburn definition of obscenity was a ready weapon in the hands of those opposed to free discussion of sexual morality and one that they were not slow to make use of. The outcome of the battle between Henry Vizetelly and Victorian prudery showed that it was an equally effective menace to creative writing. Vizetelly was a publisher who combined a taste for the realistic school of French writers with the task of popularizing Longfellow in England. He issued translations of Zola's novels which, although bowdlerized, raised a storm of vituperation in the press typical of the English suspicion of, and animosity toward, foreign (in Victorian times particularly French) literature. The Government took no action but Vizetelly was prosecuted in 1888 by the National Vigilance Association. This anti-vice society had been formed a few years earlier at the time of the "Maiden Tribute" scandal by John Kensit, the Protestant zealot. The prosecution was in respect of Zola's *La Terre* and Vizetelly was fined. A leader in *The Times* commented on the case as follows:

Between prudery and pruriency in such matters there is a wide debatable ground, and it is not always easy to draw the line which separates what is permissible from what is not. But if the line is not to be drawn so as to exclude translations of such works of Zola as "La Terre" and "Pot Bouille" it is plain that it cannot be drawn at all. Other French works of fiction published in translation by Mr. Vizetelly, such as the novels of Gaboriau and du Boisgobey, are not always very healthy reading; but their main interest lies in the elucidation of mystery or in the play of intrigue, and not in mere and sheer obscenity, naked, shameless, and unutterably vile. . . . We cannot but rejoice, therefore, that Mr. Vizetelly has acknowledged his offence and been punished for it. In future, as the Solicitor-General intimated, anyone who publishes translations of Zola's novels and works of similar character will do so at his peril, and must not expect to escape so easily as Mr. Vizetelly.

When we remember that *The Times* is here voicing the educated opinion of the day on the work of a man now acknowledged on all sides to be one of the masters of French literature, we have an outstanding example of the fallibility of the judgments of even the best opinion on contemporary works of art which should teach us the danger and unwisdom of giving such judgments the force of law.

The next year Vizetelly repeated the offence and, although an old man of seventy suffering from stricture, was made to serve three months in prison. He died in 1894 a ruined man.

During the latter part of the nineteenth century the influence of men like Edward William Lane and Sir Richard Burton aroused considerable interest among educated Englishmen in oriental customs and literature. Owing to the prudery of the times, however, oriental attitudes to sex could only be presented with either reticence or restriction of publication. The original and unexpurgated version of Burton's famous translation of *The Arabian Nights* was published to private subscribers in 1885 and 1886. Although numerous reprints followed, this work, the only integral translation into English of the great Arabic classic, has never been made available for the ordinary reader. The translation from the French of J. C. Mardrus by E. Powys Mathers, published to subscribers in 1929, does not reflect the tone of the original so accurately as Burton's translation.

Ar Raud al atir wa nuzhat al Khatir, by Muhammad al Nefzawi, a sixteenth-century Tunisian sheikh, received similar treatment. The book is a manual of sex instruction containing a great deal of curious information erroneous and otherwise. Various coital positions are described and the author's statement that a not uncommon one may cause sciatica is of medical interest. In his introduction he reports an interview he had when an earlier version of the book came into the hands of the Grand Vizir:

Three days after he came to me and, showing me my book, said, "This is your work." Seeing me blush, he added, "You need not be ashamed; everything you have said in it is true; no one need be shocked at your words. Moreover, you are not the first who has treated of this subject-matter; and I swear by Allah that it is necessary to know this book. It is only the shameless boor and the enemy of all science who will not read it, or make fun of it."

This work was fully translated into English via the French and published privately under the title *The Perfumed Garden* in 1886, but has never been available to the general reader. A manuscript translation by Sir Richard Burton was destroyed by Lady Burton after his death, together with his journals and some of his rare books.

The *Kama Sutra* of Vatsyayana may also be mentioned. The work is a Sanskrit classic written about 300 B.C. and greatly prized by the educated classes in India. The tender anxiety for the susceptibilities and pleasure of women displayed by the author throughout the work is very appealing. This solicitude stands in marked contrast to the views expressed by that Western pundit, W. Acton, a surgeon, whose book, *Functions and Disorders of the Reproductive Organs*, was regarded as a standard authority in the nineteenth century. In it he declared the supposition that women possess sexual feeling to be "a vile aspersion." In 1883 the *Kama Sutra* was translated into English, but the circulation was private and the price fifty shillings for half a dozen paper-covered pamphlets. Although the work has never been generally available in England, Sir Richard Burton's translation was published by E. P. Dutton & Company in America in the fall of 1962. Vatsyayana's work, and that of the good Sheikh Nefzawi, are, one suspects, sometimes the unacknowledged source of a good deal of popular modern sexology. But generally speaking, the sexual aspect of oriental literature is quite unknown in its true colors in England except by experts and those having access to limited editions.

Another factor in the law relating to obscene publication during the later part of the nineteenth century was the influence of the British Customs, a body which would play a conspicuous part in interference with the work of reputable authors in the twentieth century. The British Customs authorities have powers dating from 1853 in respect of obscene importations which in their present form are embodied in the unrepealed sections of the Customs Consolidation Act, 1876, and in the Customs and Excise Act, 1952. The importation of indecent or obscene articles is prohibited and it is an offense to import such articles with intent to avoid the prohibition. The articles may be seized; but if the seizure is not from the owner the Customs authorities must advise him of the seizure unless he is resident abroad. Seizures can be contested in the courts. These powers are used not only in respect of books imported as merchandise, but in respect of single copies found in the baggage of passengers which are their private property.

Besides being used to prevent the import of trashy pornography the powers of the Customs were invoked against more reputable publications. The increasing pressure of law and public opinion put restrictions on the reading matter of the well-to-do and the scholarly which all of them were not prepared to accept with quiescence. There was a demand for books which did not conform to the prevailing taste and this demand was met to some extent by publication in France. For instance, Isidore Liseux, a nineteenth-century publisher in Paris of scholarly and historical works with an erotic flavor, issued many of his wares in English translations and many of his customers for both his French and English books were Britishers and Americans. His place as a thorn in the side of the British Customs was taken by Charles Carrington who carried on an even less reputable trade, adding scientific works as well as sheer pornography to his English titles. His publications were well edited and printed and many of them of legitimate literary or scientific interest. Many of his books were smuggled into England in sheets and bound with a title page showing "The Imperial Press" as the publisher.

Carrington was a secondhand bookseller of Portuguese origin, his real name being Paul Ferfinado. By reading his own wares he graduated into the company of men like Dowson, Beardsley, and Wilde. In the Paris of the early twenties he was a pathetic figure not without a little dignity of tragedy. Blind as the result of syphilis he was no match for his predatory mistress and was helpless before the follies of his five children. They and their hangers-on swarmed over his house and stole his books. A shop was even opened specially to dispose of the thefts. He endured five years of this misery before perishing in a lunatic asylum at the age of sixty-five. His mistress provided a magnificent funeral and his tortured body was consigned to earth by the Catholic Church.[10] The end of Isidore Liseux was also sad: he starved and froze to death in the winter of 1893-94.

As the nineteenth century drew to its close the position of reputable literature in relation to possible allegations of obscenity worsened. Oscar Wilde's trial in 1895 inflamed popular prejudices and made the London publishing houses very jumpy. When Edward Carpenter's publisher found that his author had privately printed a pamphlet called *Homogenic Love,* he broke his contract to publish *Love's Coming of Age* and turned *Towards Democracy* out of doors.[11] Fortunately, the books found better treatment elsewhere, and ran into edition after edition. *Love's Coming of Age* (1896) is a book putting humane and liberal notions about sex to the general reader, which did much to enlighten public opinion in the new century.

Before the new century dawned, however, an obscenity prosecution occurred which, because of the nobility of the real victim and the importance of the book involved, is perhaps the most outstanding and most disgraceful of English obscene publication cases. The victim was Havelock Ellis and the book the first volume to be published of his monumental *Studies in the Psychology of Sex.* A survey of Ellis's life and work will exemplify better than anything the grave implications of a body of law developed from nothing by judges, law book writers, and an uncritical legislature in the space of about two centuries.

Havelock Ellis

W HAT LUCK for a little boy of seven to go around the world in
his father's ship, and that a sailing ship, too! Such was Havelock Ellis's good fortune in 1866. His father was a sea captain, and
his home a happy one. This felicity was perhaps assisted by the
nature of his father's occupation. A sailor's spasmodic returns to
the domestic circle are often more eagerly welcome than the regu-
lar appearances of husbands who follow more sedentary callings.
His mother was an Evangelical Christian of a severe school. Her
convictions forbade the theater, and alcohol was never served at
her table. This latter abstention did not, however, prevent Captain
Ellis from drinking his little son's health with his officers in cham-
pagne when the news of the birth reached his ship at Singapore.
Havelock was an only son, but he had four sisters.

On his return home he was sent to a small school, where among
other things he learned dancing. In later life he attributed to the
dance an important place in the scheme of life. His pacific nature
was demonstrated in a very early incident. One day he came home
with a noticeable hole in the back of his neck. By questioning him,
his mother learned that it had been made with a sharp slate-pencil
by one of his companions. Indignantly she said, "I hope you paid
him back." "No," replied Havelock, "for then I should have been
as bad as he was."

Next he attended the French and German College at Merton,
where he remained until he was twelve. Here he acquired an early

54

acquaintance with modern languages which was later to prove a
great boon to him. Although European thought could still be regarded as a unity, it was a unity which diversity of language made
it extremely difficult for one man to master. This was particularly
so in the field of study that Ellis was to choose for his own. Only
a small proportion of first-rate sexological works were translated
into English; and the translations that were made were frequently
poor and unscholarly.

From twelve to sixteen he was a weekly boarder at an exclusive
school at Mitcham. He showed early signs of promise and became
an indefatigable note-taker. It is worthy of remark that sport had
no interest for him. According to Houston Peterson's biography:
"At best he was a serious youth, apparently destined for an honourable career in a conservative church. At worst he was a sententious,
unworldly little prig too much concerned with God and duty."

At sixteen his sex curiosity was awakened. Such curiosity was by
no means easy to satisfy at the time. Even the great Huxley's *Elementary Physiology* dared not make mention of the processes of
human reproduction. At this age Havelock was ignorant of girls, he
had experienced nothing of the corruption frequently associated
with boarding schools, and his reading had been entirely conventional. However, anxiety about his health caused him to be placed
once more on board his father's ship, this time for a rest cure.
During the long voyage to Australia he read extensively. Under the
influence of Shelley his orthodox faith began to crumble and was
soon gone.

He plunged into Swinburne, but it is characteristic that the
poet's revolutionary enthusiasm moved him little. In after-life
Ellis was never bitterly hostile to any religious expression nor
bound up in any political issue. As a result of reading Rabelais, he
took a long farewell of prudery and became free of that famous
Abbey of Thelème, "in whose rule," he tells us in *Affirmations*,
"was but one clause, *Fay ce que vouldras*, a rule which no pagan
or Christian has ever set up before, because never before, except
as involved in the abstract conceptions of philosophers, had the
thought of voluntary co-operation of the unsolicited freedom to do
well appeared before European men."

In the South Atlantic an incident occurred which illustrates the quiet courage which always distinguished Ellis. An exceptionally heavy wave broke over the stern, destroying instruments and furniture and flooding the cabin occupied by Havelock and his father. Had they been in it at the time they would probably both have been killed. The son's only comment was: "Does this often happen, father?"

When the ship reached Sydney it was decided that, considering the state of Havelock's health, it was undesirable that he should continue the voyage on to Calcutta. So it was arranged that he should remain and await his father's return. As things turned out, he stayed four years.

For a great deal of this time he earned his livelihood by teaching, and much of it was spent in small settlements where he was almost alone. Erotic physical manifestations began to obtrude themselves on his notice, particularly, he tells us, in association with a reading of Brantôme's *Vie des Dames Galantes*. He was more and more tormented by the problems of sex, and one evening, in 1875, under the eucalyptus trees in the school grounds of Burwood, he made the most important resolution of his life. He would devote himself to a study of the matters that perplexed him in order that future generations of young people should be spared his sufferings. In the preface to the first published volume of his celebrated *Studies* he wrote:

The origin of these studies dates from many years back. As a youth I was faced, as others are, by the problem of sex. Living partly in an Australian city where the ways of life were plainly seen, partly in the solitude of the bush, I was free both to contemplate and to meditate many things. A resolve slowly grew up within me: one part of my life-work should be to make clear the problems of sex. That was more than twenty years ago. Since then I can honestly say that in all that I have done that resolve has never been very far from my thoughts.

His self-appointed task could not be said to be completed until fifty years after, when he finished the seventh and supplementary volume of the *Studies*.

Ellis's early steps on this long road were facilitated by a fortunate chance. He came across a copy of George Drysdale's *Elements of Social Science* in the window of a Sydney bookshop. This work was first published in 1854 under the title *Physical, Sexual and Natural Religion*, and had been issued in a third and enlarged edition in the year of Ellis's birth. The book never attracted a great deal of popular attention, and during the lifetime of its author it did not bear his name. Nevertheless, it went quietly from edition to edition, and was translated into every European language. It was an early attempt to face the problems of sex in an honest, scientific, and rational spirit. In spite of some inaccuracies due to its early date, it is a most valuable treatise, and Ellis was indeed lucky to possess it.

But Ellis was by no means entirely occupied with his chosen subjects. His reading included the great novelists of European literature, and *Wilhelm Meister* was his great consolation. He matriculated at Sydney University; and by study and literary exercise laid the foundations of his career as an author. He started the commonplace books which he industriously compiled for ten years, and began writing poetry which he continued until 1885.

The extent to which poets have dedicated their lives to the muses has greatly varied. There are those who are poets before all else, who had steeped themselves in the poetic tradition, and whose highest ambition has been to weave from an essentially literary experience further additions to, and developments of, that tradition. Of such Swinburne, Pound, and Eliot are outstanding examples. At the other end of the scale are men, commoner in less specialized ages than our own, who have been pre-eminently something other than poets, but whose experiences have been so vital that their expression has been forced to assume poetic form. Havelock Ellis is of that order. Many of his sonnets (together with some charming translations of Spanish folk songs) were published in 1925 and some of the sonnets reprinted in 1937. They express the depth and breadth of an apprehension of beauty and form which fired a young man "to maintain the causes of freedom and order" (his own words) in a field where chaos and superstition reigned supreme.

During Ellis's absence abroad he was much influenced by the work of James Hinton, a medical man and philosopher in the line of William Blake, who had died the year that Ellis set foot on

Australian soil. Ellis saw that he, too, must study medicine, and so great was the effect of Hinton's philosophy on his mind that he described it as a "conversion." This is not the place to examine this remarkable psychological phenomenon. We can only compare it with the effect of Spinoza on Goethe, of Wordsworth on J. S. Mill, and of Schopenhauer on Nietzsche; and say that so profound were its repercussions that in no fundamental sense did Ellis develop after 1878. His view of the nature of the universe and of his own place in it was settled when he was nineteen.

This period of exile, solitude, and germination came to an end in 1879 when he returned home. A short novel entitled *Kanga Creek*, written after his return and published in 1922, describes in poetic fashion his life in Australia.

Returning to his home at the age of twenty, he was not unnaturally something of a hero to his mother and four sisters. The subsequent decade up to the publication of his first book in 1890 was a period of intense activity in which it seemed that energy stored up during the previous four years came to flower and fruit.

He managed to secure the means to finance a medical training and worked hard, walking St. Thomas's Hospital for nine years. Here he obtained firsthand knowledge of the evils of poverty, and saw bitter evidence of the need for the spread of birth control among the masses of the people.

The eighties were a time of great social ferment and Ellis moved among the advanced socialist and progressive society of the day. He assisted in the formation of two progressive associations. One of these made a collection of secular hymns for use at their meetings. Ellis made a contribution beginning:

> Onward, brothers, march still onward,
>   March still onward hand in hand;
> Till ye see at last Man's Kingdom,
>   Till ye reach the Promised Land.

Ellis sometimes playfully suggested that this inanity would survive all his other works. The other association, The Fellowship of the New Life, attempted an experiment in communal living; and some of its more politically minded members, including Bernard Shaw, left to found the Fabian Society. It is worthy of note that in spite of activity of this type, Ellis hardly ever gave a lecture or an address in his life.

While Ellis was living in the Australian bush, far away on the Great Karroo of South Africa another genius was maturing. Olive Schreiner, the daughter of a German missionary, grew up in a wild and pioneer environment. She used her leisure and alleviated her solitude by writing novels. By saving her earnings as a governess she was able to come to England in 1881. One of her novels, *The Story of an African Farm*, was published three years later. The book found a responsive reader in Ellis; he wrote to the authoress and soon after they met. The meeting resulted in a relationship which illumined this period of Ellis's life, and continued by correspondence after she returned to South Africa in 1889. It was an intimate association of intense affection which embraced intellectual as well as emotional interests. They worked together and inspired each other; but both agreed that marriage would have been inimical to their careers. After her return, Olive's genius seemed to fade. In 1894 she married an athletic sheep farmer who was Ellis's opposite in every way. In 1917 she distressed Ellis by demanding the return of her letters to him. Ellis set a high literary value on these letters, but in the end he agreed to burn the later ones.

At the beginning of this period Ellis discovered Walt Whitman. He met Edward Carpenter through reading *Towards Democracy* and formed a warm friendship which lasted until Carpenter's death in 1929.

In 1886 Ellis obtained from Henry Vizetelly a commission as general editor of a series of unexpurgated texts of the old English dramatists. The first volume of the Mermaid Series, as it was called, appeared the following year. It consisted of Marlowe's plays and a general introduction by John Addington Symonds. An appendix contained a British Museum manuscript consisting of an information laid against Marlowe by an informer to the Privy Council. Marlowe is charged with a series of highly scandalous, blasphemous, and immoral sayings and views, and the document is generally known as "Marlowe's damnable opinions." It had previously been ignored by writers on Marlowe, and Ellis printed it for the first time. Ellis added a sensible note in which he put forward the suggestion that the information was a crude and ignorant version of acute and audacious utterances actually made by Marlowe and now "substantially held, more or less widely, by students of science and of the Bible in our own days." The "damnable opinions" were the cause of Ellis's experiencing a preliminary brush with the censorial mind. Many people were shocked, and even Swinburne and J. A. Symonds wrote expressing their disapproval. A well-meaning woman protested vigorously against the publication. Vizetelly (without consulting Ellis) replaced several words and phrases by asterisks in subsequent issues of the book, and the booksellers were provided with sets of the new leaves so that they could correct their stock.

The second volume of the series was the plays of Massinger, and Ellis secured the services of Arthur Symons as editor. Symons was a self-educated man of considerable brilliance, and Ellis formed a close friendship with him. A rather typical *fin de siècle* decadent and aesthete he provided a valuable counterpoise to Ellis's excessively idealistic and impractical nature. They traveled together a great deal: to Spain (for which country Ellis conceived a great love), to Russia, and of course to Paris where Ellis met Verlaine, Rodin, Huysmans, Rémy de Gourmont, and other choice spirits.

When the Mermaid Series had run into ten or fifteen volumes, Vizetelly was ruined by the prosecution in 1888 for publishing translations of Zola. Fisher Unwin took over the series, mangled the texts, removed Ellis's name, and dispensed with his further services without explanation or apology. Ellis was more fortunate as editor of the Contemporary Science Series. This series continued until the war of 1914 put an end to it. Many of the volumes were of the highest merit, and a considerable proportion of Ellis's modest income came from this source.

Ellis had resolved not to write a book of his own until he was thirty. According to plan, in 1890 his first book, *The New Spirit*, appeared. The new spirit was the change that had come into the world with the French Revolution, and the book consisted of studies of Diderot, Heine, Whitman, Ibsen, and Tolstoy. The *Spectator* gave him a foretaste of the sort of treatment he might expect from orthodox critics. The notice began: "Mr. Havelock Ellis—if 'Mr.' be the proper title of which we have considerable doubt," and ended, "We cannot imagine anything of which it would be more necessary for human nature to purge itself than the 'New Spirit' of Havelock Ellis."

The same year his *The Criminal*, a study written at white heat in reaction against some of Lombroso's doctrines, appeared.

In 1891, Ellis married Edith Lees, with whom he had been associated in his work for the Fellowship of the New Life and who had acquired a modest literary reputation. Of the exaltations and the corresponding frustrations of that marriage Ellis has told much in his autobiography. He speaks of his wife in these words:

What I experienced with this woman—I feel now many years after her death—was *life*. She was the instrument that brought out all those tones which the older I grow I feel to be of the very essence of life, tones of joy sometimes but oftener of anguish, not happiness. I smile when I find people cheerfully talking of "happiness" as something to be desired in life. I do not know what happiness may be, but it is not life. I have lived. And this woman by her peculiar temperament, by her acute sensibility, by her energy of impulse, by her deep hold of my most sensitive fibres, struck out the notes of joy and anguish which are love and which also are life. For love as I have known it is a passion more of what we call the soul than of the body; unlike the passion that is alone of the flesh, it is a flame that continues to burn even long years after the body that may seem to have inspired it is turned to dust. But it is because I have known love that I have lived and that my life and my work in the world have been one. My work, I am often told, is cool and serene, entirely reasonable and free of passion, but without that devouring passion of the soul my work would have been nothing.

I speak of a flame. Yet when I inhale the scent of a flower this woman loved, or gaze on a picture or a book that meant much to her, I am wrapped away from the world and caught up into another sky. I realize what are the only things in life that have any value for us and I know—what all our science as well as our art has so often asserted—that the so-called "realities" are nothing, that it is the things that are made of space and time, out of emptiness, our symbols and our pictures, that are alone the eternal things.

The marriage made no difference to his friendship with Arthur Symons. The Ellises had agreed not to live continuously under the same roof, and Havelock spent a good deal of his time sharing rooms with Symons in the Temple, at Fountain Court. Symons was editing *The Savoy*, the rival of *The Yellow Book*, and Ellis contributed an article on Zola. This, together with studies of Nietzsche, Casanova, Huysmans, and St. Francis of Assisi, was published under the title *Affirmations* in 1897.

All this time Ellis had been collecting material for his great work. In 1894 he published a preparatory volume entitled *Man and Woman*. The manner in which he started off the *Studies* was to a large extent fortuitous. John Addington Symonds had always been interested in the subject of sexual inversion. Although the prudery of the time forbade him doing justice to this theme in the works on classical and Renaissance literature which made his name famous, he had privately published two essays on the subject. As a result of his association with Ellis over the Marlowe volume, he proposed that they should collaborate in a full-size work. Ellis was naturally flattered, and decided to make the book Volume I of his *Studies in the Psychology of Sex*.

From the beginning, the book, entitled *Sexual Inversion*, was ill-fated. A few months after Symonds had made his contribution to the joint work he died. The Wilde case made rational discussion of homosexuality in England even more difficult than ever. Failing an English publisher, the book appeared in German from Leipzig in 1896. The great value of the book lay not so much in any original suggestion or discovery as in the example it gave of patient and scientific treatment. The detailed case histories it contained were an important addition to knowledge. They were the first British cases unconnected with asylums or prisons ever recorded.

The difficulties of publishing the original English version drove Ellis in all innocence to a publisher who was far from satisfactory, the pseudonymous "Dr. Roland de Villiers," an engaging but shady character. No sooner had the book come from the press than Symonds's literary executor, his old friend Horatio Brown, forbade the use of his name and material. So the edition had to be withdrawn and another with only Ellis's name and contribution printed.

The great calamity that overtook *Sexual Inversion* and its author arose, however, from a quite fortuitous connection with a body known as the Legitimation League. The League's main object was the obtaining of legal status for illegitimate children, but it was naturally interested in the principle of divorce by mutual consent and other sexual problems. The secretary of the League was a certain George Bedborough who also edited its monthly organ *The Adult*. The League had obtained a great deal of notoriety because adherence to its tenets had seemed in the eyes of two doctors sufficient evidence for certifying a young lady as a lunatic. An appeal to the Commissioners in Lunacy by the not unnaturally outraged League had secured her release and initiated a "boom" in its activities. So much so, that the respectable began to agitate for its suppression and Sir Theodore Martin (biographer of the Prince Consort and author of *Queen Victoria as I Knew Her*), in a letter which appeared in the press on December 20, 1897, suggested that "the strong hand of the law should crush a teaching which would turn Society into groups of harlots." Detectives began to attend the League's meetings. Bedborough's flat, the living room of which he used as the League's office, was watched in the hope of raiding a homosexual orgy.

Ellis became involved in this situation because his publisher handled *The Adult* and in consequence the League had copies of *Sexual Inversion* on sale. The police were interested in "de Villiers" for reasons connected with swindling and company promoting, and the authorities were only too glad of an opportunity to kill two birds with one stone.

On May 27 a detective bought a copy of *Sexual Inversion* from Bedborough and he was shortly afterward arrested and charged with "publishing an obscene libel." Certain copies of *The Adult* were also alleged to be obscene, as well as a print of a lecture delivered at one of the League's meetings. The character of "de Villiers" provides the only vestige of excuse or explanation for the attack on the book. Ellis had no connection with either Bedborough or the League and he had not contributed to *The Adult*.

The prosecution raised a storm of indignation and a Defense Committee was formed which included Robert Buchanan, Shaw, J. M. Robertson, George Moore, and Edward Carpenter. A circular was drawn up and sent all over the country. A fund was raised and Horace Avory briefed for the defense.

The case was due for trial at the Central Criminal Court on October 30, 1898, and the stage was set for a grand vindication of the principle of freedom, but at the eleventh hour Bedborough, who had been released on bail, lost his nerve. Without consulting the Defense Committee or the lawyers they had engaged he went to Scotland Yard and made his peace. He was promised complete immunity if he pleaded guilty to the substantial part of the charges in regard to both Ellis's book and *The Adult*. On the great day he appeared in court without counsel and carried out his part of the bargain. Counsel for the prosecution rose and said that, as a result of the defendant's voluntary confession and the assistance he had given the police in their inquiries, the authorities were satisfied that his position was an entirely subordinate one in regard to the publications complained of. He had undertaken to sever himself from all such traffic and from the Legitimation League. The prosecution therefore desired no more than that he should be bound over. Sir Charles Hall, the Recorder, assented to this suggestion and in giving judgment allowed himself to address the following remarks to Bedborough:

You have acted wisely for it would have been impossible for you to have contended with any possibility whatever of being able to persuade anybody that this book, this lecture, and this magazine were not filthy and obscene works.

I am willing to believe that in acting as you did, you might at the first outset perhaps have been gulled into the belief that somebody might say that this was a scientific work. But it is impossible for anybody with a head on his shoulders to open the book without seeing that it is a pretence and a sham, and that it is merely entered into for the purpose of selling this obscene publication.

The result will be this—that so long as you do not touch this filthy work again with your hands and so long as you lead a respectable life, you will hear no more of this.

John Sweeney, the detective who was in charge of the case, gives an amusing and simple-minded account of it in *At Scotland Yard*. He is very pleased with himself:

From the date of Bedborough's trial, five years ago, until now, no one has ever attempted to resuscitate the Legitimation League, and I think I may claim some credit for having carefully handled a delicate case, full of pitfalls, where the least slip would have meant one of two things—the growth of a Frankenstein monster wrecking the marriage laws of our country, and perhaps carrying off the general respect for all laws; or, on the other hand, of raising about the ears of the authorities a shriek of popular objection to our interference with the rights of free speech.

The day after the trial the *Daily Chronicle*, of which Henry Massingham was editor, came out with a leader that while giving Ellis credit for "scientific intentions" substantially supported the Recorder. Ellis in *My Life* comments as follows:

Law and the Press were indeed well matched, and between them they thought that they had dismissed me and my book from the world. Yet I—rather the spirit of Man I chanced to embody—have overcome the world. My "filthy" and "worthless" and "morbid" book has been translated into all the greatest living languages to reach people who could not say what a Recorder is, nor read the *Daily Chronicle* even if they saw it. Unto this day it continues to bring me from many lands the reverent and grateful words of strangers whose praise keeps me humble in the face of the supreme mystery of life.

Shortly afterward copies of another volume of the *Studies* were seized and an order made by the Watford magistrates for them to be "burnt." It is said that this really meant that the books were distributed among police officers who were thus in a position to study them with a view to dealing with similar books. Dean Inge made a little *auto-da-fé* on his own. He boasted to the readers of the *Evening Standard*:[1] "I bought the first and second volumes, and burnt them."

"Roland de Villiers" we may note came to a bad end. Subsequently arrested, he died in custody. The coroner's inquest found a verdict of death from apoplexy but it is believed that he poisoned himself melodramatically from a ring he carried with him.

Walter M. Gallichan gives some interesting information about the Watford case:

At the second indictment of Havelock Ellis's works, one of my own books, *Chapters on Human Love*, written in 1898 under the pen-name "Geoffrey Mortimer," was seized by the police, and an order was made by the Watford magistrates that it should be destroyed. This book would now be considered old-fashioned in its reticence and propriety. I may remark here that the prohibition created a considerable demand for this volume, and that a London bookseller, who by some occult means obtained copies, sold them at two guineas each. For some years I often saw the title of my con-demned book among the list of "wanted" in second-hand book-sellers' catalogues. Had the volume been sold unmolested in the ordinary way, and at ten shillings, the original price, it would have probably attracted very little notice.[2]

An English translation of Charles Féré's *La Pathologie des Emotions* was condemned at the same time.

The prosecutions in relation to the first two volumes of *Studies in the Psychology of Sex* of course made the publication in England of subsequent volumes impossible. Happily publication in the United States was not interfered with though imports of the German edition were stopped. Volume after volume appeared in America and Germany and copies percolated all over the world, even into Great Britain. At last the sixth volume was published in 1910. In his pocket diary for August 7 of the previous year, Ellis recorded the completion of the manuscript by a quotation from the great Elizabethan, George Chapman: "The work that I was born to do is done."

In the postscript to the great work he comments with restraint and nobility on the persecution to which he was subjected in the land of his birth:

I supposed that such a student was at all events secure from any gross form of attack on the part of the police or the government under whose protection he imagined that he lived. That proved to be a mistake. When only one volume of these *Studies* had been written and published in England, a prosecution instigated by the government put an end to the sale of that volume in England and led me to resolve that the subsequent volumes should not be published in my own country. I do not complain. I am grateful for the early and generous sympathy with which my work was received in Germany and the United States, and I recognize that it has had a wider circulation, both in English, and the other chief languages of the world, than would have been possible by the modest method of issue which the government of my own country induced me to abandon. Nor has the effort to crush my work resulted in any change in that work by so much as a single word. With help, or without help, I have followed my own path to the end.

For it so happens that I come on both sides of my house from stocks of Englishmen who, nearly three hundred years ago, had encountered just these same difficulties and dangers before. In the seventeenth century, indeed, the battle was around the problem of religion, as today it is around the problem of sex. Since I have of late years realized this analogy I have often thought of certain admirable and obscure men who were driven out, robbed, and persecuted, some by the Church because the spirit of Puritanism moved within them, some by the Puritans because they clung to the ideals of the Church, yet both alike quiet and unflinching, both alike fighting for causes of freedom or of order in a field which has now for ever been won. That victory has often seemed of good augury to the perhaps degenerate child of these men who has today sought to maintain the causes of freedom and of order in another field.

It is important to appreciate that Ellis was able to carry on with his work only by taking advantages of the legal diversities caused by nationalist divisions. The evils caused by these divisions have been greatly stressed of recent times. But we must not lose sight of the fact that freedom sometimes flourishes through diversity and lack of logic. One of the minor aims of the League of Nations (in which it was more successful than in the pursuit of its major aims) was the uniform enforcement of obscenity laws all over the world. The success of this aim would have rendered the remedy that was open to Ellis in his trouble no longer effective.

Ellis regarded the sixth volume of the *Studies* as completing his task. The twenty years between his first book and this sixth volume may be said to be the summer of his life. At fifty Ellis experienced a curious impression of premature old age. This impression was enhanced by the failure of his wife's health in 1915 and her death in the following year. In fact, in 1909 Ellis had thirty years of life before him; but these years must be regarded as his autumn. But they were a prolific autumn. Besides a seventh and supplementary volume to the *Studies*, published in 1926, he produced a mass of other work. He wrote *Little Essays of Love and Virtue* in 1922 for the youths and girls whose welfare was always before his mind when engaged on the more difficult *Studies*. In 1928 he summarized his philosophy in *The Dance of Life*, and in 1934 he published an introductory textbook entitled *The Psychology of Sex*.

During the autumn of his life he was rewarded by acknowledgment of his merits and international fame. The Royal College of Physicians, to their credit, made a tardy tribute to his lifelong devotion to scholarship by making him a Fellow. But no English university, it is worthy of note, honored itself by honoring him. The appraisement of a foreigner is often more significant than that of a fellow countryman. This is what H. L. Mencken, the distinguished American critic, said[3] about Ellis:

If the test of the personal culture of a man be the degree of freedom from banal ideas and childish emotions which move the great masses of men, then Havelock Ellis is undoubtedly the most civilized Englishman of his generation.

He is a man of the soundest and widest learning, but it is not his positive learning that gives him distinction; it is his profound and implacable scepticism, his penetrating eye for the transient the disingenuous and the shoddy. So unconditioned a scepticism, it must be plain, is not an English habit. The average Englishman of science, though he may challenge the Continentals within his specialty, is only too apt to sink to the level of a politician, a greengrocer, or a suburban clergyman outside it. The examples of Wallace, Crookes, and Lodge are anything but isolated. Scratch an English naturalist and you are likely to discover a spiritualist; take an English metaphysician to where the band is playing, and if he begins to snuffle patriotically you need not be surprised. The late war uncovered this weakness in a wholesale manner.

In 1938 Havelock Ellis suffered a severe illness. Although he recovered he seemed to realize that the end was not far off, and he employed the small measure of his recovered health and strength in setting his affairs in order.

One task was the disposal of his extensive collection of books. I write "collection of books" rather than "library" because Havelock Ellis had little of the bibliophile about him. Although he possessed hundreds of volumes from all over the world, he appeared to care little for books as books. He kept them in no formal order, but relied on his remarkable memory to guide him to any reference he required. It was in connection with this disposal that I was privileged to see something of him during the following year, when his health made him more of a recluse than ever. He asked me to help in disposing of his rarer sexological books, and in carrying out his wishes with regard to some hundred volumes I had to visit him both at his house at Herne Hill and at his country cottage near Haywards Heath. Soon after, he gave up both places and retired to Suffolk, a county in which many of his forebears had spent their lives. The hope that he would there enjoy a long and tranquil evening to his life was unhappily disappointed and he died on Saturday, July 8, 1939.

I had met him previously in connection with my own work, and received most generous assistance including loans of books and little gifts of pamphlets. His last kindness to me was an autographed copy of his poems.

During these last years, his bodily weakness did not impair the interest of his conversation. Over lunch one sunny day at Haywards Heath he recalled his childhood, and how he once stole pennies to buy pears, his favorite fruit. On another occasion he talked about his voyages, ending up by saying: "I liked the sailing ships best." He spoke very sadly of Edward Carpenter's last days of infirmity, and mentioned that Mrs. Ellis used to go and stay with him, adding (characteristically): "But I would never stay away anywhere." He once complained that the French translation of his great work was a little too light in tone. I ventured to observe that it was difficult to be unduly solemn about love in the French tongue.

There was no trace of "anecdotage" in his talk. He showed a

keen appreciation of present trends and controversies. Only about the Surrealists he once shook his head in a puzzled way and said: "They are beyond me." He displayed not the least bitterness with regard to the indignities to which his work had been subjected, but seemed to have a simple and complete faith in the ultimate triumph of reason and intellectual freedom.

Humbug and misrepresentation pursued Ellis to the grave. *The Times* obituary represented him as first and foremost an essayist and critic "who will also be remembered for his pioneer work in the psychology of sex." His sexological work and the trial which was such an important event in his life were only dealt with in small print in the lower part of the column. In point of fact, his essays and criticisms, elegant and stimulating as they are, were the by-products of his great work and of his courageous and unflinching demand for order and reason in a field which was still taboo to the columnists of *The Times*.

The Times Literary Supplement of October 4, 1940, devoted several columns to the centenary of J. A. Symonds's birth without mentioning Symonds's connection with Ellis over his work on inversion. Elsewhere, throughout the press of the world his greatness and his triumphs received their due meed of appreciation.

I have dealt with Havelock Ellis at some length in order to show what manner of man it was that the law of obscene libel chose for its most distinguished victim; and what manner of work it was in which the English legal profession could see nothing but pornographic abnormality.

The Victorian anti-sex obsession of which the persecution of this great man was the supreme manifestation resulted in a lopsided and frustrating pattern of social progress. During the nineteenth century the more enlightened members of all classes learned to think for themselves about religion, politics, and economics. This spread of liberalism had results in the amelioration of social injustice and in the improvement of physical, educational, and cultural opportunity for the people. But in regard to sexual conduct, and the vast social questions related thereto, society was in no appreciable degree freed from primitive taboos and their evil consequences.

The New Century in England

W ITH THE TURN OF THE CENTURY the façade of Victorian propriety began to crumble under the impact of new ideas. The plays of Ibsen were affecting educated people's ideas about the relation of the sexes, and English people gradually became acquainted with Freud's work although the great *Die Traumdeutung*, published in 1900, did not appear in English until 1913. H. G. Wells was introducing emancipated ideas to the novel-reading public and Bernard Shaw was doing the same for London theater audiences. Even women novelists like Elinor Glyn, Victoria Cross, and Marie Corelli allowed themselves a breadth of subject matter and a frankness of expression which would not have been permitted to their Victorian sisters.

Political radicalism and religious skepticism, however, still continued to be chary of squarely facing the sexual problems of the age. Even leaders of popular thought such as Shaw and Wells were discreet and evasive when they came to deal with the sexual aspects of reform. If they advocated changes in sexual ethics the reform was reserved, either explicitly or by implication, for some utopian future. The result of this tendency was that young men and women who grew up in the formative years of the present century became obsessed with the solution of economic and political problems as the means of ushering in the better world that was so confidently predicted by liberal prophets. The equally fundamental problems concerning population, eugenics, birth control, marriage, the family, and sex education were sidetracked, or if considered at all, considered without subjecting the assumptions of orthodox opinion to the searching analysis which was breaking it down in other spheres.

Naturally, the mind of officialdom and established authority conformed very slowly to the changing climate of taste. Augustine Birrell, a literary critic of eminence who became President of the Board of Education in 1906, is typical of the mentality all too frequently found in the men who were coming to positions of power and influence in Parliament, on the bench, and the world of the press. His finicky and asexual attitude to life is exemplified by his treatment of Dean Swift in *Essays about Men, Women and Books* (1894):

No fouler pen than Swift's has soiled our literature. His language is horrible from first to last. He is full of odious images, of base and abominable allusions. It would be a labour of Hercules to cleanse his pages. His love-letters are defaced by his incurable coarseness. This habit of his is so inveterate that it seems a miracle he kept his sermons free from blackguard phrases. It is a question not of morality, but of decency, whether it is becoming to sit in the same room with the works of this divine. How the good Sir Walter ever managed to see him through the Press is amazing. In this matter Swift is inexcusable.

Elinor Glyn's flamboyant novels were never attacked under the criminal law in England, but the popularity of *Three Weeks* (1907), a tale of very high romance in very high society, was the occasion of a dangerous intrusion of the conception of literary obscenity into the civil law. This best-seller was widely admired and equally widely condemned. The furor attracted imitators and parodists. In 1915 a film crudely burlesquing the novel appeared and the authoress sued for infringement of copyright. She lost the action, and in the course of his judgment Mr. Justice Younger said:

But there is another, and from the public point of view, a much more important aspect of this case which in my judgment entirely debars the plaintiff from obtaining relief in this court. The episode described in the plaintiff's novel, which she alleges has been pirated by the defendants, is, in my opinion, grossly immoral both in its essence, its treatment and its tendency. Stripped of its trappings which are mere accident, it is nothing more nor less than a sensual, adulterous intrigue. . . . It is enough for me to say that to a book of such a cruelly destructive tendency no protection will be extended by a court of equity.

This judge-made doctrine that there can be no right of property in "obscene" matter still holds, though little has been heard of it of late. Insurance companies, however, can and do refuse to pay claims under fire and similar policies if their assessors find evidence that "insured books and pictures can be stigmatized as legally obscene."

"Indecent literature" was included in the terms of reference of the Joint Select Committee on Lotteries and Indecent Advertisements of 1908. The minutes of the Committee contain a lot of evidence about the trade in pornography going on at the time including details of the activities of "Roland de Villiers" and Charles Carrington. In their report the Committee recommended an overhaul of the law of obscenity in the form of a comprehensive statute under which all offenses would be dealt with summarily. They expressly recommended that a provision should be inserted in the statute exempting from its operation any book of literary merit or reputation or any genuine work of art. Nothing came of these recommendations.

The National Vigilance Association continued its activities and in 1908 at its instigation the Government prosecuted Messrs. John Long for publishing a novel entitled *The Yoke* by Hubert Wales. The book must have been considered "advanced" at the time since it tells the story of a woman who becomes the lover of the son of her deceased fiancé and contains a good deal of propagandist moralizing. The case was settled by the publisher agreeing to stop publication and a destruction order was made.

In 1910 a Scotland Yard detective called on John Lane, the publisher of an English translation of Hermann Sudermann's *Das Hohe Lied*, who agreed to withdraw the book from publication. It tells at great length the story of a prostitute who does not come to a bad end.

After the outbreak of World War I the authorities attacked a publisher who did not prove so amenable to their attacks. In 1915 an emissary from Scotland Yard called on Mr. (now Sir) Stanley Unwin, who had taken over Edward Carpenter's books, the early publishing troubles of which we have already noticed. The officer was carrying one of the books which had been published for seven years (it was *The Intermediate Sex* in which certain passages were marked). He explained that these passages were objected to and asked whether the book would be withdrawn. Mr. Unwin pointed out among other things that the author had only recently received from nearly all the leading literary people in the country a most wonderful testimonial on the occasion of his birthday. He was particularly puzzled by one passage which was doubly underlined, and it transpired in a subsequent interview at Scotland Yard that the official had completely misunderstood it. He at once admitted the mistake and added that he was dealing with so much "evil" that he tended to see it where it did not exist. Nothing happened in this case and the book continues to be sold to this day, but with a less courageous publisher things might well have been different. Sir Stanley Unwin comments:

They were taking anonymous complaints much too seriously and had succeeded with some publishers in getting books suppressed without anyone hearing about it, a great grievance, by the way, for the authors, who were surely entitled to be heard.[1]

D. H. Lawrence, James Joyce, and Others

D. H. LAWRENCE, who started his career as a novelist in 1911, became one of the most distinguished victims of the "censor-morons" as he called them. Although his first novel *The White Peacock* appeared in the integral text in America, his British publishers, William Heinemann Ltd., required him to make a last-minute alteration after the book had been printed.[1]

The Rainbow, perhaps the most important of his novels, was severely handled. It was first published on September 30, 1915, by Methuen and Co., and was greeted with some clamor in the press in which the voices of James Douglas and Clement Shorter were loudly heard. On November 14 the publishers were summoned before Sir John Dickinson at Bow Street under Lord Campbell's Act to show cause why 1,011 copies of the book should not be destroyed as obscene. They offered no defense and consequently a destruction order was made.[2]

Lawrence was not even notified of the case and the suppression was a heavy blow to him financially at a time when he was already in low water. In spite of representations in the House of Commons he could obtain no redress. He and his friends believed that the real reason for the prosecution was his denunciation of the war.[3] The book was reprinted in America in 1916 but did not reappear in Great Britain until 1926. These and subsequent editions are expurgated.

Lawrence said he would have been better pleased if the novel had not been reprinted and only the surviving copies of the condemned text had remained.[4] Penguin Books, however, published the integral text in 1949.[5]

Another important novel by D. H. Lawrence, *Lady Chatterley's Lover* (about which more will be said later) was published from Florence in 1929. The version which appeared in Great Britain and America was heavily expurgated.

In January 1929 two sealed and registered packets sent by Lawrence from Bandol in France to his publishers in England were seized by the British postal authorities. One packet contained his introduction[6] to a volume of reproductions of his paintings subsequently issued by P. R. Stephenson under the imprint of the Mandrake Press. The other contained the manuscript of Lawrence's collection of poems *Pansies*. Both packets were detained for some time, but eventually, after questions had been asked in the House of Commons, they were delivered.

The poems were accompanied with a recommendation that fourteen[7] of them should be omitted on publication. This recommendation was complied with by the publisher concerned and the censored poems have never appeared openly in Great Britain or America. The complete collection with a special introduction by the author was, however, published privately in London and reprinted on the Continent. This time the publicity given to the book by the censor-morons was of financial benefit to Lawrence.

Later in 1929 Lawrence's paintings were shown at Dorothy Warren's art gallery in London. After the exhibition had been open for a few weeks it was raided by the police. Thirteen of the twenty-five pictures on show were seized together with four copies of the volume of reproductions already mentioned. The persons responsible for the exhibition, Mr. and Mrs. Philip Trotter, appeared before the octogenarian Mr. Mead at Marlborough Street police court to show cause why the seizures should not be destroyed as obscene. The case was adjourned *sine die* with costs against the defendants on their undertaking to withdraw the thirteen pictures, and the volumes of reproductions were ordered to be destroyed.

In *Pornography and Obscenity*[8] Lawrence writes:

When the police raided my picture show, they did not in the least know what to take. So they took every picture where the smallest bit of the sex organ of either man or woman showed. Quite regardless of subject or meaning or anything else: they would allow anything, these dainty policemen in a picture show, except the actual sight of a fragment of the human pudenda. This was the police text. The dabbing on of a postage stamp—especially a green one that could be called a leaf—would in most cases have been quite sufficient to satisfy this "public opinion."

This pamphlet is a passionate rejoinder to all the persecution to which he was subjected by "the grey ones," as he called them:

This is one of the disasters of young life today. Personally, and among themselves, a great many, perhaps a majority of the young people of today have come out into the open with sex and laid salt on the tail of the dirty little secret. And this is a very good thing. But in public, in the social world, the young are still entirely under the shadow of the grey elderly ones. The grey elderly ones belong to the last century, the eunuch century, the century of the mealy-mouthed lie, the century that has tried to destroy humanity, the nineteenth century. All our grey ones are left over from this century. And they rule us. They rule us with the grey, mealy-mouthed, canting lie of that great century of lies which, thank God, we are drifting away from. But they rule us still with the lie, for the lie, in the name of the lie. And they are too heavy and too numerous, the grey ones. It doesn't matter what government it is. They are all grey ones, left over from the last century, the century of mealy-mouthed liars, the century of purity and the dirty little secret.

The British Customs authorities played their part in the persecution to which James Joyce was subjected and which he so stubbornly resisted. His *Ulysses* was first published by Sylvia Beach under the imprint of Shakespeare and Company. The edition of 1,000 copies was printed in Dijon and distributed from Paris to subscribers all over the world.

A second edition of 2,000 copies, also printed in Dijon, was pub-

lished in October 1922 by Harriet Weaver[9] under the imprint of
the Egoist Press and distributed to individual purchasers, bookshops, and agents. A number of packing cases full of copies reached
London safely. I made my first acquaintance with the afterward
familiar large volume with its Greek blue-and-white lettered cover
in Bagdad about this time. Another 500 copies were printed by Miss
Weaver in January 1923. One of these was sent to London; the remaining 499 were seized at Folkestone harbor under the Customs
Act of 1867 and burned in "the King's Chimney" before Miss
Weaver, who hurried to their rescue, could take any legal action.

Sylvia Beach continued to reprint the book, which was in con-
stant demand, especially by tourists in Paris. Any copies found in the
baggage of passengers arriving at British ports were seized, and
the book was persistently pursued in England. A broadcast about
the book was canceled after letters of protest from Alfred Noyes
and James Blackwood, who was President of the Publishers' Association at the time, had appeared in *The Times*. When Lord Birken-
head died in 1930, Alfred Noyes in collaboration with Lord Darling
secured the withdrawal of a sumptuously bound copy from the auc-
tion sale of the deceased's effects. Later, fear of the law prevented
Sotheby's from selling the corrected proofs in London.[10] Nevertheless the book was freely discussed in literary circles and the universities, and a number of unbanned books were written about it. As
more and more copies were smuggled into the country the blue volume became a familiar sight on the shelves of private libraries.

The sorry farce of banning went on until 1933, when after the
book had been cleared of obscenity by the American courts its publication in England was quietly ignored by the authorities. An edition was issued in 1960 at twenty-five shillings—a fairly normal
price for a book of its size.

Unofficial censorship, however, still pursues Joyce. A 1960 recording in the Caedmon Records Literary Series of the soliloquies of
Molly and Leopold Bloom, characters in *Ulysses*, was bowdlerized
without any indication of the fact being given by the publishers of
the record.[11]

After World War I the law of literary obscenity did not confine
its attention to Lawrence and Joyce. Freudian ideas about sex be-

came widely known and even popularized, and as a consequence open and intelligent discussion of sexual problems, including those related to abnormalities, gradually became possible. As usual, however, the attitude of authority was slow to adapt itself to the new atmosphere. In 1921 a serious psychoanalytic study entitled *The Autobiography of a Child* by an anonymous author was condemned under the Act of 1857.

Sir Archibald Bodkin, who was Director of Public Prosecutions from 1920 to 1930, was an outstandingly obscurantist official. In 1921 the house of George Allen and Unwin published an English translation of *A Young Girl's Diary* which Sigmund Freud had recommended for its psychological interest and usefulness. In an interview with Mr. (now Sir) Stanley Unwin[12] he described the book as "filth" and took particular exception to an entry in which the diarist describes how she witnessed an act of sexual intercourse from a window in a room opposite. The incident, which profoundly affected her outlook on sex, is essential to the whole book. The Director agreed not to prosecute only if booksellers ordering the book, which was already restricted to the legal, medical, and educational professions, were required to supply the name, address, and occupation of their customer.

In 1923 an International Conference for the Suppression of Obscene Publications was held at Geneva under the auspices of the League of Nations. Sir Archibald, who represented Great Britain, quickly made his crusading spirit felt. When the delegates had all assembled, a Greek speaker tentatively suggested that it might be desirable to define the meaning of the word "obscene" in order that they might know what they were talking about. Sir Archibald rose and made objection. He pointed out that there was no such definition in English statute law and persuaded the conference that no definition was possible. He also boasted that the English law was so wide in regard to what constituted publication that he had got two people into prison for merely exchanging indecent books and pictures between themselves.[13]

In 1922 Frank Harris published his *Life and Loves* from France and, ever since, the Customs and postal authorities have been much exercised to keep the autobiography of this amusing old sexual braggadocio from being read in Britain. It is of interest to note that in his *Bernard Shaw* the author relates that a copy was burned in the Shaw household because Mrs. Shaw did not care to have it lying about the house for her servants to read, and Shaw did not scruple to acquaint Harris of the fact, to the latter's pain and indignation—surely curious conduct on the part of one who was so indignant about stage censorship. But Shaw was somewhat of a puritan who could not, for example, really stomach *Ulysses*.

A number of remarkable literary court cases occurred during the Home Secretaryship of Sir William Joynson-Hicks from 1924 to 1929. He was a notorious puritan jokingly known as "Jix," and during his tenure of office it was not difficult for busybodies to stimulate official action against books that offended their sense of propriety.

In 1926 Messrs. Chatto & Windus published a sequel to Shane Leslie's *The Oppidan* (1922) entitled *The Cantab*. The book attracted the censure of the Roman Catholic bishops, and the author, a devout member of the Church, withdrew it from publication. This did not, however, prevent a prosecution and copies were solemnly destroyed. Of this book the late E. S. P. Haynes wrote:

There were two passages—one rather disgusting about a rape which could not have excited anyone—and the other about an encounter with a lady who wore some very precious jewel in her navel. That struck me as bizarre but not indecent.[14]

The author submissively prepared a second edition in which the incriminated passages were innocuously overwritten, and he destroyed the manuscript of an unpublished sequel. When the final volume of the trilogy appeared as *The Anglo-Catholic*, in 1929, it was a very different work. Since Shane Leslie had attacked *Ulysses* on religious and moral grounds[15] there was perhaps some poetic justice in the fate meted out to his own work.

It was principally through *The Well of Loneliness* case that "Jix" became famous or infamous. This novel by Radclyffe Hall is a very restrained and reasonable plea for the toleration of female homosexuality. When it was published in England by Jonathan Cape in the summer of 1928, it was highly praised by responsible critics but the popular press was very upset. James Douglas in the *Sunday Ex-*

press for August 19, 1928, adopting the false analogy used long ago by Lord Campbell, declared that he would rather put a phial of prussic acid in the hands of a healthy girl or boy than the book in question. Later, a consignment of copies published by the Pegasus Press in Paris was seized by the British Customs and both publishers were summoned under Lord Campbell's Act to show cause why the book should not be destroyed as obscene.

The case came before Sir Chartres Biron at Bow Street on November 9, 1928, and the defendants put up a full-dress defense and were prepared to call men of letters, ministers of religion, social workers, magistrates, and doctors as expert witnesses. They were all, however, rejected by the magistrates. It is said that had he admitted their evidence the prosecution would have produced another array on the opposite side. It is certain that "Jix" suggested to the new Archbishop of Canterbury, Cosmo Lang, that he should ask Hensley Henson, the Bishop of Durham, to testify against the book. The invitation was accordingly made but declined.[16] The magistrate condemned the book, and an appeal to quarter sessions under the chairmanship of the aged Sir Robert Wallace was unsuccessful. The *Manchester Guardian* of November 22 contained a letter of protest signed by a number of distinguished authors, including Bernard Shaw, Rose Macaulay, John Buchan, Arnold Bennett, Lytton Strachey, and Laurence Binyon. The book was republished in 1949 and it has been left unmolested.

The next year a reviewer sent his copy of a novel entitled *Sleeveless Errand* by Norah C. James, the publicity and advertising manager of Jonathan Cape, to the Home Secretary. In consequence the police seized copies at the premises of the publisher, Eric Partridge of the Scholartis Press, who was summoned to show cause why the book should not be destroyed. In the meantime, glowing reviews of the novel appeared in the Sunday press. The story concerned two young people, typical of the twenties, who had been hurt in love and formed a suicide pact. It was difficult to understand what was objected to except the use of some expressions like "bloody," "balls," and "poor little bugger." It has been suggested that personal motives played a part in the prosecution.[17] The case was heard at Bow Street on March 3, and Sir Archibald Bodkin, as Director of Public Prosecutions, was present. In spite of a vigorous defense the book was condemned. It was subsequently published by the Obelisk Press and (with the deletion of only three words) in America. It has been translated into many languages; but it has never been republished in Britain.

The reign of prudery for which Sir William Joynson-Hicks was partially responsible made the publishers of the most reputable authors very nervous. Richard Aldington is an example of a novelist affected by this situation. The prefatory note to his first novel, *Death of a Hero* (1929), a powerful delineation of the tragedy of World War I, is illuminating:

This novel in print differs in some particulars from the same book in manuscript. To my astonishment, my publishers informed me that certain words, phrases, sentences, and even passages, are at present taboo in England. I have recorded nothing which I have not observed in human life, said nothing I do not believe to be true. I had not the slightest intention of appealing to anyone's salacious instincts; if I had wanted to do that I should have chosen a theme less seriously tragic. But I am bound to accept the opinion of those who are better acquainted with popular feelings than I am. At my request the publishers are removing what they considered objectionable, and are placing asterisks to show where omissions have been made. If anything "objectionable" remains, the responsibility is, of course, mine. In my opinion it is better for the book to appear mutilated than for me to say what I don't believe.

En attendant mieux.

R.A.

An integral text was published in Paris.

Later, Mr. Aldington wrote to me as follows:

Each of my novels has been more or less mutilated in the interests of prudery by my English publishers. I don't in the least blame them, they are only doing what I should do in their position, i.e., trying to guard themselves against the working of a law which is vaguely worded and capriciously administered. Recently the United States have permitted authors much more liberty. For which reason I shall henceforth issue the complete text of my books in America, and with indifference allow the English to make what cuts their absurd prejudices demand.

Potocki of Montalk

Soon after the passing from their respective offices of Sir William Joynson-Hicks and Sir Archibald Bodkin, a sensational obscenity case brought home to the public the fantastic lengths to which the law of obscene libel could be stretched.

On January 13, 1932, two young men went up to a constable on duty outside the Old Bailey. They wanted to know where they could find a typesetter who would set up some spicy poems containing two of the most taboo words in the English language. Shakespeare makes play with the French equivalents of the words in question in the English lesson which Katherine receives prior to her marriage with Henry V. The constable did not appear to be shocked by their enunciation in plain English, and directed the inquirers to a nearby printing house. Either through ignorance or through puckishness on the policeman's part, this direction was not altogether satisfactory. The two prospective customers were politely bowed out with an apologetic "I'm afraid we couldn't undertake a job of that sort, sir," and the firm subsequently turned out to be the printers of the *Methodist Recorder*.

The two young men then continued lightheartedly on their way to find a more accommodating establishment. Before following them further, however, it would be well to make their closer acquaintance. One, Mr. Douglas Glass, need not detain us as he soon passes from the stage of the tragicomedy of which these seemingly trivial incidents were the prelude. His companion, however, was the protagonist of the drama—Count Geoffrey Wladislas Vaile Potocki of Montalk. He wore a voluminous wine-red cloak and leather sandals, and his long hair fell over his shoulders. These personal details are worthy of notice because they have a bearing on his subsequent misfortunes. His appearance could only create prejudice in the drab surroundings of modern London and in the gray minds of its rulers. His opinions are as remarkable as his apparel. Born in New Zealand, the son of an architect and the grandson of a Polish professor, he was educated for the law but deserted it to assert his claims to be a poet by divine right and King of Poland by heredity. Proclaiming himself pagan by religion, he edited and produced a periodical called the *Right Review* which maintained a royalist antidemocratic position of the most extreme kind.

At the end of their quest Montalk and Mr. Glass found themselves in conversation with a Mr. de Lozey, the manager of a firm of linotype operators. Montalk produced the manuscript of five short poems which he wished to have set up in linotype so that he could print copies on a hand press at home for circulation among his friends. Mr. de Lozey examined the manuscript and said that the price would be 25s. Montalk considered this too high. The discussion seems to have broadened to a consideration of *Lady Chatterley's Lover* and *Ulysses*, on the merits of which Mr. Glass delivered himself at some length, and added some expression of anti-Semitic opinion. The manager did not appear at all shocked but he seems to have become annoyed. In the end it was arranged that the manuscript should be left with him and that Montalk would return with the money if he could not get the job done cheaper elsewhere. He and Mr. Glass then left the place.

The next thing they knew of the affair was that they were both arrested and thrown into Brixton Prison. The manager had shown the manuscript to the police after his prospective customers had gone.

Now what of this manuscript? I have already indicated that it contained words that, though used by Chaucer and other masters of English, had fallen out of decent literary usage until the recent efforts of Lawrence and Joyce to restore them to respectability. But a rather closer examination is necessary to appreciate the subsequent development of this case. This examination is possible because the manuscript was pirated during the proceedings and unauthorized copies are not uncommon.[1]

Of the five poems, the last is easiest to dispose of. It is a translation of Rabelais's *Chanson de la Braguette*. Urquhart's unvarnished rendering of this little pleasantry into seventeenth-century English can be obtained in any bookshop. I think Montalk's version an improvement on Urquhart because it retains the meter and rhyme pattern of the original. The fourth poem, entitled *In the Manner of Paul Verlaine, Roman Catholic Poet*, is a parody or free translation of Verlaine's "Idylle High Life" which begins *"La galopine à la pleine main."* . . . Montalk's version seems to me to capture something of the sparkling (and grossly improper) gaiety of the French. The poem comes from *Femmes*, one of the three collections of erotic verse published by Verlaine *sous le manteau*. The other two are *Amies* and *Hombres*. Most editions of these collections appeared under Verlaine's pseudonym: Pablo de Herlagnez. When Montalk's little pamphlet came into the august presence of the Court of Criminal Appeal, as it ultimately did, Mr. Justice Acton, one of the judges, said that he read Verlaine himself and the poet never wrote anything like this alleged translation. In his *ex parte* account of the proceedings, published under the title *Whited Sepulchres*, Montalk makes great play with his lordship's ignorance without mentioning the surreptitious nature of the publication of "Idylle High Life." This is hardly fair, since one could read the whole of Verlaine in the collected edition of his works without knowing that this poem existed. On the other hand, Verlaine's erotic trilogy was freely discussed and quoted from in a French biography published in 1929 and translated into English during the year of the trial.[2]

The two poems we have dealt with take up forty-five of the total of the sixty-three lines contained in the brochure. So far it can be said that the brochure, although not everyone's meat, could be of legitimate interest to anyone whose tastes were literary without being prudish. Neither Rabelais's vigor nor Verlaine's delicate mastery of French verse are in any way diminished, even when they deal with subject matter normally found repulsive.

The remaining eighteen lines of the brochure make up a poem, "For — and his Girl on leaving them the key of my room," and two other short original pieces. It must suffice to say that these are in the same vein as the translation of Rabelais and the parody of Verlaine, and by that token quite unsuitable for polite society in twentieth-century England. But it must be remembered that Montalk did not intend the brochure for general publication but for private circulation among his friends, whose literary tastes presumably were similar to his own.

As soon as Montalk and Mr. Glass were in Brixton Prison they found what a net of difficulties enmeshes anyone who falls foul of the law. Although in theory an accused person is innocent until proved guilty, his lot is far from happy. It would have been easy for both prisoners to have found bail, but they were not allowed to use the telephone. Furthermore, their friends could not telephone them because the number of Brixton Prison was not in the directory and could not be obtained on inquiry. One humorous episode, however, enlivened the Count's captivity. His celebrated cloak was taken away from him. He demanded it back, and ended with an interview with the governor. The governor decided that, as unconvicted prisoners are entitled to their own clothes, he had no power to withhold the cloak. It was therefore returned to its owner, who wore it by day and used it as an extra blanket against the cold January weather at night.

On the third day Montalk's brother was successful in getting him bailed, and Montalk set about performing a similar service for Mr. Glass. The case came before the Clerkenwell police court. Mr. de Lozey in the witness-box was very strong on his moral scruples. He said that he would certainly inform if he were offered an obscene Greek manuscript to print. He looked rather foolish when he had to admit that he knew no Greek. The magistrate seemed to take a reasonable view of the case. The Count, however, was very angry and indignant at what he considered to be wrongful arrest, and insisted on trial by jury. His bail was renewed, and Mr. Glass was discharged from the proceedings on the ground that no jury would convict him.

The trial came on at the Old Bailey on February 8 before Sir Ernest Wild, the Recorder of London, who at the age of fifty-nine had published a volume of very adolescent verse entitled *The Lamp of Destiny* and rather fancied himself as a champion of literature.

There was little dispute as to the facts against Montalk. The prosecution had to prove that the character of the poems was such that their "publication" in the admitted circumstances was a criminal offense.

In his summing-up Sir Ernest betrayed his own opinion in an unmistakable fashion. "Are you going to allow a man, because he calls himself a poet, to deflower our English language by popularizing these words?" he asked, and continued, "Remember, the standard of morals has advanced. It used to be," etc. The Recorder apparently held the curious, but not uncommon, view that the prudery which distinguished the comparatively short and quite exceptional period of English history from the death of Smollett to World War I was somehow an "advance" on what had gone before and in the nature of a permanent, rather than a temporary, addition to the national culture. At another point in the summing-up Sir Ernest said: "A man must not say he is a poet and be filthy. He has to obey the law just the same as ordinary citizens, and the sooner the highbrow school learns that, the better for the morality of the country."

In spite of this very one-sided summing-up, the jury were some time considering their verdict, and wished to retire from the box, but Sir Ernest prevailed upon them to stay where they were. At last the foreman came forward and those in the court formed the opinion that he would have given a qualified verdict had not the Recorder interrupted him. Anyhow, a verdict of "Guilty" was entered to the satisfaction of Sir Ernest who observed: "No decent-minded jury could have come to any other decision than that the defendant had attempted to deprave our literature."

During the trial Montalk's indignation at what he considered the injustice of the whole proceedings continued to rise. He refused to make any statement in mitigation of sentence, and he was given six months' imprisonment, a sentence which W. B. Yeats, the Irish poet, described as "criminally brutal."

An appeal fund was raised and subscriptions came in from all quarters. Among the subscribers were Aldous Huxley, H. G. Wells, J. B. Priestley, Walter de la Mare, Laurence Housman, Lord Esher, T. S. Eliot, and Hugh Walpole. The appeal was heard on March 7. The Count had spent the intervening time in prison. Appellants to the Court of Criminal Appeal who have not obtained bail pending appeal suffer considerable disabilities. For one thing, the lowering effects of prison diet makes it very difficult for them to give a good account of themselves unless friends outside send a dinner in to them on the day of the trial. This was not done in the Count's case, and there is no doubt that he made a poor showing. So far as he was concerned the appeal was a complete failure. The unlucky prisoner could only console himself with the fact that the case went some way to establishing that in "obscene libel" cases:

It is a good defence to the charge that the publication of matter prima facie obscene was for the public good, as being necessary or advantageous to religion, science, literature or art, provided that the manner and extent of the publication does not exceed what the public requires.[3]

I am not sure that Count Potocki was not in some degree the victim of law reform. Before the Indictments Act of 1915, the indictment in obscene libel cases was worded thus:

that (so-and-so) being a person of wicked and depraved mind and disposition, and unlawfully and wickedly devising, contriving and intending, to vitiate and corrupt the morals of the liege subjects of our said Lord the King, to debauch and poison the minds of divers of the liege subjects of our said Lord the King, and to raise and create in them lustful desires, and to bring the said liege subjects into a state of wickedness, lewdness and debauchery, on the ... day of ... in the year of our Lord, etc., and within the jurisdiction of the said court, unlawfully, wickedly, maliciously, scandalously, and wilfully did publish, etc., a certain lewd, wicked, bawdy, scandalous, and obscene libel, in the form of a book entitled ... in which said book are contained among other things divers wicked lewd impure scandalous and obscene libels . . . To the manifest corruption of the morals and minds of the liege subjects of our said Lord the King, in contempt of our said Lord the King, and his laws, in violation of common decency, morality, and good order, and against the peace of our said Lord the King, his Crown and Dignity.

I scarcely think that even Sir Ernest Wild could have persuaded a jury that Montalk was guilty of this dreadful crime. There is a suggestion of public and widespread disturbance of a sensational nature. The Indictments Act of 1915 did away with this picturesque phraseology in regard to obscene libel and many other matters. The charge became simply that of having published "an obscene libel." The purpose of the Act was to save time and trouble, and it did not in any way alter the offense; but it allowed a judge to explain to a bewildered jury that the cryptic words "publishing an obscene libel" can cover a communication made to one other party only and which has done no harm to anyone.

The Nineteen Thirties
in England

DURING THE YEAR following Montalk's case a young man who had written a long poem in Spenserian stanzas, entitled *Guido and the Girls,* had it privately printed and advertised by postal circulars. Besides recounting his love struggles, the poem aimed a good deal of Chaucerian abuse at priests and lawyers. It received kindly treatment from the press though *The Times Literary Supplement* administered a gentle rebuke for coarseness. A third and extended edition issued in 1934 satirized the late Lord Halifax (in very thin disguise) as a religious maniac. The authorities then decided to suppress the book. The author was charged with publishing an obscene libel and fined £500 at Leeds Assizes.[1]

The same year a raid was made on the premises of the Fortune Press, a London firm which had been combining the publishing of the work of promising young authors with the issue of older books, generally translations. Some of the latter class were reprints of Charles Carrington's issues and the sole excuse for the attack was that the firm's list was rather heavily weighted with erotic interest. None of the items concerned, however, could be said to be without serious literary or historical interest.

Proceedings in respect of a wide range of titles were taken under Lord Campbell's Act at the Westminster police court on October 10 and the case dragged on into the New Year.[2] The magistrate, Mr. A. Ronald Powell, said[3] he had not to consider whether a work was of literary or of other merit, and delivered himself of the memorable dictum: "A classical author might lapse into obscenity." He ruled out expert evidence to show that the authors were considered persons of importance or classical authors in their own country. The result was a veritable holocaust and a glance at the list of condemnations will illustrate the contempt of the law for creative, historical, and scientific books if they could be held by any stretch of imagination to fall within a wide and vague definition of obscenity.

Four contemporary novels were condemned. The authors were chiefly motivated by youthful indignation against the prevailing atmosphere of oppression and humbug in educational and social affairs. One of the novels was *Little Victims* by Richard Rumbold. The author, a Roman Catholic, had been repelled from Communion at Oxford on account of this book, but he had had the courage to refuse to withdraw it from circulation at the behest of his spiritual pastors.[4]

Other books in original English were *Sane Sex Life and Sex Living* by H. W. Long, a sensible and straightforward approach to its subject, and a book called *Don Leon*. The latter contains two poems published in the last century, the name of Lord Byron being falsely given as the author. They were probably written by George Colman the younger and have recently been seriously studied by Mr. G. Wilson Knight in an attempt[5] to elucidate the mystery that surrounds Byron's relations with his wife.

Four French novels in translation were condemned: three by Pierre Louÿs and one (*Là-Bas*) by J.-K. Huysmans. The classics were represented by a very scholarly annotated translation of the *Satyricon* of Petronius (originally published by Carrington) and a translation of the twelfth book of the *Greek Anthology*. The only seizure to escape condemnation was Plato's *Symposium*, but plates by Jean de Bosschère were destroyed.

Of historical interest was a translation of *Les Vies des Dames galantes* by the Seigneur de Brantôme, a nobleman who accompanied Mary Queen of Scots from France to Holyrood in 1561. Translations by Montague Summers of two books dealing with witchcraft were condemned. One was the *De Daemonialitate* of Ludovico Maria Sinistiari, a distinguished seventeenth-century Italian ecclesiastic. The other was the *Histoire de Magdelaine Bavent*, a book published in Paris in 1652 and dedicated to the Duchess of Orleans. On January 23 expert testimony was given to the standing of the translator as an authority on witchcraft, and to the anthropological value of this book.[6] Finally, a bowdlerized *Perfumed Garden*[7] was condemned.

The working of the obscenity law in relation to imaginative literature with social implications is well illustrated by the case of a novel by James Hanley entitled *Boy*. It is a tale of a working-class boy of thirteen who runs away to sea, of the hardships and sexual assaults to which he is subjected on board ship, of his introduction to the brothels of Alexandria by a shipmate, and of his murder by the captain of the vessel because he has contracted syphilis. There is some true-to-life sailors' and dockers' talk and the brothel scenes are unvarnished; but the moral tone of the book is rather on the " 'orrible warning" plane. The publishers, Boriswood Ltd., first issued it in an expensive limited edition. In 1931 an ordinary edition appeared in which certain words and sentences were replaced by asterisks. In a third edition these were filled in by euphemisms and certain passages were omitted altogether. In 1934 a cheap reprint of this doubly mutilated text was issued.

In November 1934 copies of the reprint were seized by the police at a lending library in Manchester and the librarian, who pleaded guilty, was prosecuted for obscene publication. The directors of the publishing firm were prosecuted for aiding and abetting and later the company was arraigned as principal. Pleas of "Guilty" were entered on legal advice[8] and fines totaling £400 inflicted.

In a paper entitled "Liberty in England"[9] read to the International Congress of Authors in Paris in June 1935, Mr. E. M. Forster deplored the use of the law to crush this book, which he described as "a novel of much literary merit." It was subsequently published by the Obelisk Press in Paris.

A novel somewhat similar to *Boy*, but gay instead of gloomy in tone, is *Bessie Cotter* by Wallace Smith, published by Heinemann in January 1935. The following April, after six thousand copies had been sold, the publishers were prosecuted at Bow Street for obscene publication.

The book, which has been highly praised as literature, depicts the sordid life of a prostitute in realistic and unsentimental terms. The scene is not specified but I am informed that it is Chicago in the early years of the present century. Perhaps the authorities moved against it because it cuts across conventional theories of what a prostitute ought to be and think. Bessie is neither trapped, drugged, nor brutally treated. She is neither tragically miserable nor dramatically wicked. She is a most lovable character with a simple philosophy. She does not particularly like the "sporting life" but she prefers twenty-five dollars a night at Miss Myrtle's "parlour house" to ten dollars a week in a factory. And so do her colleagues. There is nothing in particular to distinguish the book from many others which have escaped prosecution except one page on which two waiters clearing up in the early morning use the sort of words which such waiters do in fact use. It was because of this page (I imagine) that a plea of "Guilty" was entered. A fine of £100 was imposed.

The Attorney-General, Sir Thomas Inskip, who led for the Crown, in opening the case made the very illuminating statement: "The book deals with what everybody will recognize as an unsavory subject—gratification of sexual appetite."

Although occasionally a book on sex instruction may have been included almost unnoticed in omnibus condemnation as in the Fortune Press case, after the prosecution of Havelock Ellis's book the authorities had made no serious attempt to interfere with sex manuals and similar works of nonfiction. It is true that many of these books were protected by claims to restricted publication and by high prices, but many books dealing frankly with sex were sold to the general public at normal prices. Both authors and publishers had begun to take it for granted that any scientific study of sex and marriage was safe from attack on the ground of obscenity. This complacency was rudely shaken in 1935[10] by proceedings in respect of *The Sexual Impulse* by Edward Charles.

The publishers were again Boriswood Ltd. and this second prosecution gave rise to a suspicion that they were being specially watched and discriminated against because of their Communist leanings. *The Sexual Impulse* had been favorably reported on by their medical reader, Dr. Jeneen of Westminster Hospital. Galley proofs were sent to Professor Julian Huxley and Mrs. Janet Chance, who contributed forewords, to Lord Horder, who agreed with the main thesis of the book, and to Dr. Voge of Edinburgh University, who contributed some medical tables. The publication had been advertised in the medical journals and the largest order received was from a well-known medical bookseller.

A great deal of the book was devoted to philosophical speculation and the technicalities of biochemistry, but the important part was an exposition of coital technique intended for the ordinary man and woman. This was an important and novel contribution to English sexual literature. The late Dr. Norman Haire once said that descriptions of coitus in sex books leave the reader informed on every point except why anyone should ever want to do what is described, and even writers of the standing of Havelock Ellis have thought it necessary to adopt a special and solemn tone when writing on the subject. Edward Charles dealt with the matter *con amore* and his tone was gay and often poetical.

At the hearing of the charge and at the subsequent appeal the defense was allowed to call expert witnesses with regard to the educational and scientific value of the work. These included Julian Huxley, Maude Royden, J. B. S. Haldane, Janet Chance, who was the author of *The Cost of English Morals*, Robert Briffault, the author of *The Mothers*, and Bronislaw Malinowski, the author of *The Sexual Life of Savages*. The case came before Mr. A. Ronald Powell at the Westminster police court on October 1, 1935. It was clear that besides a general objection to the tone of the book, particular exception was taken to descriptions of variety of coital position, and suggestions regarding the possibility of coitus in the open air, and during menstruation. The magistrate asked Mrs. Chance, who ran a sex education center, whether she had ever given the book to a member of the working class and whether she considered some verses quoted from Aldous Huxley's *Brave New World* fit and decent for working-class people to read. He convicted the publishers of obscene publication and ordered the book to be destroyed. An appeal opened at the London Sessions House on December 10 was unsuccessful.

The Sexual Impulse has never been republished and in my opinion its loss prevented a step forward being taken in the effectiveness and value of current sex education.

During the nineteen thirties the Public Morality Council was very much to the fore. This body had formed itself in 1899. It came under the influence of Winnington-Ingram when he was made Bishop of London in 1901 and continued to be led by him during the twenty-five years of his episcopate. His mentality may be judged from his contribution to the debate[11] on Lord Dawson's bill to restrict the sale of contraceptives: "I would like to make a bonfire of them and dance round it," he declared, somewhat exaggerating the inflammability of the commodities in question. The Council's activities covered all sorts of "vice." A campaign against semi-nudity on the stage evoked a protest from Marie Tempest against "any attempt to revive the activities of the Prudes on the Prowl, the spying of the Stigginses, and the chortling of the Chadbands."[12] In 1934 the Council sent twenty-two books and two deputations on allegedly obscene publications to the Home Secretary.[13]

In March 1938 hostile clamor was raised in the *Daily Mail*,[14] the *Daily Mirror*, and the *Spectator* over review copies of a book called *To Beg I am Ashamed* by the pseudonymous Sheila Cousins and a copy was sent to the Home Secretary by the Public Morality Council. The book is an autobiography, about a quarter of which is devoted to the author's life as a prostitute. The publishers, Routledge & Sons, were visited by the police and, being threatened with "serious consequences" if the book were published, decided to withdraw it.[15] In their annual report the Council took considerable unction to themselves for the part they played in this banning, but it is a pleasure to record that this sober and enlightening contribution to a subject of universal interest was republished in 1954 without any interference.

The annual report of the Council for 1959 showed that they enjoyed an income of over £2,500 and continued to include "obscene" literature among the matters with which they concerned themselves. In his address to the annual general meeting on October 26, 1960, the General Secretary, Mr. George Tomlinson, said that the Council were watching the *Lady Chatterley's Lover* case with great interest.

Sydney Smith voiced a fundamental objection to all societies of the Public Morality Council type:

It is hardly possible that a society for the suppression of vice can ever be kept within bounds of good sense and moderation. . . . Beginning with the best intentions in the world, such societies must, in all probability, degenerate into a receptacle for every species of tittle-tattle, impertinence and malice. Men whose trade is rat-catching love to catch rats; the bug destroyer seizes upon the bug with delight; and the suppressor is gratified by finding his vice.

In 1931 Jack Kahane founded the Obelisk Press in Paris with the object of combating British prudery and in the not illegitimate hope of commercial profit. Of the novels by reputable authors banned in England he reprinted *The Well of Loneliness, Sleeveless Errand, Boy,* and *Bessie Cotter,* as well as the autobiography *To Beg I am Ashamed.* The Press also published English novels of merit whose authors could not find publishers because of prevailing fear of the obscenity laws. The Hogarth Press were about to publish Cyril Connolly's *The Rock Pool* when they took fright over the *Bessie Cotter* prosecution and the book was issued by the Obelisk Press in 1936. When at last a new edition was issued by a London publisher, the author in an introductory note paid a charming tribute to Jack Kahane who had died in 1939. In 1938 the Press issued a novel entitled *The Black Book*—an early work of Lawrence Durrell who has since become famous. The Press also reprinted Frank Harris's *My Life and Loves.*

It is as the publisher of Henry Miller's great autobiographical sequence of novels, however, that Jack Kahane will be remembered. In 1932 he received the manuscript of *The Tropic of Cancer* and recognized the genius of the chaotic and erotic writing. The book appeared in 1934 and was treated as a serious contribution to literature by writers no less eminent than Aldous Huxley and T. S. Eliot, and also by Ezra Pound, who remarked: "At last an unprintable book that is fit to read." *Black Spring* and *The Tropic of Capricorn* followed in 1938 and 1939. These three titles have, of course, been eagerly pounced upon by the British Customs; but the books have nevertheless become widely known and written about the world over.

England in Wartime
and After

JUST AS THE AUTHORITIES during World War I found time to attack D. H. Lawrence's *The Rainbow*, so they were not idle during the momentous events of 1939 to 1945 in banning "obscene" books. The year 1942 in particular was noteworthy from this point of view for one of those "cleaning-up" drives which from time to time employ the time and attention of the police. This occasion may not have been unconnected with a desire to present a superficially good face to the American Forces being drawn into Britain. Most of the cases were, of course, concerned with trashy books of no literary or educational significance, but two of them are important because of their relation to the question of sex instruction.

In November 1940 Dr. Eustace Chesser published a book entitled *Love Without Fear*. The author was a psychological and gynecological specialist whose professional work had impressed upon him the enormous amount of matrimonial misery brought about by sexual ignorance and by the fear and nervousness born of that ignorance. The book was published to remedy this state of affairs and it was written in a style calculated to appeal to ordinary men and women without any special knowledge of the subject or remarkable scholastic achievements. The vocabulary was plain and straightforward and the author at no time took refuge in Latin or in medical terms incomprehensible to the layman. Nearly all the factual part of the book was made up of quotations from Havelock Ellis, Magnus Hirschfeld, Ivan Block, Van der Velde, Krafft-Ebing, and Marie Stopes. In all, forty-four authors were directly or indirectly quoted.

In 1942, after 5,000 copies had been sold, the author and the publishers were jointly prosecuted at the instance of the Director of Public Prosecutions for publishing an obscene libel. It would have been possible (under the Criminal Justice Act, 1925) to have arranged for the common law offense to have been tried summarily. The option of trial in a magistrate's court instead of by a jury, however, faces the accused with an awkward dilemma. Summary trial makes an adverse decision on the issue of obscenity something like a certainty, especially if the Director of Public Prosecutions is behind the case; but the penalties are comparatively light and an author or publisher prepared to pocket his pride and display a proper penitence before some ignorant magistrate can reasonably hope to escape with a moderate fine. On the other hand, there is always a chance that a jury may be impressed by a man's sincerity or bring a healthy man-in-the-street common sense to bear on the case; but if acquittal is not secured, heavy penalties may be expected. In this case the accused courageously insisted on trial by jury.

The trial opened at the Central Criminal Court on June 2, 1942, before the Common Serjeant, Mr. Cecil Whiteley, K.C. The prosecution drew the attention of the court to passages in the book particularly objected to. They included descriptions of genital kissing and manual stimulation of women, various coital positions, and methods of defloration, as well as stories related to the fear of impotence and to the psychological mechanism of fetishism, Lesbianism, flagellomania, voyeurism, and other deviations. It was agreed on all sides, however, that the book (copies of which were given to the jury to take home to read) must be judged as a whole and not condemned on the evidence of isolated passages taken out of their context. Dr. Chesser went into the witness-box and the trial hinged on his ability to justify in the eyes of the jury his policy of drawing the attention of the ordinary man and woman to these subjects. Some of his most significant replies to examination and cross-examination were as follows:

Mr. Curtis-Bennett (for Dr. Chesser): What caused you to sit down and write the book? A. One cannot be in practice for long without realizing that the physical ailments of people are nothing as compared with mental troubles and difficulties. A large proportion, if not the greatest proportion, of these mental difficulties are the direct result of sexual difficulties.

Q. In your industrial practice in Salford, the years you were there, did you learn a lot about that? A. A terrific amount.

Q. What was the evidence you found there as to people's regard for the sexual act? A. There was no real regard for it at all, with the result that there was an utter lack of knowledge as to what it was meant for. The wives complained that the husbands regarded them as merely there for their benefit when they came back from work. . . . I felt that these sexual difficulties would, in a great many cases, never have arisen if there had been anything like a proper amount of sex teaching or sex books read on the subject.

Q. Did your practice in London confirm what you had found at Salford? A. Very much so.

Q. Why did you write the book? A. In order to attempt to help those people who, I felt, needed it.

Q. Were you aware of various other publications, including Van der Velde's *Ideal Marriage?* A. Without them, this would not have been written.

Q. I was coming to that; but in your view are they suitable for the ordinary man and his wife to read? A. No, not for everyone, because they will not be understood by everyone.

The Common Serjeant: Your whole object was to make this understandable by the ordinary man? A. Yes.

Q. What do you say generally about this book? A. My answer to it all is that if you are discussing sex, or if you are attempting to teach sex to anyone, you must include everything which is included in sex.

Mr. Curtis-Bennett: I want to know why, for example, you put in flagellation? A. Flagellation is something very much more common than most of us quite care to believe.

The Common Serjeant: Well, will you explain it? A. None of us like to feel that we are absolutely unique, and that we stand alone in possibly having a sex deviation or abnormality. If, on the other hand, on reading a book like this, patients find that there are quite a large number of people suffering from it, they are much more likely to seek aid than they might otherwise be.

Mr. Curtis-Bennett: Throughout your book, in all chapters almost you are dealing with the various matters and saying repeatedly "Go and see a doctor!" A. Yes, quite. It encourages them to seek medical treatment if they feel that these are conditions which are being medically treated, and not absolutely hush-hush and not being talked about. That is the whole point. It is the whole point of a number of these things that complaint has been made about.

Mr. Byrne (for the prosecution): Why did you give in this book so many stories, anecdotes, and so forth? A. It makes a book much more readable, and it makes it easier to bring together a point.

Q. Did you think it was necessary that married people should really know anything about Lesbianism? A. Most definitely.

Q. Can you tell me why you want to describe what goes on in a licensed brothel on the Continent? What has that got to do with married people? A. It has a great deal to do with married people. It very vividly brings home the point that practices which are committed in these brothels are obviously done as a result of a great deal of experience and a great deal of knowledge of sex and the attraction and stimulation of love, and if more of that were known among married people, these proceedings might never have been in question.

Q. In your passages in which you deal with kissing extending down to the thighs, genital kissing, and so forth, was there any idea at the back of your mind that such passages might stimulate the reader who happened to pick up this book? A. Definitely not.

Q. Do you say it is really necessary for husbands and wives and people who are going to be married to know such techniques? A. Very strongly I say yes.

The Common Serjeant: You had better say why, because that is really most of this book. A. The genital kiss is something which is practiced by a large number of us, and yet a large number of us think that the genital kiss is something which is abhorrent, something which should not be done, something which may give rise to a tremendous amount of guilt and shame, so that if a man attempts to practice it it may easily break up the marriage; and genital kissing is regarded as a perfectly normal procedure by all, more or less, who are in a position to write about it.

Q. That part of the book on "voyeurism" where you tell of husbands having persuaded their wives to have intercourse with other men while they looked on—how is that to assist the married couples you were catering for? A. That is not an uncommon state of affairs, much more common than an average person would think; and let us assume that the readers were unaware of it, and see it written, it gives them a certain amount of confidence to realize that what their husband is suffering from is an abnormality, and one which can be treated if he went to see a doctor about it, as against an attitude in which she was saying "Well, I am going to claim a divorce, or ruin the married life."

The Common Serjeant: How many wives have complained to you, apart from what you have read? A. I should say at least, probably, nine or ten wives in the last two or three years.

Q. Do you think it was really necessary in your last chapter to go into the minute description of the organs of sexual congress?

A. Very much so. Surely one must know the details of one's own anatomy before one can begin to understand it?

The Common Serjeant: Just explain what you mean. A. Before you can understand any subject in sex, surely it stands to reason that you must know something about your own sex organs, and exactly what happens during sexual stimulation, during orgasm, and at the love play. If I use Latin words, then you do not even know what part of your anatomy it refers to. You must be given something which describes your sexual organs to you and describes what happens during congress.

Q. Is it your experience that a large number of married couples are totally unaware of these things? A. Absolutely. In a large number of married women they merely give themselves to their husbands as a duty, and very often a most unpleasant duty, and regard their husbands as good husbands if they do not make what they consider unnecessary claims.

Mr. Byrne: You say, inside the dust cover: "The author has written this book for those who are married or about to be married, and in this connection the bookseller's co-operation is requested." What steps did you take to see that this book was not sold to persons who either were not married or were not contemplating matrimony? A. The only steps that I can take are (1) to put a price on the book which will, one hopes, keep it out of younger people's hands, such as typists and others, where 12s 6d would be quite a consideration, and (2) to put this note into the book. If a young person went into a bookseller's shop, the bookseller should not sell it; beyond that I am not in a position to take precautions. I can only hope that they will be careful.

The Common Serjeant: Under what age would you regard it as undesirable that this book should be read? A. About eighteen.

In relation to this question of the author's responsibility for the type of person to whom the book was sold we may anticipate events to note that, before retiring to consider the verdict, the foreman and a juror addressed some very close questions to the judge in order to ascertain whether the book was for sale only or whether it was available in subscription and public libraries. They were assured that it was available on sale only. Earlier in the case a detective who had purchased the book was cross-examined as to the respectability or otherwise of the shop in which he made the purchase. This raises the serious question as to the extent to which an author can be justly held responsible for all the "circumstances of publication" of his work. Granted that he selects a reputable publisher, is he to be made responsible because his book is lent out by libraries to unsuitable readers or because copies find their way into disreputable shops? It is only fair that in such cases the prosecution should have to prove not only that he is the author but that he has some responsibility for any circumstances of publication influencing the case. Failing such proof the prosecution should be confined to the bookseller, librarian, or other person directly concerned.

Three doctors then gave evidence that they had found the book useful in their practice and had recommended it to their patients. An answer of Dr. Harold Avery is of particular interest:

Mr. Curtis-Bennett: Is there any other book you know which it is possible to recommend to the ordinary layman and laywoman who is married or about to be married that they would understand?

A. Well, that is a matter that depends entirely on the type of patient who comes along. In the consulting practice which I carry on
I have patients who vary from dockyard laborers, probably, to members of royalty. I would not recommend that to members of royalty,
who could understand Van der Velde or Norman Haire, but the
large fifty per cent or more of the population would understand
this book far more than they would understand the others.

The Common Serjeant's summing-up was lucid, dispassionate,
and scrupulously fair, and in marked contrast to the moralistic
harangues delivered by some judges in similar cases which have almost been speeches for the prosecution. This piece of good fortune
for the defendants combined with Dr. Chesser's obvious sincerity
in the witness-box was perhaps more than anything else responsible
for the fact that after a retirement of less than an hour the jury returned a verdict of "Not Guilty" in respect of both defendants.[1]

When the trial was over Dr. Chesser showed that although he
had been adamant in resisting the unwarranted claims of the law to
dictate to a writer on questions of subject matter and style, he was
quite willing to bow to the opinion of those qualified to judge such
matters and whose duty it is to do so. Out of deference to literary
critics and the views of his intellectual peers, some changes were
made in the edition of the book issued after the trial. A story about
a bumble bee, which few could have found either helpful or enter-
taining, was omitted, together with a description of an oriental
mode of defloration. Rather surprisingly a translation of the celebrated description of coitus by the French physician Felix Roubaud
was also omitted.

There is no doubt that Dr. Chesser made a splendid fight for
responsible freedom in matters for sex education which went some
way to reverse the unfortunate effects of *The Sexual Impulse* case.

Dr. Chesser's victory was followed by a case which showed that
the gain for freedom in sex education was limited in extent. If he
had vindicated his right to publish his book, it still remained most
hazardous to widen the circle of readers of similar books by lending them on hire.

The case concerned a "one-man" company called the Economy

Educator Services Ltd. which carried on a commercial lending library business, mainly dealing in books of sex instruction, on a mail-order basis, first from Plymouth and then from Bodmin. In 1942 the police raided the company's premises in Plymouth and obtained destruction orders under the Act of 1857 in respect of ten titles. These orders were quashed on appeal[2] to quarter sessions except as regards two books: *The Power to Love* by Edwin Hirsch and *Lifelong Love* by Rennie MacAndrew, published in 1935 and 1938 respectively. Raids were then made by the Cornwall police on the company's premises which had moved to Bodmin, and a prosecution[3] was launched for publishing or procuring with intent to publish the books already mentioned and also *The Encyclopedia of Sexual Knowledge* (1934) and *The Encyclopedia of Sex Practice* (1938). The first of these encyclopedias was edited by Norman Haire and the second partially so.

The case[4] came before Mr. Justice Macnaghten at the Bodmin Assizes on October 29, 1942. The principal director of the company and his wife, who was a nominal director, were personally indicted as well as the company. To spare his wife, and because of the legal advice he had received, the male defendant pleaded guilty except as regards *Lifelong Love* in respect of which the judge accepted a plea of "Not Guilty" saying that the book was in a very different category from the other three. The plea was probably misguided because it might have been difficult to persuade a Cornish jury that Cornishmen should not be allowed to read books freely available all over the country.

Mr. J. D. Caswell, K.C., on behalf of the defendant, said that his client had had no desire to circulate anything that was obscene in the eyes of the law and put his case as follows:

The only way in which a bookseller can decide whether a book is obscene is to consider who are the publishers, for how long it has been published, and who are the authors. In the case of *The Encyclopedia of Sexual Knowledge* the general editor was a well-known physician and surgeon. It had been reviewed by Professor Huxley and in *The Listener* and *The New Statesman* and 50,000 copies had been sold throughout the United Kingdom since it was published in 1934. When the book was published there was a prosecution in respect of a circular advertising it[5] which was regarded as obscene so that the attention of the authorities must have been called to the book which was dealt with by well-known booksellers. In fact, my client has never sold or dealt with any book in respect of which there has been a prosecution. I submit to your lordship that when a bookseller finds that a book has been circulated and published openly and noticed in respectable journals it is *prima facie* evidence for him that that book is not considered by the authorities to be wrong.

The judge, however, was not impressed. In passing a sentence of six months' imprisonment and £100 costs with a fine of like amount on the company, he addressed the prisoner as follows:

The magnitude of the evil which flows from such publications is shown by the calendar of prisoners at these present assizes. Of the twelve other prisoners who will stand after you in the dock no less than five stand charged with crimes of obscenity. You published obscene words: they did obscene acts—according to the allegation of the prosecution. The obscene acts which they did in most cases were with children of tender years. You, for your own personal profit, were willing to publish these incitements to acts of obscenity. No one who reads the books in question can doubt that that was the intention of the writers of parts of these books. Whether he who incites to obscenity or he who commits obscenity is the worse it is unnecessary to enquire; both deserve the contempt of mankind, both deserve and must receive punishment.

Leaving aside the question of the intention of the authors of these books, it may be noted that the suggestion of a causal relation between obscene books and sexual crime is by no means uncommon. Yet, as we shall see later, there is little evidence that even admittedly pornographic books incite their readers to crime, and it may be that such reading acts as a catharsis for antisocial emotions.

The sentence was confirmed on appeal to the Central Criminal Courts;[6] but many people considered that it was unjust to single out the prisoner for prosecution from all the thousands who had handled the books, and others were appalled at the severity of the sentence. They did what they could by writing to the governor of the prison, to Members of Parliament, and to the Home Secretary, the Rt. Hon. Herbert Morrison. On August 19, 1943, Mr. T. L. Horrabin, M.P., was informed by the Home Secretary that the remainder of the imprisonment had been remitted, but by that time the prisoner was almost due for release under the good conduct regulations.

The Prosecution of Offences Regulations made in 1946 require all obscene publication prosecutions to be reported by the police authority concerned to the Director of Public Prosecutions. The reason for this regulation is that prosecutions often concern a provincial bookseller or library and the report enables the Director to consider whether others should not be prosecuted, for example, a London publisher or the author of the book. The regulation does not result in any uniformity or even good sense being introduced into the administration of the law, as we shall see when noting some of the cases in which the Director has been involved.

Another "clean-up" drive seems to have been inaugurated in anticipation of the Festival of Britain which was held in 1951 and which was expected to attract many visitors from abroad. The resulting court cases included another prosecution affecting the question of sex education.

In June 1950 the proprietors of a Blackpool shop trading in birth control requisites and similar articles were summoned by the local police under the Act of 1857 in respect of certain books they had been selling, and at the same time similar summonses were taken out against a number of local booksellers. The serious books concerned were all works of sex instruction and included: the *Encyclopedias*, which were the subject of the Economy Educator Services indictment; five books by Rennie MacAndrew including *Lifelong Love, Sexual Anomalies and Perversions*; a posthumous summary published in 1946 of the work of Magnus Hirschfeld, the German sexologist; and A *Plain Talk on Sex Difficulties* by F. B. Rockstro, which had been sponsored for many years by the British Sexological Society.

When the case[7] was heard on July 24, the Director of Public Prosecutions had taken it up and instructed Mr. C. James to prosecute. He opened by emphasizing the importance of the place where the books were sold and suggested that they might be obscene if sold in Blackpool whereas if sold in, say, Kensington High Street, they would not be obscene. He soon got away from this point, however, and quoted extensively and verbatim from the texts. The passages included a quotation from Havelock Ellis about a husband who tries to be considerate to his wife during the early days of his marriage, a description of a youth's misery because of his ignorance about masturbation, and a diagrammatic representation of the organs of reproduction.

Mr. R. S. W. Pollard gave expert evidence for the defense. He said he was a practicing solicitor, appointed a magistrate in 1946, and had been chairman of a matrimonial court since 1947. He was also chairman of the Marriage Law Reform Society. He testified that from his knowledge of divorce and separation the books were of educational value and for the public good.

In spite of a vigorous and lengthy defense by Mr. Leslie Harris, who stressed the long-standing and widely-distributed publication of the books, they were all condemned except *Lifelong Love*, which was exonerated in deference to the remark of Mr. Justice Macnaghten in the Economy Educator Services case.

The following year the Hirschfeld book was included among over a hundred titles which the police at Newcastle asked to be destroyed. Dr. Norman Haire, however, gave expert evidence in favor of the book and the magistrates refused to condemn it.[8]

Secondhand booksellers have generally enjoyed a considerable degree of immunity from police interference; but a lamentable case occurred at Poole, Dorset, in May 1951.[9] The police seized twenty-four books and a portfolio of original watercolors from a private house from which an antiquarian book business was carried on. Nine were returned, and one other minus four original watercolors with which it was extra-illustrated. The magistrates ordered the rest of the seizure to be destroyed. Apart from two copies of *Lady Chatterley's Lover* all the books destroyed were in French. At the suggestion of the defendant one of the books, a rare and unrecorded edition of a book printed in 1816, was sent to the British Museum instead of being actually destroyed. In evidence he said that many of his customers were medical men and psychologists, and he himself had been commissioned by Prof. Alfred C. Kinsey to send material to an American institute.

On January 17, 1952, the Smethwick magistrates made an order for the destruction of a number of books and magazines seized by the police from a shop under the Act of 1857. The shopkeeper raised no objection to the destruction. The order, however, included copies of the *Sun Bathing Review* and *Health and Efficiency*, the leading sunbathing periodicals in England. The publishers were not notified of the proceedings, but when the matter came to their notice an appeal was lodged at their instigation so far as these magazines were concerned.

At quarter sessions on March 11 Mr. G. K. Mynett for the prosecution said:

As I put the case it is in this form: you have here a bookseller carrying on a business in a back street in a single room who had a great mass of other books which are, I am told, obviously indecent and obscene. If a boy or girl or young person came into the shop for an ordinary youth magazine or perhaps a comic paper and happened to see one or other of these two sunbathing magazines, the effect might be to deprave that young person's mind. In neither of these magazines is it suggested that there is any indecent or obscene matter; it is purely a question of photographs of nude men, principally of nude women, in decent postures; but in practically all the cases the figures are completely naked, and the two sexes in the company of each other.

Mr. Ryder Richardson for the appellants contended that the exposure of a photograph of a nude body was not obscene, and he called the editor of *Health and Efficiency* and the president of the British Sunbathing Association to testify to the value of the nudist movement and the healthy nature of the attraction of the magazines for their readers. He contended that the magazines should not be destroyed merely because they happened to have been in bad company in a bad place; and he pointed out that it was impossible to be sure where magazines would be exposed for sale.

The Recorder allowed the appeal; but he said he must not be

taken to be acceding to the views put forward by the witness called for the appellants. He contented himself by saying that in his view it was not established beyond all doubt that the magazines were obscene publications.

Later in the year four consignments of continental nudist magazines were seized by the Customs at the Port of London. The importer objected, and the case[10] came before Sir Frederick Wells at the Guildhall on September 24. Evidence was given on behalf of the British Sunbathing Association of the hygienic, educational, and moral value of nudism; and the president of that body explained that its members were interested in the seized magazines because of the international character of the movement. Nudist magazines of the type involved in this case had been cleared of obscenity by legal decisions in Denmark, Norway, Sweden, and Switzerland. Mr. Eric Falk for the importer referred to the Norwegian judgment as embodying his own argument. It contained the following passage which must surely commend itself to all sensible people:

The representation of a nude human being is in itself not indecent or obscene and this applies whether the representation has the form of pictures, sculpture or photographs. This conception must be said to be generally recognized today. In order that such a representation shall be considered obscene or offensive such circumstances must be present that give it an obscene character, *i.e.* a strong emphasis on the genital parts or region, or by placing human beings together or the like . . . of course, a difference of opinion as to nudism exists, but followers of this cult ought in the opinion of the court to be allowed to make unhindered propaganda of their views, when it takes place in a way that does not outrage public decency.

In spite of Mr. Falk's advocacy the magistrate ordered all the magazines before him to be destroyed. As the law then stood, there was no appeal from the decision of a court of summary jurisdiction in cases of Customs seizures, and it was open to the Customs to choose whether the matter should be tried summarily or by the High Court. This curious state of the law was commented on by Lord Chief Justice Goddard in R. v. *London (County) Quarter Ses-*

sions ex parte Bowes (1950), a case concerning a seizure of dia-
monds, where he expressed regret that the Customs authorities had
elected to take the case, which involved a great deal of money, before a magistrates' court. The Customs have still the choice of
jurisdiction in these cases but the Customs and Excise Act of 1952
gives a right of appeal from a magistrates' court to quarter sessions.

The only essential difference between the British magazines
which were exonerated in the first of the above cases and their
continental counterparts which were condemned in the second
was that the British illustrations were touched up to delete the
sexual organs and the continental illustrations were not. If we neglect the fact that appeal was impossible in one case and consider
the vagaries of decisions in all obscene publication cases, it might
appear that this matter of touching up was the criterion which decided the difference in treatment. Undoubtedly the police have a
rule of thumb that all integral nude photographs are obscene
whereas the most salacious pictures of women in which the pudenda are concealed are not. But this work-a-day rule has no basis
in statutory or decided law. It may be noted that the edition of
Maurice Parmelee's *Nudism in Modern Life* published by John
Lane in 1933, which contains untouched photographic reproductions of activities in nudist camps, has never been interfered with,
and it is unlikely that the responsible publication of photographs
whose sole purpose was the illustration of healthy nudist activity
would ever be held to be illegal. Unfortunately the position is complicated by the fact that some nudist magazines are associated with
"art" supplements of a dubious character, and by the disinclination
of the commercial British nudist press to encourage the importation of rival publications.

The seizure of nudist magazines is by no means the full extent of
the use by the Customs of their powers for the purpose of interfering with the circulation of serious literature in recent times.

In 1946, when Kathleen Winsor's monumental and repetitive
novel *Forever Amber* was being attacked in the American courts,
copies were burned at British ports. Certain public libraries, including that of Birmingham, treated the book in the same way.[11]

When Samuel Beckett's *Molloy* and Vladimir Nabokov's *Lolita* were originally published in Paris in 1955, they were also seized by the British Customs.

The most astonishing example of Customs interference with fictional literature occurred in 1957 when a two-volume edition of the novels of Jean Genet in French, which had been ordered from Paris by the Birmingham Public Library for their reference department, was seized. Genet is a very realistic depicter of low life and his characters express themselves, often in argot, in true-to-life terms. He is, however, reviewed by reputable critics and his view of life is discussed in literary circles throughout Western Europe. If the books had reached their destination they could have been understood only by advanced students of the French language, and the librarian would have been responsible that they were issued only to responsible readers. The Birmingham authorities, however, took a very pusillanimous line. A deputation, apparently ignorant of French, visited the Customs and Excise offices in London and were persuaded not to challenge the seizure in the courts. The chairman of the Public Libraries Committee, who was one of the party, was dreadfully shocked at passages translated for their benefit which dealt with homosexual incidents.[12]

The attention of the British Customs may have been drawn to Beckett, Nabokov, and Genet because *Molloy, Lolita*, and an English translation of Genet's *Journal du Voleur* (with an introduction by Jean-Paul Sartre) were published by the Olympia Press. This publishing house devoted mainly to books in English succeeded the Obelisk Press as the particular thorn in the side of British censors.

When Jack Kahane, the owner of the Obelisk Press, died in 1939, the Press was inherited by his son Maurice, who during the German occupation of Paris took his mother's name of Girodias to avoid anti-Semitic persecution. In 1951 he sold the Obelisk Press and its subsidiary, the Editions du Chène, and set up the Olympia Press in 1953.

Although M. Girodias has been responsible for printing a great deal of rubbish, some of his publishing ventures have been very commendable. He has followed his father in publishing Henry Miller and has to his credit a revised version of *The World of Sex* and *The Rosy Crucifixion* trilogy. In 1955 he published a very good novel, *The Ginger Man* by J. P. Donleavy, which was subsequently bowdlerized by the author for publication in Britain. More recently his press has published *The Naked Lunch* by William Burroughs (a novel which received serious attention as literature from an international conference of writers at the Edinburgh festival in 1962 and which has since been published in America by Grove Press), the Casement diaries (also published in America by Grove Press), and reprinted an erotic work by Aubrey Beardsley.

The novel *Lolita* was completed by Vladimir Nabokov in 1954. He is a Russian aristocrat who exiled himself in 1919 to live first in France and then in the United States where he taught literature at Cornell University. *Lolita* followed a series of writings in Russian, French, German, and English. From an international and sophisticated angle the novel deals with the seduction of a twelve-year-old girl by a middle-aged man. Not surprisingly it failed to find a publisher in America, and consequently the author offered it to the Olympia Press, who issued it in two volumes. Surprisingly, the United States Customs authorities decided not to regard it as obscene although (as has been mentioned) copies were seized by the British Customs.

Attempts at suppression gave Lolita Haze, the "nymphet" of the novel, a world-wide publicity somewhat in excess of her deserts as a literary creation. She was first introduced to the English public when in December 1955 Graham Greene nominated her story to the *Sunday Times* as one of his three favorite books of the year. John Gordon (on whom the mantle of James Douglas as guardian of British morality has fallen) bought the book on this recommendation and fulminated in the *Sunday Express*: "Without doubt it is the filthiest book I have ever read. Sheer unrestrained pornography."[13] When in 1958 the book was published as a best-seller in America, Lionel Trilling contributed a long and serious review in the London monthly *Encounter*.[14] The following year, after the passing of the Obscene Publications Act, the book was openly published in England. There was no prosecution and the work was treated seriously by the critics.

In 1959, the Olympia Press made a substantial contribution to the informed discussion of public affairs by publishing a copy of

the so-called "black diaries" of Sir Roger Casement, the Irish pa-
triot who was hanged for attempting to assist the Easter rising of
1916. The diaries had been seized by the police at the time of Casement's arrest and, although they were not used as evidence at his
trial, typescripts were shamefully circulated to prominent people
in Britain and America to prejudice and discredit the writer before
his trial, while he was under sentence of death, and after his exe-
cution. Alfred Noyes made use of them in a British propaganda
article published in the American press. The English Home Office,
in spite of repeated requests, had stubbornly refused to release the
diaries or to allow them to be examined. The Olympia Press publication forced them to make the originals available to scholars, and
insured that a similar but not complete British edition could not
conveniently be suppressed on the ground of obscenity. Now that
the text is available for all to read, one can only wonder that those
who were shown the typescripts seem to have been so obsessed
by the occasional homosexual entries that they were blinded to
the essential nobility of the man as exemplified by the entries recording his compassion for the oppressed and his love of tropical
animals and plants.

Another interesting publication of the Olympia Press was Aubrey
Beardsley's *Venus and Tanhauser*. In this book, of which *Under
the Hill* is a pale reflection, Beardsley fails to transform that hyper-
sexuality not uncommon in tubercular patients into art as he does
in his drawings. Nevertheless the work, crude and even pitiable
as it is, is of legitimate interest to students of the artist's life and
mind.

The printer of a book found to be obscene in law is equally
guilty with the author, publisher, and the booksellers who handled
it. This places a burden on the printing trade which it is by no
means fitted to bear. A printer who receives an order from a reputable publisher in the ordinary way of trade should not have to
anticipate the operation of a law arbitrary in its judgments and
capricious in its administration. As things are, printers are sometimes prone to play for safety and constitute themselves as unofficial
censors of a clumsy and obscurantist kind. When, in the fifties, a

publisher at last set himself to provide English readers with integral translations of Zola's novels, the issue of the translation of *La Terre* was almost prevented because a large number of printers refused to produce it, pleading fear of legal consequences.[15] When Penguin Books decided to publish the integral text of *Lady Chatterley's Lover*, they could obtain no advance information from the Government regarding a possible prosecution for obscenity and their normal printers would not fulfill their contract.[16]

It is a criminal offense to aid and abet a misdemeanor triable on indictment or any summary offense. Of recent times the police have used this provision of the criminal law to prosecute persons who order obscene books or other matter through the post.[17] Presumably they base their investigations on the mailing list and correspondence files of firms who are raided as vendors of obscenity, but it is not clear why prosecutions are launched against a few of the many customers of these merchants and not against others. A typical charge was that against a clergyman in 1955. The prosecution alleged that "by sending these order forms he has aided and abetted counselled and procured those people to publish obscene material to himself."[18]

In view of the fuss made about the "four-letter" words in D. H. Lawrence's *Lady Chatterley's Lover*, the publication in 1955 of *The Mint* by his namesake T. E. Lawrence is worthy of note in relation to our subject. The integral text was published in a limited edition, but for unrestricted publication "the coarse words automatic in barrack-room speech" were eliminated and the spaces left blank, while one passage was omitted altogether.

The Obscene Publications Act, 1959

W^E NOW HAVE TO CONSIDER a recent and important landmark in the history of the English obscenity laws—the Obscene Publications Act of 1959. Its origins go back to the early years of the decade in which it was passed when an "anti-vice drive" was associated with the Home Secretaryship of Sir David Maxwell-Fyfe. He was appointed in 1951 and became Lord Chancellor as Lord Kilmuir in 1954. The "drive" was a three-pronged affair covering the witch-hunting of homosexuals, the harrying of prostitutes, and a crusade against pornography. In 1953 alone, 197 prosecutions were instituted in respect of allegedly obscene publications.

Serious literature was not greatly affected by the "drive" though, of course, there were the usual imbecilities inevitably associated with a campaign of its nature. The expurgated edition of D. H. Lawrence's *Lady Chatterley's Lover* published by William Heinemann Ltd. was included in a lot of books brought before Mr. W. E. Batt at the Thames Police Court for destruction. The owners of the books did not defend them but a plea for Lawrence's book was put in by counsel of the publishers. Although the magistrate described the book as "absolute rubbish" and the Director of Public Prosecutions pressed for its destruction, it was excluded from the order.[1] Unsuccessful attempts were made to suppress the second volume of the Kinsey Report at Doncaster[2] and George Ryley Scott's *Phallic Worship* at Swindon.[3] In the Swindon case, however, the justices distinguished themselves by ordering the destruction of the Navarre Society's edition of J. M. Rigg's unexpurgated translation of Boccaccio's *Decameron*, although the same book was in the Swindon reference library. This ridiculous order, although supported by the Director of Public Prosecutions, was reversed on appeal on September 15.

So far as books were concerned the "drive" was mainly directed against rubbishy volumes of a pornographic or near-pornographic character obviously published with the object of making money at the expense of a salaciously minded and semiliterate public. Subliterature of this sort may be regarded as the legitimate prey of those who administer the law, and fines and occasional imprisonment may be considered as an occupational risk of the type of trade. The incidence of the law is, however, very arbitrary and an offender who is punished may well feel that his wares are no worse than other books which are not the subject of prosecution.

Such a sense of injustice drove two men who had been sentenced for publishing the works of a certain pseudonymous Hank Jansen to the Court of Criminal Appeal. It appeared that in the course of the trial in the lower court, a large number of books published by leading houses and circulated by the libraries were produced by the defense, and the jury were intended to look at them to help them to decide whether according to the standards of the day the books which were the subject of the charge should be regarded as obscene. "That seems to me," said Lord Goddard, dismissing the appeal on March 15, 1954, "absolutely wrong,"[4] and he declared that the law of England was the same as that laid down in a Scottish case in 1953,[5] namely, that the character of the offending books should be ascertained by reading them, and that the character of other books which might be in circulation was a collateral issue the exploration of which would be endless and futile. He remarked, however, that the books put in ought to be looked into by the authorities.

This last remark of the Lord Chief Justice seems to have been the originating cause of five prosecutions launched in 1954 in respect of novels issued by reputable publishers. The books were: *The Image and the Search* by Walter Baxter, *September in Quinze* by Vivian Connell, *The Man in Control* by Charles McGraw,

Julia by Margot Bland, and *The Philanderer* by Stanley Kauffman, an American author.

The last two of these books had earlier been the subject of proceedings in the Isle of Man under the Obscene Publications and Indecent Advertisements Act, 1907, a local statute, against Boots's Library for lending them out. The High Bailiff inflicting nominal fines said that, although he considered both books obscene within the meaning of the Act, he was satisfied that the library had acted in perfectly good faith in lending them.[6]

All five books were not markedly different from the general run of novels which flow from the press year after year and first-class literary importance can hardly be claimed for them, although Mr. E. M. Forster in a letter to the publisher described *The Image and the Search* as "a serious and beautiful book" and Mr. Stanley Kauffman as an American author of standing.

The results of the cases show how uncertain was the basis on which the authorities were prepared to launch prosecutions. Werner Laurie Ltd., the publishers, and the author pleaded guilty at the Clerkenwell police court in the *Julia* case.[7] Hutchinson Ltd. were convicted in respect of *September in Quinze*,[8] the Marlborough Street magistrate having sent the case for trial by jury. Heinemann Ltd., the publishers, and the author were formally acquitted after two juries had disagreed over *The Image and the Search*.[9] Arthur Barker Ltd., the publishers, were found not guilty by a jury regarding *The Man in Control*;[10] and a similar verdict was returned in respect of Secker & Warburg, the publishers, and the printers in *The Philanderer* case[11] where the defendants had exercised their right of trial by jury.

The case of *The Philanderer* was particularly important because of the summing up by Mr. Justice Stable, which was a classic exposition of the law as it then stood. He stressed the value to the reading public of accurate pictures of contemporary social conditions in other countries at a time like the present when ideas were in the melting pot, and pointed out that although the law was the same as in 1868 the jury had not to consider the effect of publishing the book at that time but its effect on society as it is today. Just because a book was not suitable reading for the decently brought-up young female of fourteen or a child in the nursery to read it was not, the judge declared, a criminal offense to make it available to the general public.

In an account[12] of his experiences in this prosecution, Mr. Fredric J. Warburg, the managing director of Secker & Warburg, said that in cases of the kind the determining factor was the judge's summing up and he expressed his gratitude to the judge for allowing him to leave the dock and sit with his solicitor during the trial.

These five cases aroused an unprecedented degree of interest and uneasiness in the public mind about the law relating to obscene publications. *The Times* and other influential papers printed correspondence and editorials about the matter, the B.B.C. devoted two Third Programme broadcasts to it, and questions were asked in the House of Commons. This agitation was in marked contrast to the equanimity with which the public had regarded the persecution under the same law of men like Havelock Ellis, to instance a scientific writer, and D. H. Lawrence, to instance a creative literary artist. There was widespread apprehension throughout the literary world because it was felt that the social pioneer and the highbrow novelist were not alone in being threatened by the uncertain incidence of an arbitrary law. The ordinary commercial publisher was shown to be in danger and the novelist appealing to the average circulating library public "had to write under the shadow of the Old Bailey," as a number of successful men of letters put it in a letter to *The Times*.[13] The British public are much more sensitive about a threat to anything they regard as a legitimate commercial activity than about the troubles of intellectual speculation or artistic creation.

Public opinion was clearly ripe for some measure of reform of the law. The Society of Authors took the initiative by setting up a committee to consider the matter. The committee, originally presided over by Sir Alan Herbert and subsequently by Sir Gerald Barry, consisted of nearly a score of authors, critics, journalists, publishers, printers, a literary agent, a lawyer and representatives of the P.E.N., the Society of Authors, and the Arts Council. Shortly before Christmas 1954 the committee submitted its findings to Major Lloyd-George, Sir David Maxwell-Fyfe's successor at the Home Office. The principal recommendations took the form of a bill, drafted by Mr. Norman St. John-Stevas,[14] the legal member of the committee, to amend and consolidate the existing law. The text was introduced in the House of Commons as the Obscene Publications Bill, 1955, by Mr. Roy Jenkins on March 15, 1955, as a Private Member's Bill. He duly stressed the alarm of the publishing world about the five prosecutions of the previous year; but like most Private Members' Bills it got nowhere.

At this stage the question of the reform of the law of obscene libel was mixed up with the related but rather different problem of what are known as "horror comics." The comic is a paper for children consisting mainly of strip cartoons. Originally, these publications were innocent enough, but of late years some have appeared which are devoted to horror, crime, and cruelty. The situation caused considerable anxiety to those interested in the welfare of children and adolescents. The Government elected to deal with this problem with some promptitude by a special measure, and secured the passage of The Children and Young Persons (Harmful Publications) Act, 1955.

Agitation for some reform of the law of obscene libel continued both inside and outside Parliament. The Obscene Publications Bill, 1957, introduced in the Commons by Lord Lambton, obtained a second reading and was referred to a Select Committee of the whole House. Although the committee could only make a formal report before the 1956–57 parliamentary session killed the bill, the committee was reconstituted at the beginning of the 1957–58 session with general terms of reference "to consider whether it was desirable to amend and consolidate the law relating to obscene publications."

The reconstituted committee continued the hearing of evidence and eventually testimony from representatives of Government departments, the police, authors, publishers, printers, and the Public Morality Council and other voluntary societies was collected. Mr. T. S. Eliot and Mr. E. M. Forster were among the distinguished persons examined.

The committee's report appeared before the 1957–58 session and when Parliament reassembled in October 1958 it was confidently expected that some Government action would be taken. Nothing, however, was announced; and the Obscene Publications Bill, 1959, a Private Member's Bill introduced by Mr. Roy Jenkins, embodying the recommendations of the report, failed to get a second reading. At this point Sir Alan Herbert complained that the supporters of reform were back to the beginning again in what he called a long game of snakes and ladders.[15]

Pressure in and out of Parliament (including a threat by Sir Alan to intervene in a contested by-election as an Independent), however, proved effective in inducing the Government to find time for the bill. After many delays and much bargaining over some amendments, it became law as the Obscene Publications Act, 1959, on August 29, 1959.

The Obscene Publications Act, 1959, is an important landmark in the history of the English law relating to obscene publication. The preamble states that it is an Act "to provide for the protection of literature; and to strengthen the law concerning pornography." In general its provisions abolish the old common law offense of publishing an obscene libel and set up a new statutory offense in its place. The Cockburn dictum is replaced by a new definition of obscenity. The Obscene Publications Act, 1857, is repealed and its provisions re-enacted with substantial modification. And, finally, the defense of public good and the relation of expert evidence thereto is given statutory definition.

The Act makes it an offense to publish, whether for gain or not, an obscene article. The offense is triable summarily or on indictment and is punishable by fine or imprisonment. Prosecution on indictment must be commenced within two years of the commission of the offense; and summary prosecution within twelve months. Cases on indictment would be tried by jury and, since the possible sentence of imprisonment on summary conviction exceeds three months, a person charged summarily has a right to trial by jury.[16]

An "article" means any matter to be read or looked at and includes sound records and films. A person publishes an article who distributes, circulates, sells, rents, gives, or lends it, or who offers it for sale or rent. Publishing covers the playing of records, the projecting of films, and the showing of pictures, sculpture, and other objects intended to be looked at.

A person cannot be convicted of an offense if he proves that he had not examined the article concerned and had no reasonable cause to suspect that his publication of it would make him liable to conviction. Nor can he be held responsible for the subsequent publication by another person of an article he has published unless the republication could be reasonably expected by him.

Perhaps the most important provision of the Act is a new test of obscenity which reads as follows:

an article shall be deemed obscene if its effect or (where the article comprises two or more distinct items) the effect of any one of its items is, if taken as a whole, such as to tend to deprave and corrupt persons who are likely, having regard to all relevant circumstances, to read, see or hear the matter contained or embodied in it.

If a magistrate is satisfied on oath that there is reasonable ground for suspecting that on any premises, stall, or vehicle obscene articles are being kept for gain, he may issue a search warrant enabling a constable to search the premises and seize any articles which the constable has reason to believe to be obscene and kept for publication for gain.

When articles are seized under the above procedure the occupier of the premises, or user of the stall or vehicle, may be summoned to a magistrate's court to show cause why the articles should not be forfeited, and if the court is satisfied that they were obscene articles kept for the purpose of gain they may be forfeited. In addition to the person summoned, "the owner, author or maker of the articles brought before the court, or any other person through whose hands they had passed before being seized," shall be entitled to appear before the court on the day specified in the summons to show cause why they should not be forfeited. Appeal to quarter sessions is provided for.

No person can be convicted, and no forfeiture order made, under the Act

if it is proved that publication of the article in question is justified as being for the public good on the ground that it is in the interests of science, literature, art or learning, or of other objects of general concern.

The opinion of experts for or against the literary, artistic, scientific, or other merits of an article may be admitted in any proceedings under the Act.

The new Act was regarded with considerable satisfaction by the supporters of reform and it has been generally greeted as a remarkably progressive piece of legislation. Indeed, it is a great step forward to have this branch of the law brought out of the uncertain realm of common law and judicial decision and practice. A detailed examination of the Act, however, will reveal that it does not go much farther than to give statutory authority to what was already held to be the law by enlightened judges and to what had already been practiced by the better courts.

The new test of obscenity is certainly an improvement on the old Cockburn dictum under which almost any book touching on sexual matters, including the Bible and the plays of Shakespeare, could have been condemned. It should prevent, in future, oratory from the prosecution or from the bench that all books must be suitable reading for "a callow youth, or a girl just budding into womanhood," to use the words of the summing up in the *September in Quinze* case. It should also give some legal sanction to the restricted publication of books not suitable for general circulation. All the same, it is little more than a statutory expression of the exposition of the old common law as made by Mr. Justice Stable in *The Philanderer* case. It has been fairly generally recognized of late that books must be taken as a whole. Where the issue of obscenity has been contested, juries have as a rule been provided with copies to read and the prosecution has not been allowed to tear isolated passages out of their context.

It is right and proper that authors and other interested parties in forfeiture cases besides the occupier of the premises concerned should be heard; but such intervention was allowed when it was sought to destroy Magnus Hirschfeld's book at Newcastle in 1952. The enactment of the defense of public good is welcome but it was recognized as available under common law by the Court of Criminal Appeal in Montalk's case. Similarly, it is well that the admissibility of expert evidence on literary, artistic, and scientific issues (as distinct from the issue of obscenity itself) should be put beyond all doubt; but such evidence was allowed in *The Sexual Impulse* and *Love Without Fear* cases.

The above improvements, however, have to be balanced against a retrograde step, other defects, and the omission of reforms which appear to be clearly called for, some of which were included in the Government and earlier bills. For example, a serious step in the wrong direction is the abolition of an important safeguard contained in the repealed Act of 1857. Before a search warrant could be issued under that Act, the police had to swear to the actual sale of one or more obscene articles at or in connection with the premises concerned. Under the forfeiture provisions of the 1959 Act the police will only have to satisfy the issuing justices that there is reasonable ground for suspecting that obscene articles are kept on the premises for publication for gain. The omission of the 1857 safeguard was recommended by the Select Committee in 1958 in response to police evidence complaining of the difficulty of effecting a purchase from wholesale stores holding obscene books. No doubt the requirement did put an obstacle in the way of pursuing commercial pornography, but it was also a valuable protection for scholarly and private libraries which, in the nature of things, often contain books that would be considered obscene if publicly circulated, and the requirement was inserted into the 1857 Act expressly to secure this protection. Such libraries are now liable to raids at the instance of suspicious and overzealous police officers. It is small consolation that the owners may be able to establish their innocence of commercial activities when seized books are brought into court, because seizures are sometimes retained for months and, when exonerated, returned thumb-marked, dog-eared, and otherwise damaged.

The Act contains no directions as to the disposal of forfeited matter, which as a general rule will be destroyed. There is nothing to prevent the destruction of rare and valuable books and objects of art by ignorant and morally zealous magistrates. Such forfeitures should always be offered to a suitable library, art gallery, or museum.

Up to a late stage the 1959 bill defined "publication" as "distributing, circulating, selling, offering for sale or letting on hire." This definition would presumably have excluded private and noncommercial transactions from the offense of publishing obscene articles. The Act brings giving, lending, and showing within the compass of the offense; and it appears that Montalk could still be sent to prison for trying to get a Christmas card printed, and that prosecutions can still be based on purely private letters. Before the Select Committee[17] the police objected to any restriction of the legal meaning of "publication" which would prevent them from prosecution in cases such as one where obscene post cards were shown to young men with a view to homosexual seduction. There seems no reason why such cases should not be covered by the general law concerning sexual offenses.

The 1957 bill gave a right to be heard in court to authors and other parties interested in all obscene publication cases. Under the Government's bill this right was confined to forfeiture cases and did not extend to prosecutions of persons for the offense of publishing an obscene article, and this restriction is embodied in the Act. Consequently, the sort of injustice done to Havelock Ellis could be repeated today if a second Bedborough chose to plead guilty to publishing a book like *Sexual Inversion* or failed successfully to defend his action. But a conviction for obscene publication or a destruction order does not only concern the author, publisher, and distributors of the book; the reading public should also be considered and questions of public interest are involved. This point would only be satisfactorily met if the court was bound, as in divorce cases, to take the public interest into consideration whatever the attitude adopted by the defendants.

The 1957 bill provided that all destruction of obscene matter should be subject to court order. This provision was objected to in the evidence submitted to the Select Committee[18] by the Customs on the ground that it would involve them in unnecessary work and place a heavy additional burden on the courts. Neither the Customs nor the Post Office are mentioned in the Act, so seizures of imported goods and detentions of postal packets without court order will continue, and interference with personal possessions and private correspondence will still be legal.

The 1959 bill provided that no prosecutions for publishing an obscene article should be commenced without the consent of the Director of Public Prosecutions. This provision did not become law. The loss was not great for, as we have seen, experience does not suggest that it would have brought either uniformity or common sense to the administration of the law. This end could probably only be attained by giving special statutory protection to books that have been openly published for a number of years, to classics and foreign books of repute in their countries of origin, and to public corporations, learned libraries, and noncommercial art galleries.

The Act does nothing to relieve in any degree the responsibility of printers regarding obscene literature—a responsibility which tends to drive them to become censors of literature. This omission is not surprising because in their evidence before the Select Committee[19] the British Federation of Master Printers confined themselves to suggestions for general reforms of the law and repudiated any suggestion that they should be specially protected.

It should be noted that there is no right of trial by jury when the issue of obscenity is contested in forfeiture proceedings, although the result may be as important to those concerned and to the interests of literature, art, and science as the outcome of a prosecution for the offense of publishing an obscene article.

Finally, nothing has been done to clarify the legal position of nudist magazines. The evidence of the Customs given to the Select Committee on their attitude to foreign magazines was very confused and suggested that they were somewhat a law to themselves.[20]

The Act may be seen as a useful but modest piece of law reform which should introduce some degree of certainty and predictability into the law relating to obscene publications and prevent some of the worst abuses for which morally indignant judges, crusading officials, and ignorant magistrates have been responsible in the past. To what extent apprehensions about its defects are justified only experience of its operation can determine. It would, however, be unduly optimistic to think that opportunities for abuse at the instance of ignorant moral fanatics will never be taken advantage of where they exist, for such people are all too frequently found in the ranks of English legal, official, and political life. There is no doubt at all, however, that many problems left untouched by the Act will have to be tackled by future legislation if the law on this subject is to be brought into harmony with the requirements of intellectual and artistic freedom.

The shortcomings of the Act both as regards its scope and structure may perhaps be found in the nature of its genesis. It is essentially the reply of the literary professions and industries to what was felt to be a threat to its legitimate commercial rights. Like so much legislation resulting from the British political machine, it is a producers' rather than a consumers' measure.

The history of the movement for reform suggests that those who supported it, for all their undoubted public spirit, were mainly concerned that successful authors, the great publishing houses, the booksellers, and the printers should be left to pursue their callings in peace. The interests of the reading public, particularly the more scholarly and forward-looking section of it, did not receive so much consideration. The public is anxious to keep in touch with literary, sociological and scientific developments abroad as well as at home; but the home producers of books may put the free international exchange of ideas after more domestic interests. Finally, the work of the pioneer, whether in speculative thought or artistic achievement, so important to the scholar and the social reformer, may not loom very large in the vision of those principally concerned with commercial success.

Welcome as the new Act was, it obviated neither the need for present vigilance nor the urgency for further reform.

Censorship in America

ENGLISH COMMON LAW as it stood at the Revolution was taken over into American law. There seems to be some doubt whether the offense of obscene libel was part of this heritage. At any rate, little was heard of it till the beginning of the nineteenth century. But in the case of the *Commonwealth of Pennsylvania* v. *Sharpless* in 1815, certain yeomen, "being evil-disposed persons," were charged on indictment with exhibiting in a private house "a certain lewd, wicked, scandalous, infamous and obscene painting, representing a man in an obscene, impudent and indecent posture with a woman, to the manifest corruption and subversion of youth, and other citizens of this Commonwealth, to the evil example of others in like case offending, and against the peace and dignity of the Commonwealth of Pennsylvania." The common law was strengthened by statute in some of the states—Vermont (1821), Massachusetts (before 1835), and Connecticut (1834). There was also federal legislation against the importation of indecent pictures and articles (1842) and against the transmission of obscene books and pictures by mail (1865).

The sensitiveness of the American judges, and particularly the federal judges, to English legal opinion caused the American courts to follow English developments very closely. They readily turned to the Cockburn judgment after 1868 to help them to define such terms as "lewd," "lascivious," "indecent," and "obscene" when used in statutes and common law indictments.

The gradual stiffening of the law enabled the game of literary "smut-hunting" to develop with transatlantic exuberance. Charles Knowlton was fined in one Massachusetts town and imprisoned in another for publishing his *Fruits of Philosophy* in 1832. This pamphlet was subsequently made famous the world over by the Bradlaugh-Besant trial. Even that great figure in American literature, Walt Whitman, was attacked. At one time *Leaves of Grass* was banned; and in 1865 the author was dismissed from a post in the Department of the Interior because he was "the author of an indecent book." Chief Secretary Mr. James Harlan, the head of the Department, appears to have used his position to inspect Whitman's desk, and found there an annotated copy of *Leaves of Grass*, at that time out of print.[1]

It was left, however, to a perverted genius to bring the operation of American puritanism to its highest pitch so far as obscene publications were concerned. Anthony Comstock was born in 1844. He was the embodiment of Protestant Christianity at its narrowest and cruelest—a fanatic to whom everything was obscene that savored of sex. He started his career as a vice crusader by making arrests under a State of New York Act dealing with obscenity which was passed in the year of the Cockburn dictum, 1868. By 1872 he was working for the Young Men's Christian Association which had set up a Committee for the Suppression of Vice. The next year he managed to get through Congress a comprehensive Act, popularly known as the Comstock Act, which tightened up the federal law regarding obscene publications and which, most notably, brought contraceptive literature within the scope of its prohibitions. Comstock was appointed a special agent of the Post Office for enforcing this Act— a position which he held until his death in 1915.

The Committee of the Y.M.C.A. became the Society for the Suppression of Vice. It should be noted that this Society postdated its English namesake by seven decades. Indeed, Comstock did little more than add American efficiency and pep to the discoveries of English prudery. During a long and energetic life he waged a relentless campaign against what he deemed "obscenity." His professed criterion was possible harm to a child. Neither literature nor art was spared: his slogan was "Morals, not Art or Literature." As *agent provocateur*, he boasted of the number of his victims driven to suicide. For more than forty years he conducted a sort of reign of terror in the publishing world.

In 1905 he attacked *Mrs. Warren's Profession* as "one of Bernard Shaw's filthy productions": Shaw retaliated by adding the word "Comstockery" to Anglo-American speech. Elinor Glyn's *Three Weeks*, which escaped the attention of the criminal law in England, was barred from the mails and banned altogether in one state. In 1920, James Branch Cabell's *Jurgen* was the subject of a prosecution, but Judge Nott directed the grand jury in New York County to acquit it of obscenity.

In 1906 Theodore Schroeder wrote of the American Titan of vice suppression:

Mr. Comstock is also an unconscious witness to the harmlessness of obscenities. In a recent report he informs us that for thirty years he has "stood at the mouth of the sewer," searching for and devouring "obscenity" for a salary; and yet he claims that this lucrative delving in "filth" has left him, or made him, so much purer than all the rest of humanity that they cannot be trusted to choose their own literature and art until it has been expurgated by him.

It is perhaps worthy of note that in 1915, the year of his death, Comstock, who was by then becoming a figure of fun to the younger generation of Americans, was appointed by President Wilson to represent the United States at the International Purity Congress at the San Francisco Exhibition.

In the year of his death, Comstock had a brush with a woman who was to go a long way toward undoing his life's work so far as the prevention of the spread of contraceptive information was concerned. Not only had he brought contraceptive literature within the scope of the Federal Act of 1873, but he had succeeded in making the conveying of contraceptive information an offense in the State of New York, and other states followed suit. Such was his bigotry on this subject that he frequently referred to dealers in contraceptives as "abortionists."

The woman referred to was Margaret Sanger. In 1912 she awoke to a sudden realization of the now familiar evils that ensue from the withholding of contraceptive advice from the poorer classes. She journeyed to Paris to obtain the latest information on technique and henceforth the imparting of that information to her fellow-countrywomen became her life work. In her book, *My Fight for Birth Control*, she writes:

It was at this time I began to realize that Anthony Comstock was alive and active. His stunted, neurotic nature and savage methods of attack had ruined thousands of women's lives. He had indirectly caused the death of untold thousands. He and a weak-kneed Congress which, through a trick, in 1872 had given him the power of an autocrat, were directly responsible for the deplorable condition of a whole generation of women left physically damaged and spiritually crippled from the results of abortion. No group of women had yet locked horns with this public enemy.

In 1914 her paper *The Woman Rebel* was obstructed by the federal law on mailing. At the same time she wrote a pamphlet entitled *Family Limitation* and made arrangements for the distribution of 100,000 copies. She writes:

Within its covers was contained all the practical advice I could give, including the names and description of the devices used for contraception which I had obtained in France. It was simply and plainly written, and was dedicated to the wives of working men.

She was then indicted for articles which had appeared in *The Woman Rebel* and left the country in October 1914. In December a man presented himself at her husband's studio and said that he was personally acquainted with Mrs. Sanger and wanted a pamphlet on family limitation for his own use. Sanger gave him one. The man was a decoy sent by Comstock and in due course that gentleman arrived himself and arrested Sanger. He was brought to trial in September 1915 and promised acquittal if he would reveal the whereabouts of the author of the pamphlet. Sanger declined the offer. On conviction he served a term of imprisonment in default of paying a fine. Comstock gave evidence at the trial, took a chill, and died.

Margaret Sanger returned to the United States to stand her trial, but early in 1916 the Government entered a *nolle prosequi* and she went free.

During her visit to England before her trial Margaret Sanger visited Marie Stopes's house in Hampstead and imparted the information obtained from France. The subsequent propaganda of these two courageous women belongs to the history of contraception rather than to the subject of this book. Marie Stopes, it is pleasant to record, was not harassed by the law of obscene libel in England. Since the Bradlaugh-Besant case prosecutions of those advocating contraception in Great Britain have not been many. They have generally depended on accessory circumstances and have not been direct attacks on the subject itself.

The mantle of the great Comstock fell on John S. Sumner, his successor as Secretary of the New York Society for Suppression of Vice. This Elisha did his best to follow in the steps of his Elijah, but he lacked Comstock's perverted genius, his cruelty, and his vindictiveness. Very slowly public opinion and the legal atmosphere of the time was turning against all he stood for, and he was not nearly so successful as his predecessor in interfering with serious literature on the ground of obscenity.

As early as 1917 he experienced a serious reverse. He unsuccessfully prosecuted a bookseller for selling an English translation of Gautier's *Mademoiselle de Maupin*. A New York jury awarded damages against him for malicious prosecution and the judgment was upheld by the highest court of appeal in the State of New York.[3]

In September 1925 he was successful in effecting the seizure and confiscation of a thousand copies of the second volume of Frank Harris's *My Life and Loves* from a firm of American binders and Harris's chief agent in New York was prosecuted.[4] His attacks on books of repute, such as works by Flaubert and Gide, were, however, dogged by failure. Even more notable defeats were sustained over prosecutions in respect of *The Well of Loneliness*, *Let's Go Naked* (a translation of a book on nudism by Louis Charles Royer entitled *Au Pays des hommes nus*), and above all Erskine Caldwell's *God's Little Acre*, the case against the American publishers which was dismissed by Magistrate Benjamin Greenspan in New York on May 23, 1933.[5]

Comstockery was, however, still a force to be reckoned with. An amazing wave of censorship swept over Boston in the latter part of 1929, and a holocaust was made of over threescore books. The condemnations included the following list: *The Wayward Man* by St. John Ervine; *What I Believe* by Bertrand Russell; *Oil* by Upton Sinclair; *From Man to Man* by Oliver Schreiner; *Power* by Leon Feuchtwanger; *Twilight* by Count Keyserling; *The World of William Clissold* by H. G. Wells; *The Hard-Boiled Virgin* by Frances Newman; *Elmer Gantry* by Sinclair Lewis; *Doomsday* by Warwick Deeping; *The Sun Also Rises* by Ernest Hemingway.

The following year the Massachusetts Supreme Court upheld the conviction of Donald S. Friede for selling Theodore Dreiser's *An American Tragedy*. (The same author's *The Genius* had been suppressed in 1916.) At the same time the court upheld the conviction of a reputable Boston bookseller who had been trapped into selling a copy of D. H. Lawrence's *Lady Chatterley's Lover* to an *agent provocateur* employed by the New England Watch and Ward Society. The method of obtaining commission of the crime was adversely commented on by the court, the prosecuting counsel, and the Boston press. Mr. Sumner, who claimed to have instigated the whole thing, justified the use of the *agent provocateur* on the ground that he had information that the bookseller was supplying copies of *Lady Chatterley* to Harvard professors!

The Boston convictions focused public attention on the Massachusetts obscenity law. The relevant statute forbade the public sale of any book "*containing* obscene indecent language." Enlightened opinion forced a change to the words "a book which *is* obscene, indecent." This presumably meant that the book must be considered in its entirety.

Some reform was also obtained in relation to the powers of the Customs in relation to "obscenity." Prior to 1930 they were able to behave in a very arbitrary manner. Anything which the officials judged "obscene" could be confiscated without trial. A trial was necessary only if an aggrieved person was sufficiently wealthy and persistent to bring the case into court himself. This is still substantially the position in England. The American officials used their power to exclude such authors as Aristophanes, Defoe, Petronius, Rabelais, Boccaccio, Balzac, Rousseau, Casanova, and Voltaire in a most wholesale fashion. At the same time scientific works of recognized European reputation were seized. At last a young Baltimore attorney carried a case of seizure of *Daphnis and Chloë* by Longus and other books into court. He won a brilliant victory. Further indefensible seizures caused public agitation and finally the law was amended by the Tariff Act of 1930. In the first place, if seizure was contested, the Government and not the aggrieved person had to press proceedings in the courts. Secondly, the Secretary of the Treasury was given discretion to admit classics or books of recognized literary or scientific merit, even if obscene. As a result the Customs lifted the ban on Voltaire, Rabelais, Boccaccio, and many other authors without judicial compulsion. Shortly afterward the consignee of 120 seized copies of Dr. Johanne Rutgers's *The Sexual Life in Its Biological Significance* forced the issue to litigation and won a favorable verdict from the jury. In spite of improvements, however, the American Customs frequently perpetrated amazing follies. In 1933 they seized reproductions of a copy of the famous frescoes in the Sistine Chapel made before Daniele da Volterra had, at the command of Pope Paul IV, painted loincloths on Michelangelo's heroic figures.

There was also considerable improvement in relation to books of sex instruction. The Dennett case is very instructive. In 1918 Mary Ware Dennett, a well-known social worker, made a short compilation of elementary sex information for her two adolescent sons. The material subsequently appeared in the *Medical Review of Reviews* and was so enthusiastically received that it was reprinted in 1919 as a pamphlet entitled *The Sex Side of Life, an Explanation for Young People*. In 1922 the pamphlet was declared unmailable by the Post Office. Six years later the author fell into a trap set by the authorities and she was indicted for mailing the pamphlet to a fictitious "Mrs. Miles." A motion to quash the indictment failed and in 1929 she was convicted. The following year the conviction was reversed on appeal.[6]

In April 1931 a ban on Marie Stopes's *Married Love* was lifted by the enlightened decision of Federal Judge Woolsey[7] and the following year the same judge refused to find her *Contraception* obscene.

Toward Freedom in America

THE TIDE may be said to have turned definitely against Comstockery when James Joyce's *Ulysses* was cleared of obscenity by Judge Woolsey in 1933.

The troubles of *Ulysses* in America began when it was being serialized in *The Little Review*. Copies of the periodical were seized by the Post Office in 1919 and 1920. In December 1920 John S. Sumner's society initiated a prosecution in New York and after several postponements the case came up for trial on February 14, 1921. In the result Margaret Anderson, the editor of the review, was fined. She wanted to go to prison rather than pay, but a woman who did not approve of *Ulysses* saved her from jail by paying the fine herself.

When the work was first published in book form by Sylvia Beach in 1922, many copies posted to subscribers from Paris got through to their various destinations in the United States in spite of a Customs ban. Ernest Hemingway arranged for a friend to smuggle a consignment across a ferry from Canada (where the book was not banned) by making repeated journeys with copies hidden in his trousers.[1] At the end of the year the American post offices began holding up copies and finally an accumulation of 400–500 copies of Harriet Weaver's edition were confiscated and destroyed.[2]

It was impossible to copyright the work in the United States and pirated and bowdlerized editions were issued to meet the heavy demand for it. It is said[3] that no less than 30,000 copies were sold by clandestine methods in America and elsewhere. From these sales the unfortunate author, who was becoming more blind, derived no royalties.

The situation changed, however, when in 1933 Random House, Inc., who were publishing an American edition, challenged a seizure by the United States Customs of an imported copy under Section 305 of the Tariff Act, 1930. The clearance of the book by Judge Woolsey and the subsequent majority opinion[4] of the United States Court of Appeals delivered by Judge Augustus Hand in the following year which upheld the clearance made an important contribution to American law in regard to obscene publication. Four points were established:

1. . . . in any case where a book is claimed to be obscene it must first be determined whether the intent with which it was written was what is called, according to the usual phrase, pornographic—that is, written for the purpose of exploiting obscenity. If the conclusion is that the book is pornographic that is the end of the inquiry and forfeiture must follow. (Judge Woolsey)*

2. The meaning of the word obscene as legally defined by the Courts is: tending to stir the sex impulses or to lead to sexually impure and lustful thoughts. . . . Whether a particular book would tend to excite such impulses and thoughts must be tested by the Court's opinion as to its effect on a person with average sex instincts—what the French would call l'homme moyen sensuel—who plays, in this branch of legal inquiry, the same role of hypothetical reagent as does the "reasonable man" in the law of torts and "the man learned in the art" on questions of invention in patent law. . . . It is only with the normal person that the law is concerned. (Judge Woolsey)

3. It is settled at least so far as this court is concerned that works of physiology, medicine, science, and sex instruction are not within the statute, though to some extent and among some persons they may tend to promote lustful thoughts. We think the same immunity should apply to literature as to science where the presentation, when viewed objectively, is sincere and the erotic matter is not introduced to promote lust and does not furnish the dominant note

* For the complete text of Judge Woolsey's opinion see Appendix, p. 218-222.

of the publication. The question in each case is whether a publication taken as a whole has a libidinous effect. (Judge Hand)

4. We believe that the proper test of whether a given book is obscene is its dominant effect. In applying this test, relevancy of the objectionable parts to the theme, the established reputation of the work in the estimation of approved critics, if the book is modern, and the verdict of the past if it is ancient, are persuasive pieces of evidence, for works of art are not likely to sustain a high position with no better warrant for their existence than their obscene content. (Judge Hand)

In the appeal court a dissenting judgment by Judge Manton followed closely the Cockburn criterion.

The *Ulysses* case was applied by the federal courts, and many of the state courts adopted its standards wholly or in part, but some state courts still adhered to the Cockburn rule.

The federal statutory law on obscene publications is now embodied in the United States Code, Title 18, 1461–1463, and Title 19, 1305.

The long war against the Comstock Act of 1873 in its relation to contraceptive literature, begun by the courageous Margaret Sanger in the lifetime of its author, was brought within sight of a victorious conclusion in April 1938. In that month a decision of the United States Circuit Court of Appeals was given against the Government in *U.S.* v. *Certain Magazines* (*Marriage Hygiene*). The Court held that contraceptive literature could enter the United States under the Tariff Act without interference on the part of the Collector of Customs, provided the consignee, even though a layman, was a person qualified to receive it. The lawyers for the defense made the following statement:

We have won a very important legal victory, and one that is likely to have a highly salutary effect on the treatment accorded by lower courts to contraceptive books and materials. Prior to this decision, it was the policy of the Government to stop all contraceptive literature at the Customs regardless of the identity of the consignee. We now have an adjudication that such literature may freely enter, *provided* the consignee is a person qualified to receive it. The qualifications of the consignee may be established by a mere affidavit, and the procedure is very simple.

Subsequent decisions relating to contraceptives themselves have made artificial birth control fairly generally available in the United States, though the Roman Catholic Church keeps up a stubborn fight for the exclusive use of her harmful and unreliable "rhythm" method. Legally contraceptives can be supplied only for "the prevention of disease" in parents or offspring, but this is a very elastic phrase which is often very liberally stretched.[5]

American law in relation to nudist literature received some clarification from the outcome of protracted litigation concerning Maurice Parmelee's classic book on the subject. The book was first published in America under the title *The New Gymnosophy*. This edition was threatened with legal proceedings by the Federal District Attorney for the County of New York in spite of the fact that the American Customs authorities gave a favorable opinion upon it. There was, however, no prosecution. The plates of this edition did not show the sexual organs. A revised edition with integral plates was published in America in 1931 and in Great Britain in 1933. In 1934 the District Court of Columbia ordered copies seized by the Customs under the Tariff Act of 1930 to be destroyed because of the illustrations. The American Civil Liberties Union assisted in the defense, and on appeal the United States Court of Appeals of the District of Columbia[6] cleared the book on May 4, 1940, by a majority decision. The opinion, after declaring that it cannot be assumed that nudity is obscene per se and under all circumstances, said:

The picturization here challenged has been used in the libelled book to accompany an honest, sincere, scientific and educational study and exposition of a sociological phenomenon and is, in our opinion, clearly permitted by present-day concepts of propriety.

Nudist magazines have not received consistent treatment by the American courts and a magazine condemned in one state has sometimes been exonerated in another. Generally speaking condemnations have not been made on the ground of nudity per se but because in the opinion of the court the illustrations have been designed to appeal not to the legitimate interests of the nudist movement but to salacious tastes among the general public.[7]

In 1940 a distressing incident occurred which, although it did not directly invoke the law of obscenity, is germane to the subject because it shows up the power and vigor of the forces opposed to free speculation about sexual ethics.

At this time Bertrand Russell was living in America. He was employed by the University of California and had agreed to give the William James Lectures at Harvard in the autumn. On February 26, the Board of Higher Education of New York City invited him to be Professor of Philosophy at the College of the City of New York. The appointment was to run until June 30, 1942, his seventieth birthday. He accepted the post and resigned his professorship from the University of California.

When the matter was made public William T. Manning, a bishop of the Episcopalian Church, wrote a letter to the press denouncing the appointment on the ground that Russell was "a recognized propagandist against religion and morality and who specifically defends adultery." This letter was only the first of a series of attacks, ecclesiastical and political in origin. An attempt by a member of the board, one of Bishop Manning's communicants, to have the appointment rescinded by the board was unsuccessful.

The next step took the form of what is known as a taxpayer's suit in the New York Supreme Court by a Mrs. Jean Kay, a dentist's wife, of Brooklyn. Her main plea was that Russell was an advocate of sexual immorality and that she was apprehensive of what might happen to her daughter, Gloria, if she became one of his pupils. It was not revealed who was paying the costs of the suit.

Mrs. Kay's lawyer, Joseph Goldstein, in his brief described Russell's writings as "lecherous, libidinous, lustful, venerous, erotomaniac, aphrodisiac, irreverent, narrow-minded, untruthful and bereft of moral fiber." He alleged that Russell had gone in for salacious poetry, had conducted a nudist colony in England, and approved of homosexuality.

The suit was heard before Judge John E. McGeehan, a Roman

Catholic who had previously distinguished himself by trying to have a portrait of Martin Luther removed from a courtroom mural illustrating legal history. On March 30 he delivered judgment voiding the appointment on three main grounds. Two were technical, concerning noncitizenship and the absence of a competitive examination, and would have excluded almost any distinguished foreigner from the College. The third ground was that the appointment sponsored or encouraged violations of the criminal law in regard to abduction and seduction of persons under eighteen, adultery, and homosexuality; and adversely affected public health, safety, and morals. In support of this ground the judge quoted passages dealing with premarital and extramarital relationships from Russell's *Education and the Modern World* (1926), *Marriage and Morals* (1929), and *What I Believe* (1925).

It was naturally expected that this preposterous decision would be appealed against. Distinguished individuals and enlightened bodies rallied to Russell's support from all sides. By a majority the Board of Higher Education decided to appeal; but Fiorello La Guardia, a cautious politician who was mayor at the time, wanted to avoid further trouble and the New York City Corporation supported him. All Russell's efforts to associate himself with the suit and to defend his work and reputation in the courts came to nothing.

A tremendous body of American opinion, however, ranged itself on Russell's side. A collection of essays[8] by eminent contributors representing very different philosophies and social viewpoints agreed on the unqualified necessity of honest and scientific discussion of human problems; and pressure brought on Harvard to cancel its invitation to Russell was firmly resisted. These reactions were evidence of the essential soundness of American opinion in relation to freedom of expression in spite of the existence of conditions which make occasional obscurantist activity too often successful.

Puritanical zeal resulted in some remarkable prosecutions. For instance Kathleen Winsor's monumental and repetitive novel, *Forever Amber*, was attacked, but in 1948 was cleared by an appeal court, the judge observing that the book, by its very repetitions of Amber's adventures in sex, acts like a soporific rather than an aphrodisiac. While conducive to sleep, it is not conducive to a desire to sleep with a member of the opposite sex.

During the earlier stages of the case copies of the book were burned by the British Customs and by certain English public libraries including Birmingham.[9]

In 1948 Ernest J. Besig, the director of the American Civil Liberties Union, attempted to import into the United States copies of Henry Miller's *Tropic of Cancer* and *Tropic of Capricorn* which, as we have seen, were published in Paris. The copies were seized by the American Customs and Mr. Besig sued for their release. The outcome showed up the less liberal side of American law and practice. The judge, Louis E. Godman, who tried the case without a jury, was unsympathetic; and brushed aside reviews of the books and other evidence of literary merit. He dismissed the suit and on October 23, 1953,[10] the Ninth Circuit Court of Appeals upheld his decision.

In the early years of this century Theodore Schroeder, an American lawyer and champion of literary freedom, had argued at length in a number of articles that laws against obscene literature in the United States of America were unconstitutional.

This issue received the highest judicial attention when a volume of stories entitled *Memoirs of Hecate County* by Edmund Wilson, a leading American critic, published in 1946, was attacked by the redoubtable John Sumner. The publishers were charged in 1948 before a New York court with publication of an obscene work, particular objection being taken to a story entitled "The Princess with the Golden Hair." Professor Lionel Trilling testified to the literary and moral qualities of the book but the prosecution succeeded and the judgment was upheld on appeal. Finally the case came before the United States Supreme Court[11] on the sole issue that the constitutional guarantees in relation to the freedom of the press had been infringed. On this matter the court was equally divided.

The book had also been condemned in Los Angeles but cleared in San Francisco. It circulates freely in Great Britain in a text which is integral except for the suppression of a nobleman's name.

The constitutional argument was taken up and applied by Judge Curtis Bok at Philadelphia in 1949[12] when he dismissed indictments brought by the police in respect of nine novels. The books were: *The Studs Lonigan Trilogy* (1932-1935) and *A World I Never Made* (1936) by James T. Farrell; *Sanctuary* (1931) and *Wild Palms* (1939) by William Faulkner; *God's Little Acre* by Erskine Caldwell; *End as a Man* by Calder Willingham (1949); *Never Love a Stranger* by Harold Robbins (1948). As we have seen, *God's Little Acre* had been cleared by a New York magistrate in 1933. *A World I Never Made* had been similarly cleared in 1937. A previous seizure of *The Studs Lonigan Trilogy* by the Philadelphia police had been successfully contested in 1948.

In a long and reasoned opinion Judge Bok said that the law did "not penalize anyone who seeks to change the prevailing moral or sexual code" and he deplored the "complete confusion between post office and the Customs over what constitutes obscenity." He then reviewed English and American developments and said that it was quite clear that the "harsh rule" laid down by Lord Chief Justice Cockburn had been supplanted in the American courts by a modern rule:

From all these cases the modern rule is that obscenity is measured by the erotic allurement upon the average modern reader; that the erotic allurement of a book is measured by whether it is sexually impure—i.e. pornographic, "dirt for dirt's sake," a calculated incitement to sexual desire—or whether it reveals an effort to reflect life, including its dirt, with reasonable accuracy and balance; and that mere coarseness or vulgarity is not obscenity.

This passage reflects a great deal of what was said by Judge Woolsey in the *Ulysses* case.

Judge Bok then proceeded to review the constitutional guarantees of freedom of expression and concluded that a statute penalizing obscenity could only be applied

where there is a reasonable and demonstrable cause to believe that a crime or misdemeanour has been committed or is about to be committed as the perceptible result of the publication and distribution of the writing in question; the opinion of anyone that a tendency reto exists or that such a result is self-evident is insufficient and irrelevant. The causal connection between the book and the criminal behaviour must appear beyond a reasonable doubt.

The decision was subsequently affirmed on appeal to the Superior Court of Pennsylvania.[13]

A striking example of the lack of uniformity as between one state and another in regard to the treatment of literature is provided by the fact that about this time *God's Little Acre* was banned in Massachusetts on appeal to the Supreme Court of that state.

In 1952 the House of Representatives set up a Select Committee on Current Pornographic Materials, under the chairmanship of Mr. E. C. Gathings of Arkansas, to investigate the extent of the trade in obscene literature and to recommend changes in the law. The Committee devoted most of its attention to cheap books, "cheesecake" magazines and "horror comics." The report recommended minor changes in the federal law, such as that the law prohibiting the transportation of obscene books should cover private as well as public transport. Otherwise the Committee contented itself with exhorting the publishing industry to put its house in order. A minority report complained among other things that the Committee had not adequately distinguished between "what may broadly be classified as obscene and what falls within the realm of free thought and creative expression."

Judge Bok's ruling as to the constitutional position of obscenity statutes and much other argument on the same lines was swept away on June 14, 1957, when the United States Supreme Court decided by a majority in *Roth* v. *United States*[14] that:

(1) obscenity, whatever it may be, is not within the area of protected speech and Press under the First Amendment, and

(2) in view of this exclusion the Court would not apply, in connection with a prosecution involving obscenity, the "clear and probable danger" test which would require a causal relationship between allegedly offending material and anti-social conduct.*

The First Amendment to the Constitution reads:

* For the complete text of the majority opinion see Appendix, p. 223-230.

Congress shall make no law respecting an establishment of religion, or prohibiting the free exercise thereof; or abridging the freedom of speech or of the Press.

This restriction applies equally to state legislatures as a consequence of the Fourteenth Amendment.

The Supreme Court decision, however, made it very plain that the area which can be excluded from constitutional protection is narrowly limited. The opinion included the words:

All ideas having even the slightest redeeming social importance—unorthodox ideas, controversial ideas, even ideas hateful to the prevailing climate of opinion—have the full protection of the guarantees, unless excludable because they encroach upon the limited area of more important interests.

With regard to the test of obscenity the opinion said:

Some American courts adopted this [the Cockburn] standard but later decisions have rejected it and substituted this test: whether to the average person, applying contemporary community standards, the dominant theme of the material taken as a whole appeals to prurient interest. The *Hicklin* test, judging obscenity by the effect of isolated passages upon the most susceptible persons, might well encompass material legitimately treating with sex, and so it must be rejected as unconstitutionally restrictive of the freedoms of speech and press.

After the Roth case the Supreme Court reversed three findings of obscenity upheld by the United States Court of Appeals. The material involved included the nudist magazines *Sunshine and Health* and *Sun* containing photographs plainly showing genitalia.

The work initiated by Professor Alfred C. Kinsey, who gave his name to the well-known "Kinsey Reports" on the sexual behavior of human beings, has not gone unhampered by American law. He founded an Institute for Sex Research at Indiana University and for years the Customs seized material sent to the Institute from abroad. Protracted litigation culminated on October 31, 1957, in a victory for freedom of scientific investigation. Judge Edmund L.

Palmieri of the United States Court, Southern District of New York, gave a decision in favor of the Institute. The gist of the decision was that the material, although unquestionably obscene were it in the hands of the general public, was not obscene in the hands of scientists. "What is obscenity to one person is but a subject of scientific inquiry to another,"[15] the judge pointed out. The Customs did not appeal and announced that they would base their future policy on the decision.

The series of enlightened court decisions which began with the *Ulysses* case, and the corresponding liberalizing of American public opinion with regard to obscenity, have secured for the United States a measure of literary freedom which compares favorably with that enjoyed in England even after the passing of the Obscene Publications Act in 1959. Of the many champions of liberty who have contributed to this happy change we may mention Morris L. Ernst, the lawyer who defended *Ulysses*. He fought case after case with ability, courage, and success, and wrote much in the cause for which he stood.

As a result of the Roth decision it appears that both Congressmen and members of state legislatures are addressing themselves seriously to the problem of devising obscenity laws which will leave serious literature alone and, at the same time, be effective against commercial pornography. Some recent state enactments display a realistic appreciation of the situation. For instance, learned, university, and public libraries are specifically excluded from the application of an Act passed by Washington in 1959. In deciding the constitutionality of such legislation the courts have been concerned to see that Acts for the protection of children do not in fact prohibit the circulation to the general public of material deemed unsuitable for minors.

Generally speaking the realities and importance of this subject seem to be better understood in the United States than in England, and the opposition to the censorship is more organized and cohesive. The American Civil Liberties Union has been quite active from time to time about this aspect of liberty, while it is largely neglected by the National Council for Civil Liberties in England.

The American Book Publishers Council publishes a periodical Censorship Bulletin which presents a unified front over attacks on genuine literature, whereas in Britain publishers seem to be left to fight their own battles individually. However, we shall see in the next chapter that the results in the critical use of *Lady Chatterley's Lover* have been the same in both countries.

Lady Chatterley's Lover

IN ENGLAND the Obscene Publications Act, 1959, marks the extent to which Parliament was prepared to go toward the reform of the law on literary obscenity and it is safe to say that it will be the statutory basis of the law for some time to come. In the United States the Supreme Court judgment in the Roth case in 1957 was the culmination of a series of judicial decisions which had liberalized and clarified the law and it is unlikely that important changes or further progress will be made in the near future.

The merits of the positions thus arrived at in the two countries were soon put to a significant and practical test in respect of a book that has been the concern of the authorities since it was written more than thirty years before.

If *The Rainbow* is D. H. Lawrence's most important novel, *Lady Chatterley's Lover* is certainly the most notorious; and Lawrence valued it highly as an expression of his message to the world. It was begun in 1926 when Lawrence was living at the Villa Mirenda near Florence. He wrote three versions of the manuscript during the period October 1926 to January 1928. The book does not differ markedly from Lawrence's other work as regards the sort of philosophical and moral message expounded, but it is unique in that the author employed a sexual vocabulary which had long passed out of polite usage and allowed himself great freedom in his descriptions of sexual congress and love play. A similar license had been taken by Joyce in *Ulysses* which had achieved world-wide success as a banned book. There the same vocabulary and the same freedom in description had been used to express an attitude to sex of which Lawrence did not approve: in *Lady Chatterley's Lover* he allowed himself this liberty in putting forward his own passionately held views on the subject.

This calculated challenge to convention put publication in English-speaking countries out of the question at the time. The first edition was published in July 1928 from Florence with the aid of Giuseppe Orioli, who ran a bookshop of international fame in that city. Lawrence, who was nearing the end of his life, had become a prominent literary figure. There was a considerable demand for the book which was met by the discreet distribution of copies. Richard Aldington and other friends helped by receiving consignments at their offices and country cottages in England and disposing of them according to instructions from Florence.[1] The British and American Customs authorities, however, soon began confiscating copies; and Lawrence, who could establish no copyright in the work, suffered grievously from the rivalry of pirated editions. To combat this robbery he issued a cheaper but integral edition from Paris in 1929. This edition has an introduction entitled "My Skirmish with Jolly Roger"[2] in which Lawrence gallantly defends his book and scorns the pirates. The expurgated editions published in Great Britain and America after Lawrence's death were, in the very nature of the circumstances, no more than emasculated ghosts of his work. It was lamentable, however, that, as in the case of other works by Lawrence expurgated by the publishers, the volumes contained nothing which revealed the fact that the author's text had been mangled.

This situation continued substantially the same for thirty years. Lawrence's reputation as one of the great literary figures of the century was firmly established, every serious student of his work had to obtain by hook or by crook a copy of the unexpurgated *Lady Chatterley's Lover* which was given serious and detailed attention by his numerous biographers and critics. I remember myself, in the early thirties, hurriedly finishing my reading of a copy I was bringing from Paris before reaching Dover for fear that the Customs might find it in my baggage. Odd copies brought before the courts in England and the United States were always held to be obscene.

This dreary scene was suddenly changed when in 1959 the Grove Press of New York, with the approval of Frieda Lawrence Ravagli, Lawrence's widow, distributed an unexpurgated edition through a book club named Readers' Subscription. The volume had a preface by Archibald MacLeish, former Librarian of Congress and a distinguished man of letters, and an introduction by Mark Schorer, Professor of English Literature at the University of California, a leading scholar of D. H. Lawrence and his work.

Copies of this edition were detained in the mails and on June 11 the Postmaster General, Arthur E. Summerfield, declared the book nonmailable on the ground of obscenity. He also banned circulars advertising the work. The publishers brought an action[3] seeking to restrain the Post Office from enforcing this decision and asking for a declaration that the book was not obscene within the meaning of the statute barring obscene matter from the mails, or if it were that the statute was unconstitutional as violating the guarantees of the First and Fifth Amendments.

On July 21, 1959, Federal Judge Frederick van Pelt Bryan delivered a decision* in favor of the book. The judge made it clear that the Postmaster General had no discretion as to what he was to treat as obscene. He could only apply the current legal standard and his decisions could always be challenged in the courts.

The opinion referred to the reputable manner in which the book had been published and to the fact that Readers' Subscription subscribers were relatively small in numbers and drawn largely from academic, literary, and scholarly fields. After reviewing the *Ulysses* case and the Roth case the judge continued:

Both cases held that, to be obscene, the dominant effect of the book must be an appeal to prurient interest—that is to say, shameful or morbid interest in sex. Such a theme must so predominate as to submerge any ideas of "redeeming social importance" which the publication contains.

It is not the effect upon the irresponsible, the immature or the sensually minded which is controlling. The material must be judged in terms of its effect on those it is likely to reach who are conceived of as the average man of normal sensual impulses, or, as

* For the complete text see Appendix p. 231-248.

Judge Woolsey says, "what the French would call l'homme moyen sensuel."

The material must also exceed the limits of tolerance imposed by current standards of the community with respect to freedom of expression in matters concerning sex and sex relations. Moreover, a book is not to be judged by excerpts or individual passages but must be judged as a whole.

All of these factors must be present before a book can be held obscene and thus outside constitutional protections.

Judged by these standards, "Lady Chatterley's Lover" is not obscene. The decision of the Postmaster General that it is obscene and therefore non-mailable is contrary to law and clearly erroneous. This is emphasized when the book is considered against its background and in the light of its stature as a significant work of a distinguished English novelist.

After outlining the plot of the novel the judge continued:

The book is replete with fine writing and with descriptive passages of rare beauty. There is no doubt of its literary merit.

It contains a number of passages describing sexual intercourse in great detail with complete candor and realism. Four-letter Anglo-Saxon words are used with some frequency.

These passages and this language understandably will shock the sensitive minded. Be that as it may, these passages are relevant to the plot and to the development of the characters and of their lives as Lawrence unfolds them. The language which shocks, except in a rare instance or two, is not inconsistent with character, situation or theme.

Even if it be assumed that these passages and this language taken in isolation tend to arouse shameful, morbid and lustful sexual desires in the average reader, they are an integral, and to the author a necessary part of the development of theme, plot and character. The dominant theme, purpose and effect of the book as a whole is not an appeal to prurience or the prurient minded. The book is not "dirt for dirt's sake." Nor do these passages and this language submerge the dominant theme so as to make the book obscene even if they could be considered and found to be obscene in isolation. . . .

The tests of obscenity are not whether the book or passages from it are in bad taste or shock or offend the sensibilities of an individual, or even of a substantial segment of the community. Nor are we concerned with whether the community would approve of Constance Chatterley's morals. The statute does not purport to regulate the morals portrayed or the ideas expressed in a novel, whether or not they are contrary to the accepted moral code, nor could it constitutionally do so.

The judge then dealt with the contention (as old as the Cockburn judgment) that the author's intention has no relevance to the question whether his work is obscene:

No doubt an author may write a clearly obscene book in the mistaken belief that he is serving a high moral purpose. The fact that this is the author's purpose does not redeem the book from obscenity.

But the sincerity and honesty of purpose of an author as expressed in the manner in which a book is written and in which his theme and ideas are developed has a great deal to do with whether it is of literary and intellectual merit. Here, as in the Ulysses case, there is no question about Lawrence's honesty and sincerity of purpose, artistic integrity and lack of intention to appeal to prurient interest.

Thus, this is an honest and sincere novel of literary merit and its dominant theme and effect, taken as a whole, is not an appeal to the prurient interest of the average reader.

The judge then referred to a finding by the Postmaster General that the book offended contemporary community standards, and continued:

I am unable to ascertain upon what the Postmaster General based this conclusion. The record before him indicates general acceptance of the book throughout the country and nothing was shown to the contrary. The critics were unanimous. Editorial comment by leading journals of opinion welcomed the publication and decried any attempts to ban it.

He pointed out that frank descriptions of the sex act and "four-letter" words frequently appear in contemporary novels; and declared:

I hold that, at this stage in the development of our society, this major English novel does not exceed the outer limits of the tolerance which the community as a whole gives to writing about sex and sex relations.

The opinion concluded by relating the case to the constitutional problem involved:

It is essential to the maintenance of a free society that the severest restrictions be placed upon restraints which may tend to prevent the dissemination of ideas. It matters not whether such ideas be expressed in political pamphlets or works of political, economic or social theory or criticism, or through artistic media. All such expressions must be freely available.

A work of literature published and distributed through normal channels by a reputable publisher stands on quite a different footing from hard core pornography furtively sold for the purpose of profiting by the titillation of the dirty minded. . . .

To exclude this book from the mails on the grounds of obscenity would fashion a rule which could be applied to a substantial portion of the classics of our literature. Such a rule would be inimical to a free society. To interpret the obscenity statute so as to bar "Lady Chatterley's Lover" from the mails would render the statute unconstitutional in its application, in violation of the guarantees of freedom of speech and the press contained in the First Amendment.

This decision was unanimously upheld by the 2nd Circuit Court of Appeals in New York on March 25, 1960, Chief Judge Charles E. Clark saying that Lawrence "writes with power and indeed with moving tenderness which is compelling, once our age-long inhibitions against sex revelations have been passed."[4] On June 2 it was announced that no appeal would be carried to the Supreme Court.[5]

Throughout this period of litigation the press was generally approving in its attitude to the Grove Press publication and even religious periodicals were not unfavorable. *The Living Church,*[6] an official Episcopal journal, said that *Lady Chatterley's Lover* was an unsmirking adult novel and the editor criticized all censorship except parental.

Since the Universal Copyright Convention of 1952 had no retroactive effect, and since under the law as it previously stood, American copyright could not be obtained for any book published outside the United States unless an edition was wholly manufactured in the States shortly after the original publication, no American copyright could be claimed in *Lady Chatterley's Lover*. The lifting of the obscenity ban stimulated the pirating of both unexpurgated and expurgated texts, and to meet this threat to their legitimate interests the Grove Press issued a paperback reprint of the volume that had been the subject of Judge Bryan's decision.

The Grove Press followed up their *Lady Chatterley* victory by announcing the open publication of Henry Miller's *The Tropic of Cancer* for June 24, 1961. Copies appeared in New York bookshops weeks before publication date and the book was banned from the mails by the United States Post Office.[7] The ban was lifted without the issue being brought to trial. On September 5, 1962, Grove Press published *The Tropic of Capricorn* without interference.

Even the expurgated edition of *Lady Chatterley's Lover* did not go unmolested in England. In 1953 the magistrate (Mr. W. E. Batt) at Thames Police Court was asked to make destruction orders in respect of a number of books, all of a rubbishy character except *Lady Chatterley's Lover* which happened to be included in the seizure. The actual defendants raised no objection but the publishers of Lawrence's novel, William Heinemann, put in a special plea for the book:

The Magistrate: I have read the book and it is absolute rubbish.

Counsel: I am not here to defend its literary merits but I do not know which edition you read—the expurgated or the unexpurgated.

The Magistrate: Whichever version, it was still rubbish, but I suppose it must have been the expurgated—I should have chucked the other on the fire.

Detective Sergeant Herbert Bird said that he had not read the book but he had been instructed by the Director of Public Prosecutions to ask for its destruction.

The magistrate decided that the book was not sufficiently obscene to justify destruction and excluded it from the order covering the other books.[8]

Encouraged by the reforms effected by the Obscene Publications Act, 1959, and also no doubt by the clearance of the book by the American courts, Penguin Books proposed to publish the unexpurgated text of the novel in their ordinary format.

Difficulties at once presented themselves. In the House of Commons the Attorney General would not say whether or not a prosecution would result and Penguin's normal printers refused to fulfill their contract in respect of the book.[9] Other printers were, however, found and publication was announced for August 25, 1960. Inquiries were then set on foot by Scotland Yard,[10] and by agreement the book was "published" by handing over a number of copies to the police, general publication being postponed indefinitely.[11]

On August 19 a summons was applied for at Bow Street on behalf of the Director of Public Prosecutions under the Obscene Publications Act, 1959.[12] No doubt because of the co-operative attitude of Penguin Books in postponing general publication, only the company was prosecuted, no charge being made (as is generally the practice) against the directors individually and personally. When the case came up before the magistrate on September 8 the defendants, who elected to be tried by jury, were committed for trial at the Old Bailey.[13] It is interesting to note, however, that before Penguin Books came up for trial the Southend magistrates distinguished themselves by anticipating the verdict. A continental unexpurgated edition of *Lady Chatterley's Lover* was among some hundreds of books and other articles seized by the police from a commercial lending library. After retiring to read passages marked by the police (a procedure contrary to the principles of the Act of 1959) the magistrates ruled the book to be obscene.[14]

The trial of Penguin Books Ltd. began at the Central Criminal Court before Mr. Justice Byrne on October 21.

Opening for the prosecution, Mr. Mervyn Griffith-Jones said:[15]

When you have seen this book and, making all such allowances in favour of it as you can, the prosecution will invite you to say that it does tend, and certainly may tend, to induce lustful thoughts in the minds of those who read it.

It goes further, you may think. It sets on a pedestal promiscuous intercourse and it commends and sets out to commend sensuality almost as a virtue, and encourages and even advocates coarseness and vulgarity of thought and language. You may think it must tend to deprave the minds certainly of some, and maybe many, of the persons who are likely to buy it at the price of 3s. 6d. and who read it, with 200,000 copies already printed and ready for release.

Outlining the plot, Mr. Griffith-Jones said that there were twelve very detailed descriptions of sexual intercourse, the only variation being the time and place of the incidents. The emphasis was always on the pleasure, the satisfaction, and the sensuality of the episode. The jury might think that the plot was little more than padding between one episode and the next. There was also the use of "four-letter" words. One word was used some thirty times, another fourteen times, another thirteen times, and others six, four, and three times. It was against that background that the jury must view the more purple passages.

Mr. Gerald Gardiner, Q.C., for the defense, submitted that the prosecution should not prejudice the jury's mind on particular passages before they had read the book as a whole; and the judge ruled the particular passages should not be read until after formal prosecution evidence and defense opening.

A police officer then gave evidence about the arrangements made with the publishers concerning the case; and was cross-examined by Mr. Gerald Gardiner, Q.C., for the defense:[16]

Mr. Gardiner asked: "Do you know any civilized country where copies of Lady Chatterley's Lover cannot be bought, except in Lawrence's Commonwealth?"

Mr. Griffith-Jones objected to this. He said what happened in other countries was not relevant.

Mr. Gardiner submitted that evidence of the book being available in all the civilized countries of the world would be evidence of its literary value, but the judge told him: "I am against that."

In opening the case for the defense, Mr. Gardiner said that the book must be taken as a whole as tending to deprave and corrupt, which obviously involved a change of character, leading the reader to do something wrong which he would not otherwise have done. The author was clearly a strong supporter of marriage and hated promiscuity. The defense would say that the book was not obscene and it would not tend to deprave anyone. It was a book the publication of which was in the public interest. The publishers relied on the status of Lawrence as an author and his place in English literature. Few would disagree that he was among the six greatest of English novelists of the century. The descriptions of physical union were necessary to what Lawrence was trying to say, and he thought that if he used words which had been part of our spoken speech for about 600 years, he could purify them from the shame which they had achieved since Victorian times.

A novel feature was introduced in regard to the reading of the book by the jury, who had each been supplied with a copy:[17]

After the luncheon adjournment Mr. Justice Byrne asked when it was proposed that the jury should read the book.

Mr. Gardiner said that the usual practice in recent years had been for the jury to take a book home for reading, but Mr. Justice Byrne replied that he was not in agreement with that.

Mr. Gardiner said that in the case heard before Mr. Justice Stable, the jury were sent home to read the book. As this had been the position in recent years, there were no special considerations in this case why the usual practice should be departed from.

"Indeed," he said, "it has these advantages: first, the jury rooms are jolly uncomfortable, with hard wooden seats, and anything more unnatural than twelve men and women sitting on hard chairs round a table, reading a book in one another's presence, is hard to imagine." Apart from these considerations, he said, some people were slower readers than others.

Mr. Griffith-Jones said he did not wish to cause the jury any discomfort, but the proper course would be for them to read the book in their room.

Mr. Gardiner: It is very undesirable.

After further consideration, Mr. Justice Byrne told the jury that he thought they should read the book at Court. "I am sorry," he said, "and I do not want to subject you to any kind of discomfort, but if you were to take this book home you might have distractions."

It was agreed that the trial should be adjourned until Thursday, October 27th, and that the jury should meet at the court each day, except Saturday and Sunday, to read the book in their room.

When the trial was resumed the defense began to call a series of expert witnesses to testify to the literary and other merits of the book as allowed by section 4 of the Act of 1959. Contrary to the usual practice in criminal trials, these witnesses were not allowed in court while evidence other than their own was being given. The witnesses included Miss Helen Gardner, Dame Rebecca West, the Bishop of Woolwich and two other Anglican clerics, Professor Vivian de Sola Pinto, Sir William Emrys Williams (the secretary-general of the Arts Council), Mr. Richard Hoggart, Mr. E. M. Forster, Mr. Roy Jenkins, M.P., Mr. Norman St. John-Stevas, Sir Alan Lane, Sir Stanley Unwin, Miss Dilys Powell, Mr. C. Day Lewis, Miss Janet Adam Smith, and Mr. Hector Alastair Hetherington.

According to their positions in life the witnesses testified to the literary, educational, sociological, psychological, and ethical merits of the book. The prosecution objected to the Bishop of Woolwich as a witness on the ground that ethical considerations were not mentioned in the Obscene Publications Act, but the judge upheld the defense's contention that the words of section 4, "literary, artistic, scientific or other merits," could include ethical merits. The judge also ruled that although the book could be compared with others for literary merit, the defense could not use evidence to show that other books were obscene. In his evidence on literary merit, Mr. Hetherington, the editor of *The Guardian*, spoke of the open sale of books dealing with sadism, Lesbianism, perversion, and various forms of violence.

Although the evidence of these witnesses was formally confined to the literary and other merits of the book and was not concerned with the issue of obscenity, a great deal of what was said went to demolish the prosecution's reasons for alleging that the work was obscene (e.g., that it put promiscuity on a pedestal, that it consisted of repetitive descriptions of sexual intercourse connected by mere padding, etc.). Much of the evidence supported the defense's contention that Lawrence was a strong supporter of marriage. Some witnesses said that expurgation ruined the book, and some spoke in favor of the use of "four-letter" words.

In all the defense called thirty-five witnesses and had available another thirty-six who were not called. The prosecution called no witnesses. Mr. Griffith-Jones explained this by saying that he conceded that Lawrence was a great writer and that the book was of some merit. There can be no doubt that it would have been impossible to find witnesses prepared to speak against the book at all comparable in number and eminence with the array produced by the defense.

In his summing-up, Mr. Justice Byrne interpreted the law as laid down in the 1959 Act. He told the jury that they had to consider the two limbs of the case. First, had the prosecution satisfied them beyond all reasonable doubt that the book was obscene—if not they would acquit—and, if it was obscene, had the defendants (on whom the onus of proof rested in this matter) established on the balance of probabilities that the merits of the book as a novel were so high that they outbalanced the obscenity so that its publication was for the public good?

The evidence the jury had to consider about whether the book was obscene was the evidence of the book itself taken as a whole, the judge explained. A book was obscene if it had a tendency to deprave and corrupt persons who were likely, having regard to all the relevant circumstances, to read it. His lordship observed:

To deprave meant to make morally bad, to pervert, to debase or corrupt morally: the words "to corrupt" meant to render morally unsound, to destroy morally the purity or chastity, to pervert or ruin a good quality, to debase, to defile. There was no intent to deprave or corrupt necessary to be proved in order that this offense should be committed. The intention was quite irrelevant.

As regards the circumstances of publication, the judge said that the jury might think that in these days of high wages and high pocket money the price of 3s 6d would put the book within the grasp of the vast mass of the population.

His lordship commented individually and somewhat critically on the evidence of a number of the expert witnesses and observed generally that "in these days the world seemed to be full of experts." He pointed out that the jury must consider the public—not so much the student of literature as the person who perhaps knew nothing about literature or the author but reads the book "during the lunch-time break at the factory, and takes it home in the evening to finish it."

On November 2, after a trial occupying five days,[18] the jury retired for three hours and returned with a verdict of "Not Guilty," which was greeted by a burst of applause from the public in court.

The result of the case was commented on with very general approval by the responsible press. *The Times* was a notable exception. A leader in that august organ entitled "A Decent Reticence"[19] declared the verdict to be "a challenge to society to resist the changes in its manners and conduct that may flow from it." A large number of letters appeared in the correspondence columns of the newspapers and weeklies. Very extreme views on either side were expressed in some instances. Lord Morrison in the *Daily Mail* displayed his ignorance of the state of the law on obscene publications during his term of office as Home Secretary.[20]

The Archbishop of Canterbury at his Diocesan Conference said that the Bishop of Woolwich was "mistaken to think that he could take part in this trial without becoming a stumbling-block and a cause of offence to many Christians."[21] The bishop made a reasoned defense of his action in *The Observer* and the *Church Times*,[22] while Canon Ronald Preston preached in his favor at Manchester Cathedral.[23] The Bishop of Hereford, on the other hand, could read no more than two-thirds of the book and said it was an offense against the moral health of the community.[24]

Some public libraries announced they would stock the book in the ordinary way, others that it would be kept off the open shelves but supplied on demand, and others that they would not have it at all. The Nottingham City Council passed, by sixteen votes to fifteen, a motion moved by an eighty-eight-year-old alderman asking their Public Libraries Committee not to implement a decision to make the book available.[25]

Mrs. Barbara Barr, Lawrence's step-daughter, no doubt spoke for a multitude of ordinary inarticulate people when, on hearing of the verdict, she said: "I feel as if a window has opened and fresh air has blown right through England."[26] She expressed the hope that she would get back her copies of the novel which had been confiscated on her return from America the previous October. May we also hope that in future the standard editions of *The White Peacock*, *The Rainbow*, and *Pansies* will appear as Lawrence intended them?

It seems to have been the celebrated "four-letter" words more than anything else in the book that provoked antagonism. Sir Charles Taylor was particularly indignant because one of them had been repeated in *The Guardian*[27] and in *The Observer*.[28] He expressed himself in an article in the *News of the World*,[29] comparing the moral influence of that newspaper favorably with that of the book. Later, the Press Council (a body that is supposed to exercise some persuasive control over the conduct of the periodical press) rebuked the *Spectator*, *The Guardian*, and *The Observer* for printing certain of these words, declaring that the course taken was both objectionable and unnecessary.[30]

The voice of established obscurantism was perhaps typified when it was announced that the words would not appear in the Oxford dictionaries—in spite of the fact that they are used in a novel now widely read throughout most of the English-speaking world.

When Parliament reassembled after the 1960 summer recess and the new session was opened, a good deal was heard of *Lady Chatterley's Lover* in the House of Commons. Mr. Ray Mawby and thirteen other Tory Members put down an amendment to the Queen's speech regretting that it contained no proposal to repeal the Obscene Publications Act "which has had such dire consequences." He was particularly concerned with the section dealing with the defense of public good. The amendment was not taken before the debate ended, but Mr. Mawby announced his intention of introducing a Private Member's Bill.[31] The following day the

Home Secretary said that he would not introduce a Government repeal bill.[32]

In answers to questions, the Attorney-General explained that the decision to prosecute Penguin Books was taken, not by the Government, but by the Director of Public Prosecutions because in his opinion the evidence available disclosed, *prima facie*, an offense under the Act of 1959. He declined to take action about the "four-letter" word in *The Guardian*.[33]

Later, the Home Secretary rejected a suggestion that he should appoint a committee to which publishers might voluntarily submit publications and whose certificates would be an absolute defense against prosecution under the Obscene Publications Act.[34]

In the House of Lords,[35] Lord Teviot drew the attention of the Government to the *Lady Chatterley's Lover* verdict and asked whether they would take steps to ban writings of that nature, particularly those of the author of the book. In an intemperate speech he abused not only the verdict and the book, but also Lawrence's *The Man Who Died* and the Wolfenden Report.

In the ensuing debate only the Earl of Craven gave Lord Teviot wholehearted support. Lord Shackleton, Lord Conesford, and Lord Boothby spoke in support of the verdict. Viscount Gage attacked the book in a lighter tone. He said that one Member of the House, who was asked how he would like his daughter to read the book, had replied that he would have no objection but that he had the strongest objection to his gamekeeper reading it. The Bishop of St. Albans felt that after so much publicity it was just as well that the book should be published openly rather than smuggled into the country and read surreptitiously. The Earl of Kinnoull and Lord Amwell would have liked the circulation of the book to have been less unrestricted.

Viscount Hailsham, Lord President of the Council, replied for the Government in a speech that was a marked contrast to the rather poor quality of the rest of the debate. He deprecated a debate which called into question a verdict in a properly conducted criminal trial. He explained the law as enacted by the Obscene Publications Act and considered it unthinkable that after being passed with so much discussion and unanimity it should be amended because of a single verdict. He said that the real question underlying the debate was whether it was legitimate to seek to prevent the publication of books simply because they embody a philosophy with which one does not happen to agree. He would have preferred to see the book between boards at 30s than in a paperback at 3s 6d, but knew of no principle of jurisprudence which could differentiate between 30s and 3s 6d or between boards and a paperback. Speaking as a Christian, he said:

It may well be that we should like to preserve the innocence of our children and of society from the disasters which we believe will follow from the adoption of false creeds, false prophets and false Christs. We cannot do so by prohibiting their work by an Act of law.

A good speech was marred by a statement that "the Bishop of Woolwich made an ass of himself."

Lord Hailsham's view that the price of a book is irrelevant to the question of obscene publication is curious in a lawyer of his eminence. The price of a book is surely one of "the circumstances of publication" which were taken into consideration in obscene libel cases; and, if we look at section 1 (1), surely price is one of "all relevant circumstances" to which regard must be given in deciding who are "likely" to read the book and consequently whether it will "deprave and corrupt." The idea that it would have been better if *Lady Chatterley's Lover* had been published at a higher price and that libraries and bookshops should not display it was not confined, as we have seen, to those who wanted the book legally banned. Some restriction of this sort was followed in the British production of *Ulysses*. The book was first published at a high price, which was gradually lowered, and even today some libraries and bookshops are cautious in handling it. Restricted publication is, of course, repugnant to democratic principles; on the other hand, there are many authors who write books which they do not wish, at first instance, to see in the hands of the half-educated and the irresponsible. By the time that the Grove Press decided to challenge authority over *Lady Chatterley's Lover*, however, any restriction on publication was impracticable in the States, and once the American paperback editions had appeared any attempt to restrict publication in Britain would only have made the English look silly.

Restricted publication has been officially recognized as confer-
ring some degree of immunity from prosecution in England on the
ground of obscenity, as in the case of A Young Girl's Diary. If
restricted publication has not proved a workable, if undemocratic,
compromise in Britain and America over a certain sort of book,
the "censor-morons" have only themselves to blame. Books addressed to the educated and responsible public have been relent-
lessly pursued in the courts, and the Customs and postal authorities
have not hesitated to seize single copies of books addressed to libraries and individual readers or in the possession of noncommercial passengers.

The verdict in the Penguin Books trial did not, of course, affect
Scotland or Northern Ireland where, as we shall see later on, the
Obscene Publications Act, 1959, does not apply; and proceedings
against the sale of the book could have taken place in spite of the
English case.

The result of the English prosecution was favorably greeted by
a leader in The Scotsman, but the case did not attract the excited
attention north of the border that it received in the south. In the
House of Commons on November 15, 1960, the Lord Advocate
said that he had considered the question most carefully and did not
propose to institute legal proceedings.[36] Questioned at a subsequent sitting of the House,[37] he would not agree that Scots law
should be brought into conformity with English law, nor that the
opinion of a Scottish jury ought to be taken on the book. On this
occasion the Member for South Ayrshire declared that his former
constituents Robert Burns and James Boswell would heartily approve of the decision.

In Edinburgh on February 3, 1961, the vice-president of the
Glasgow Union of Boys' Clubs applied to the High Court for authority to initiate a private prosecution, pleading that he was apprehensive of the effect of the book on young people for whose
moral welfare he was responsible. The application was refused on
the ground that his interest was not personal and peculiar.[38]

In Northern Ireland it was also decided to take no action against
the book.[39]

There is no doubt that the Penguin Books verdict was an instance of the not infrequent triumph of a jury's common sense over official stupidity and puritanical prejudice. But the light thrown by the case on the working of the new Act gives no ground for complacency. By the device of artificial publication to the police, something like a pre-publication censorship can be set up, and the authorities can hale before a jury a book of international literary reputation in spite of the fact that the Act declares itself to be "for the protection of literature." Apparently evidence that the book was freely published in America could not be given. Counsel could only allude somewhat obliquely to the fact that it was only in the British Commonwealth that Lawrence's work could not be read. Both the prosecution and the judge seemed to suggest, and the defense almost to concede, that there was something reprehensible in advocating any code of sexual conduct other than that of official Christianity; and the notion that the reading of the working class should be supervised by their betters dies hard. The English law of obscene publication seems to be still subjective and vague in its conception, unpredictable and chancy in its operation, and to pay little regard to freedom of speculation and artistic creation.

In the United States, as we have seen, the law is much more objective and certain and the higher courts have a very tender regard for freedom of thought and expression and are prepared to set very narrow limits to what can be suppressed on the ground of obscenity.

The Ladies' Directory

WHILE THE ENGLISH CASE OF *Lady Chatterley's Lover* was awaiting trial at the Old Bailey, another case was started which was not finally decided until after Lawrence's book was cleared. This new case has no direct literary interest, but it throws light on the interpretation of the Obscene Publications Act, 1959, and its relation to the common law and other statutes.

At this time the Street Offences Act, 1959, had enabled the police to drive the prostitutes off the London streets, and ways and means whereby they could attract business were much sought after. To further this object a Soho man put on sale a periodical called *The Ladies' Directory*[1] in which prostitutes inserted paid advertisements giving their telephone numbers and in some cases their photographs and indications of any peculiar sexual tastes for which they catered.

Although the man was quite open about what he was doing and sought the opinion of the police regarding the legality of his directory, he received no help from them and was eventually prosecuted. He was tried at the Central Criminal Court[2] in December 1960 and a jury found him guilty of (1) conspiracy to corrupt public morals, (2) living on the earnings of prostitution, and (3) publishing an obscene article. He was sentenced to nine months' imprisonment.

The three convictions and the sentence were upheld by the Court of Criminal Appeals.[3] With regard to the obscene publication charge, the Court held:

1. That the appellant's honesty of purpose was not a relevant consideration because under the Obscene Publications Act of 1959 it was unnecessary to prove intention to corrupt.

2. That the argument that persons who supplied themselves with the booklet were already corrupt and depraved was based on the fallacy that a man cannot be corrupted more than once.

3. That the evidence of prostitutes as to the meaning of words (such as "corr.") used in the directory was admissible, but (so far as the obscene publication charge was concerned) not evidence about the results of the advertisements, the age of those who responded to them, the practices indulged in, or what the police found at the premises advertised.

4. Section 2 (4) of the Obscene Publications Act did not preclude the charge of conspiring to corrupt public morals because that common law offence did not "consist of the publication" but of an agreement between the appellant and others.

The Court granted leave to appeal to the House of Lords on the conspiracy and earnings of prostitution counts but refused leave on the obscene publication count.

Since the House of Lords was not concerned with the obscene publication charge, it might be supposed that the proceedings before that court were not relevant to the subject matter of this book. In fact the finding of the lower court that the publisher of allegedly obscene matter could be convicted of conspiracy to corrupt public morals raised a problem of the gravest importance regarding the protection to literature which it was the purpose of the Obscene Publications Act, 1959, to provide.

Mr. W. R. Rees-Davies, for the appellant, drew attention to section 2 (4) of the Act which provided that "a person publishing an article shall not be proceeded against for an offence at common law consisting of the publication of any matter contained or embodied in the article where it is of the essence of the offence that the matter is obscene." He submitted:

that meant what it said, namely that a person publishing such an article should not be proceeded against for an offence at common law. If that were not the right construction of the subsection, the Director of Public Prosecutions could tomorrow morning institute proceedings against the publishers of *Lady Chatterley's Lover*, charge them with a conspiracy to corrupt public morals, have a complete rehearsing, preclude all argument as to literary merit, and thereby set at nought all the work of Parliament in the Act of 1959.[4]

The Lords, however, dismissed the appeal on both counts.[5] In his speech Viscount Simonds said:

Let it be supposed that at some future, perhaps early, date homosexual practices between adult consenting males were no longer a crime. Would it not be an offence if, even without obscenity, such practices were publicly advocated and encouraged by pamphlet and advertisement?

Lord Morris of Borth-y-Gest in his speech said that "he entertained no anxiety on the suggested peril of launching prosecutions to suppress unpopular or unorthodox views."

It is difficult, however, to share Lord Morris's complacency on this issue. Views are generally regarded as unpopular or unorthodox which attack the current code of public morals with the purpose of changing it. In the last chapter of this book reference will be made to a reputable body of opinion which holds that pornographic books may do more good than harm by acting as a safety valve for antisocial instincts. A book advocating this opinion, "even without obscenity," would no doubt increase the reading of pornography: would the author, publisher, and printer be guilty of a conspiracy to corrupt public morals? In his book *Is Chastity Outmoded?*[6] Dr. Eustace Chesser fairly states the arguments for and against prematrimonial chastity. When the material of the book first appeared in a collection of essays published by the British Medical Association, there was such an outcry from organized religion and morality that it was withdrawn. If instead of this impartial presentation of opposing views an author elaborated the very cogent case of prematrimonial intercourse, would not the practice of chastity be diminished? And would the publication not run the risk of being regarded as a conspiracy to corrupt public morals?

The challenge to literature and to the purpose of the Act of 1959 inherent in *The Ladies' Directory* case was recognized in the press[7] and it is to be fervently hoped that it will not be lost sight of. The enlightened and effective discussion of moral problems is by no means generally approved today; and, as we shall see, moralists of the standing of Sir Patrick Devlin can put forward a formidable case for regarding morals as fixed. In particular the effect of the Act in making a book like *Lady Chatterley's Lover* available to the masses was bitterly resented in certain ecclesiastical, judicial, and official circles. It would be naive to look for any sudden and overt counterattack from the forces of reaction, but we may expect that the weapon of "conspiracy to corrupt public morals" will be kept in reserve and brought into play when some favorable opportunity of stifling free discussion or restricting the scope and availability of works of art presents itself. This threat requires to be anticipated by a clear and unequivocal enactment of the legislature. In the meantime, it is some comfort to note that on June 29, 1961, the Attorney-General gave an assurance in the House of Commons that the Director of Public Prosecutions would never bring prosecutions for conspiracy to corrupt public morals in such a way as to circumvent the provisions of the Obscene Publications Act, 1959, with regard to the defense of public good and the admissibility of expert evidence.

Soon after *The Ladies' Directory* case another threat to the Obscene Publications Act, 1959, appeared. The Act did not repeal the early statutory provisions relating to obscenity, and a body called the Moral Law Defence Association (said to include forty M.P.s) issued a leaflet urging sympathizers to move the police to prosecute vendors of indecent books under the Town Police Clauses Act, 1847,[8] in order to nullify any "ill-effects" of the 1959 Act. The idea behind this suggestion appears to be that such prosecutions (and presumably similar ones under the Metropolitan Police Act, 1839) could be conducted without any of the restraints and safeguards embodied in the 1959 Act.

In 1962 it was somewhat amusingly ruled by high judicial authority[9] that the offense of publishing an obscene article cannot be committed by means of a sale to police officers because they must be assumed to be incorruptible. It was clear, however, that such sales could form the basis of proceedings for forfeiture and (somewhat alarmingly) of charges of conspiracy to contravene the Act of 1959.

Scotland, Ireland, and the British Commonwealth Overseas

AT THE UNION with England in 1709, Scotland retained its own judicial system and its law remained the same except as subsequently added to and modified by United Kingdom statutes. Scots law on obscenity is very similar to English. To publish, circulate, or expose for sale any obscene work devised and intended to corrupt the morals of the community and to create inordinate and lustful desires is an indictable offense under common law. No corrupt intention need be proved. The Burgh Police (Scotland) Act, 1892, made the publication or exhibition of obscene matter a summary offense. The Obscene Publications Acts of 1851 and 1959 were not applicable to Scotland, but Customs and Post Office legislation is common to the whole United Kingdom.

A shopkeeper was prosecuted at Stirling in 1959 because a book entitled *The House of Borgia* was sent to him from Denmark in lieu of a technical manual which he had ordered. The defendant was discharged but the book was forfeited.[1]

Nineteenth-century puritanism in Scotland was even more harsh and joyless than in England. Even in the remote Highlands native art, music, and dancing were ruthlessly crushed by dour "missionaries" from the Lowlands. In the introduction to his *Carmina Gadelica*, Alexander Carmichael records a distressing incident related to him during one of his visits to the Hebrides which is more revealing than a host of generalities. A young lady told him:

When we came to Islay I was sent to the parish school to obtain a proper grounding in arithmetic. I was charmed with the school-girls and their Gaelic songs. But the schoolmaster—an alien like myself—denounced Gaelic speech and Gaelic songs. On getting out of school one evening the girls resumed a song they had been singing the previous evening. I joined willingly, if timidly, my knowledge of Gaelic being small. The schoolmaster heard us, how-ever, and called us back. He punished us till the blood trickled from our fingers, although we were big girls, with the dawn of womanhood upon us. The thought of that scene thrills me with indignation.

The dominant spirit of puritanism did not even spare the literary remains of the national poet, Robert Burns. His letters were bowd-lerized when they appeared in print, and all editions of a collection of indecorous drinking songs and broad verse made by the poet and pirated under the title *The Merry Muses of Caledonia* were either corrupt or bowdlerized. It was not until the bicentenary of Burns' birth in 1959 that an integral version was published. The volume was compiled under distinguished editorship and issued privately.[2]

Under the Government of Ireland Act, 1920, Northern Ireland was given a Parliament of her own and a separate judiciary. She has remained part of the United Kingdom and certain matters, notably for our purposes Customs and postal services, are reserved for the Parliament at Westminster. The Obscene Publications Act, 1959, does not apply to Northern Ireland nor does the Chil-dren and Young Persons (Harmful Publications) Act, 1955, except so far as the prohibition of the import of harmful matter is con-cerned. No local legislation of a similar character has been enacted.

Southern Ireland achieved a far greater degree of independence than envisaged by the Act of 1920 and finally separated from the British Commonwealth in 1949. English law existing in 1920 con-tinued to apply until modified by the local legislature. This freedom was used so far as the control of literature was concerned to reverse the whole tradition of English-speaking peoples as regards the law of obscene publications in her territory. In 1929 the Obscene Pub-lications Act, 1857, was repealed and an administrative censorship set up. The old common law offense of publishing an obscene libel remains but it is seldom invoked.

Under the Censorship of Publications Act, 1929, a Censorship of Publications Board was set up. Either on its own initiative or acting on a complaint referred to it by the Minister of Justice, the Board may report to the Minister with regard to any book or a particular edition of a book that it is "in its general tendency indecent or obscene and should for that reason be prohibited or that in the opinion of the Board such book or edition advocated the unnatural prevention of conception or the procurement of abortion or miscarriage or the use of any method, treatment or appliance for the purpose of such prevention or such miscarriage and should for that reason be prohibited." The Board may report in a like manner on the recent issues of any newspaper or periodical, the devoting of "an unduly large proportion of space to the publication of matter relating to crime" being an additional ground of report. On receipt of such a report from the Board, the Minister may issue a "prohibition order" forbidding importation, sale, or distribution of the book or edition, or of subsequent numbers of the periodical. Infringement of the order is a criminal offense. A special part of the Act makes the printing, publishing, sale, or distribution of birth control advocacy (whether prohibited or not) an offense. Reports of judicial proceedings are severely restricted by the Act except so far as volumes devoted to bona fide law reporting are concerned.

The power of the legislature to punish the publication or utterance of "blasphemous, seditious or indecent matter" was provided for in article 40 of the 1937 Constitution.

Serious complaints about the working of the system resulted in an Appeal Board being set up by the Censorship Act, 1946, which also effected a number of less important changes.

So long as the procedure laid down in the Censorship Acts is observed, the decision of the Minister that a publication is obscene is final and cannot be challenged in the courts of law.

Under the influence of the Roman Catholic Church these Acts are enthusiastically and indiscriminatingly implemented. The Board deals with about fifty books a month and the current *Register of Prohibited Publications* contains about four thousand books and four hundred periodicals. The most distinguished British and

American writers of fiction and nonfiction are well represented and all books on birth control are, of course, included. The English Sunday newspapers are particularly liable to prohibition orders and some of them issue a special Irish edition which may serialize the life of a saint in lieu of a more lurid feature. The spirit in which the Board acts is typified by the words of a vindicating statement made in a Senate debate: "I hold the Censorship Board is quite justified in banning a book if it contains one passage subversive of Christianity or morality."[3]

It would be wearisome to particularize further the absurdities, inconsistencies, and injustices of this system. They are inherent in all administrative censorship and interference with the freedom of the press. Fortunately, the volume of traffic across the Northern Ireland frontier and the Irish Channel makes it fairly easy for determined and educated people to obtain books banned by the Board. But the mass of the people are cut off from a great deal of information, discussion, and artistic achievement freely available in the rest of the English-speaking world. To those who out of a love of liberty supported the claim of the Irish to independence, it is sad that freedom so hardly gained should have been put to such a reactionary end.

The British migrants who settled so much of the hitherto unknown parts of the world from the seventeenth century onward took the English common law with them and conformed to its subsequent development. So far as obscene publications were concerned, this basis was embodied with a great variety of additions and modification in the law of the several territories which attained independence within the Commonwealth. Legislation in the parts of Asia subjected to British rule was also modeled to a considerable extent on English law.[4]

Generally speaking, the law in the English-speaking dominions is more stringent than in Great Britain. In Canada, Australia, and New Zealand legislation against horror comics was passed in advance of the English Act of 1955.

The Canadian law on obscene publications is laid down in section 150 of the Criminal Code as enacted in 1954. Obscenity was not defined; but in 1959 the following addition was made:

For the purpose of this Act, any publication a dominant characteristic of which is the undue exploitation of sex, or of sex and any one or more of the following subjects, namely, crime, horror, cruelty and violence, shall be deemed to be obscene.

At the same time provision was made for the destruction of obscene publications and horror comics in accordance with a procedure very similar to that laid down for the destruction of obscene articles in England under the Obscene Publications Act, 1959.

On June 10, 1960, a judge in Montreal decided that *Lady Chatterley's Lover* was obscene in spite of the evidence of literary experts including Professor Harry T. Moore, America's leading authority on D. H. Lawrence.[5] The following year the Canadian Customs held up the import of four Penguin Books: *The Physiology of Sex* by Kenneth Walker, *Love in a Cold Climate* by Nancy Mitford, and the account of *The Trial of Lady Chatterley*.[6]

Obscenity is variously dealt with by the legislation of the six states comprising the Commonwealth of Australia. Customs and postal law is, however, laid down by the federal parliament and applies uniformly to all the states. Censorship boards have been set up in Queensland and Tasmania to carry out administrative censorship in regard to obscene publications. In Queensland the decisions of the board may be challenged in the courts of law: in Tasmania, objections are heard by the board itself.

Recently the Victoria police seized, on the premises of William Heinemann Ltd., books which the Minister of Customs, acting on the recommendations of an advisory board, allowed to be imported. The first was *God's Little Acre* by Erskine Caldwell, and a destruction order was upheld on appeal to the Supreme Court. The judge said that the book had been sold without an attempt to restrict its distribution.[7] Another book seized was *Carlotta McBride* by Charles Orson Graham, which had been imported in similar circumstances. The copies were ordered to be destroyed by a stipendiary magistrate in Melbourne.[8]

A sensational case began in New Zealand in 1956 when films, photographs, and books were seized from the luggage of a world-famous conductor on his arrival by plane from London after a world tour. He was charged under the Customs Act, 1913, with importing indecent articles and fined £A100.[9]

More recently the Minister of Customs banned the import of Vladimir Nabokov's novel *Lolita* under the Customs Act, 1913, which prohibits the importing of books which are indecent within the meaning of the Indecent Publications Act, 1910. The New Zealand Council of Civil Liberties subsequently imported six copies of the book and challenged without success the prohibition before the Supreme Court.[10] Delivering judgment, Mr. Justice Hutchin said that the book had been written with no pornographic intent and was obviously written for the educated reader; but that he thought it was aphrodisiac. Referring to a recommendation to the Minister by an advisory committee that individual orders should be permitted, he said that this might minimize the likelihood of the book coming into the wrong hands, but there was no legal provision authorizing such a course.[11] It appears, however, that the New Zealand Customs do in fact admit certain books which would otherwise be prohibited if there is evidence that they are addressed to suitable individuals or intended to be sold to restricted classes (e.g., medical men). Three copies of each issue of nudist publications may be imported by specified nudist clubs.

After the Nationalist Party came into power in 1948 a system of intensive censorship was set up in the (then) Union of South Africa. This has been accomplished by the enactment of new legislation and the rigid enforcement of older laws. The motive behind this movement has been fundamentally political, but the bogy of pornography has been allied to fear of Communism in seeking support for the system. In 1961, South Africa became a republic and separated from the Commonwealth.

The most effective of the measures concerned is the Customs Act of 1955, which provides for the prohibition of the import of goods which are "indecent or obscene or on any ground whatsoever objectionable." The decision as to what comes within the scope of these words rests with the Minister of the Interior. He is only required, in the case of books, periodicals, and pictures, to consult the Board of Censors who control public entertainments. There is no recourse to the courts of law. There are some four thousand books on the banned list, including *Streetcar Named Desire* by Tennessee Williams, *Aaron's Rod* by D. H. Lawrence, and *I Claudius* by Robert Graves. It is an offense even to possess an article imported in violation of a prohibition under the Act; but it is not an offense to reprint prohibited books and articles unless they offend against the Post Office Act of 1958 or provincial laws against obscenity. For instance, after Bertrand Russell's essay "Why I am not a Christian" was banned under the Customs Act of 1959, it was printed and distributed by the Rationalist Association in South Africa with impunity.

In 1956 a Commission of Enquiry in regard to Undesirable Publications (the Cronje Commission) recommended the setting up of a single system of control of local and imported printed matter. All "undesirable" publications are recommended to be prohibited, the power to decide what is "undesirable" being vested in a Publications Board in the case of books and magazines and in the courts in the case of newspapers. In 1960 the Government promoted a bill on the lines of this report but it was withdrawn. Another bill was introduced the following year with the important concession that recourse to the courts of law was available in all cases. The bill forbids the publication of "undesirable" matter; and the wide definition of "undesirable" includes anything "obscene or offensive or harmful to public morals."[12]

In Malta there appears to be an arbitrary system of book banning administered in accordance with the ideas of the Roman Catholic Church, which is a dominant force in the island. The General Secretary of the National Marriage Guidance Council in London complained in *The Times*[13] that in 1960 books ordered from the Council's recommended list by two British servicemen in Malta had been seized by the Maltese Post Office as "indecent publications," and that the reply to an application for the return of one of them stated that all matter so classified was burned. Subsequently a Maltese correspondent explained that this was the wish of the vast majority of the population, to whose will servicemen in the island were subject. He also drew attention to the prohibition of the import of contraceptives to be found in the British *Post Office Guide*.[14] Literary classics were also seized.[15]

French and Other Laws

MANY AN ENGLISH-SPEAKING MAN sees France through rosy spectacles. To him it is a land singularly free from those restrictions on alcoholic refreshment, the theater, and literature which he supports with good or bad grace at home according to his temperament. To cross the Channel or the Atlantic is to leave the reign of Mrs. Grundy behind and to enter a realm where the ideal of moral liberty is carried to its logical conclusions without compromise and without hypocrisy. He finds this contrast particularly marked in regard to questions of decency and obscenity in literature. Books suppressed in England or the United States are reprinted on Parisian presses and find a refuge in the bookshops where they appear cheek by jowl with a quantity of ephemeral pornography specially produced to meet the tastes of British and American tourists.

The facts behind this very superficial picture of paradisal literary freedom are not so simple. There have been times when the French law in regard to literary obscenity has been almost Victorian in its operation. The soil of France produced a vice crusader not far behind Comstock or "Jix" in fanaticism: and the magistrates of France have proved themselves capable of *sottises* quite comparable to the wisdom produced by English benches when they venture upon the fields of art and literature. Our judgment of the present position must wait on a review of the development of the law and on the way in which it has been administered.

Before the revolution of 1789 the preoccupation of authority in regard to the control of books was with blasphemy and sedition. If indecency was condemned it was because it attacked the clergy or the king. Song, however, held something like a privileged position and was from the time of Villon the acknowledged vehicle for sallies of Gallic wit against authority, sanctity, and propriety. This tradition is carried on today in the *chansonniers* of Paris which are noted for their ribaldry and the merciless scorn to which they expose the rulers of France. Recently the *chansonniers* indignantly refused a request by the radio and television authorities to submit the scripts of their performances for prior inspection on the ground that it would infringe the traditional freedom of expression of their artists.[1]

The license of the revolutionary period produced a spate of pornography which reached its apogee in the erotic nightmares of Sade and the counterblasts of Rétif de la Bretonne. These and similar works were consigned by the First Consul to the Enfer of the Bibliothèque Nationale which he modeled on a similar institution in the Vatican Library. The revolutionaries themselves had, however, attempted to deal with the problem. In 1791 a law, opposed by Robespierre, was passed making criminal public assaults on the modesty of women by indecent action, the exposure for sale of obscene pictures, and the corruption of young persons. Under Napoleon, in 1810, writing and songs were brought under the purview of the law.

With the restoration a reign of prudery started in real earnest. In 1819 a law created the offense of *outrage à la morale publique et religieuse et aux bonnes moeurs.*

An early victim of this state of the law was the song writer Béranger, whose liberal and Bonapartist tendencies were offensive to the monarchy. He was twice imprisoned and between his trials an enactment of 1821, among other reactionary provisions, withdrew the trial of the offense from juries.

In 1825 one of the very few prosecutions in France of a scientific work took place. Antoine Jacques Dulaure, a prolific archaeologist and historian whose works are remembered with respect today, published a new edition of his *Des Divinités génératrices* which had issued from the press twenty years before. The book is a learned

study of the phallic element in the religions of all ages. Dulaure's
trenchantly expressed republican and anti-Catholic opinions had
made him many enemies in the new regime who were only waiting
for an opportunity to settle their scores with him. The book was
seized and condemned.

Later, the law was invoked against reprints of Voltaire's *Pucelle*,
while decrees forbade works by Rousseau and l'Abbé Prévost, as
well as the *Decameron* and the *Heptameron*. During this period
Louvet de Couvray's *Amours du Chevalier de Faublas* was condemned no less than four times. First published in 1786 and 1789,
this picture of aristocratic manners before the revolution provoked
Carlyle to a typical outburst of condemnatory rhetoric. The works
of Crébillon *le fils* were condemned in 1852. In his lifetime the
author had been banished from Paris by the outraged virtue of
Madame de Pompadour. It is scarcely an exaggeration to say that
the French law attempted to re-edit the literature of previous ages;
Ronsard, Piron, Choderlos de Laclos, and Mirabeau are other
names among the authors of works condemned for obscenity.

Reaction was particularly strong during the Second Empire. In
1853 the brothers Goncourt were prosecuted over a magazine
article. The motives of the attack were really political, but an acquittal was obtained only on the personal intervention of the Emperor, who wished to avoid being made to look a fool.

One of the cases was not without its humorous side. In 1855
an ironmonger was charged before the 3rd Chambre Correctionelle
de la Seine for selling "some chambers on the bottom of which was
displayed, painted on the enamel, a large open eye accompanied
by the words 'I see you.'" The complainant was a rival tradesman
probably more jealous than virtuous. The defendant was sentenced
to a month's imprisonment. The sentence was confirmed, on appeal, where the defendant's advocate made an energetic defense.
What was culpable about either the eye or the lettering? "Bran-
dishing his chamber pot and exposing it to the audience," he
claimed that the resulting laughter came not only from the gentlemen present but also from the ladies (whose respectability was
above question). His client had only made a joke—a Billingsgate
joke, perhaps, but only a joke—and a joke was not an offense.
Counsel for the prosecution was, however, adamant. He was not

arraigning either the picture or the lettering, but their position. The court would appreciate that. And the court did.

An English and (I imagine) contemporary version of the delectable article which was the subject of the foregoing case was displayed at an exhibition of popular art entitled "Black Eyes and Lemonade" held at the Whitechapel Art Gallery in 1951. It was made of delf and had two handles. Inside on the bottom, the picture of a little man was surrounded by the legend: "I'll never tell what I see"; while outside, husband addressed wife in plain English verse on their joint use of the convenient receptacle.

Under Napoleon III, Béranger's Bonapartist admirations brought him into official favor, and he was accorded national honors. But contemporary writers who were experimenting with new methods and new subjects were less fortunate. In the year of Béranger's death (1857) two masters of the French language, one of prose, the other of verse, occupied in their turn the dock of the 6th Chambre Correctionelle de la Seine.

In January there was the celebrated prosecution of Flaubert over *Madame Bovary*, whose publication in serial form had just been completed. Flaubert was acquitted. But his counsel put forward the plea, familiar in English courts of law, that in depicting "vice" his client had done no more than seek to promote "virtue." This plea assumes that it is the business of literature to support the morality of the day, rather than "to hold as 'twere the mirror up to nature" and to subject the prevailing *mores* to intelligent criticism. In pronouncing their judgment, the magistrates made the most of their opportunity by reading the immortal Flaubert a long lecture on the relation of art to morality with little lack of assurance and less of banality.

In the summer came the turn of Baudelaire's *Fleurs du mal*. The appearance of the book had been greeted with a great deal of abuse in the press, and the first attack on a volume of verse since the case of Béranger followed. Baudelaire did all he could to defend himself. He even appealed to the influential Sainte-Beuve for help. But the great critic felt that his respectability had already been compromised by some praise of *Madame Bovary* he had published in the *Moniteur* and he could offer nothing but good advice. The prosecution adopted the procedure (not unknown in English obscenity cases) by which passages are taken out of their context and considered in isolation. Baudelaire protested and claimed that his book should be considered as a whole. At the trial, counsel for the prosecution roundly denounced everything about the book from its contents to its low price. Six poems now read the world over were condemned and the poet was fined. In spite of the courtesy of the magistrates (the decision referred to "the poet" and not "the accused"), Baudelaire was astounded and mortified. He could not be comforted even by Victor Hugo's commiseration and encouragement:

Your *Fleurs du mal* shine and dazzle like the stars. Go on. I shout Bravo! with all my strength to your hardy spirit.

Like many another author in a similar predicament he thought that he could have done better than his counsel. The plea of exposing "vice" in the interests of "virtue" had again been put forward. Baudelaire was confident that if he had conducted his own case, and had asserted the absolute independence of art *vis-à-vis* morality, he would have been acquitted. He was wise enough, however, not to put this opinion to the test on appeal, but resolved to write six new poems "much more beautiful than those suppressed." By 1861 he brought out a new edition to which he supplied not six but thirty-five new poems. He intended to preface this edition with a defense of his work, but although he made three drafts the project was not carried out. The first version begins:

It is not for my wives, my daughters or my sisters that this book has been written, any more than for the wives, the daughters or the sisters of my neighbour. I leave this office to those who are concerned to confound good actions with beautiful language.

In 1866 the condemned poems, along with fresh material, appeared in a surreptitious publication under the title of *Les Epaves*.

The year 1857 also saw the death of Eugène Sue, whose socialist and revolutionary views had been expressed in his *Mystères de Paris* and his *Mystères du Peuple*. He died while the latter work was being condemned on a large number of counts, of which obscenity was one.

Baudelaire's publisher in 1857 was Poulet-Malassis—known to his intimates as Coco-mal-perché. A rebus on his name decorated most of the books he issued, but it did not appear on *Les Fleurs du mal*. Poulet-Malassis had a flair for new and audacious talent, as well as a habit of reprinting provocative books that the authorities would rather have left forgotten. Against him the French law waged a war as bitter as that of Victorian prudery against Vizetelly. In *le grand procés de Lille* of 1868 sixty-three books, including works by Verlaine, Casanova, Mirabeau, and even Corneille were condemned.

The reign of prudery continued into the early years of the Third Republic. In 1874 *Les Diaboliques* of Barbey d'Aurevilly was condemned to destruction although the author escaped conviction. The following year prudery became unadulterated when a publisher was fined for reproducing the magnificent *fermiers généraux* edition de luxe of La Fontaine's *Contes*, in spite of the previous authorization of the Minister of the Interior.

The year 1876 saw a remarkable left-wing election victory, and an agitation for an amnesty in respect of political offenses committed during the Commune of 1870 began. Bourgeois nervousness manifested itself in prosecutions where the charge of obscenity masked political prejudices. A short story entitled "Maudite" contributed to the *Evénement* by Léon Cladel sought to further the granting of an amnesty by depicting the sufferings of the wife of a deported communarde forced into prostitution to support herself and her children. Both the author and the editor were haled before a magistrate's court in Paris and fined for obscene publication.

Later in the same year Jean Richepin was imprisoned on account of the alleged obscenity of *Chanson des Gueux*. The motive of the prosecution was largely fear of the political effects of Richepin's realistic pictures of the life of the "down and out." He published an eloquent protest in the *Tribune* on the morrow of the condemnation, concluding thus:

I have depicted the little ones, the bare-footed, and those dying of hunger. I have tried to show the mud in which society forces them to live; I have stirred up this mud with a cynical but compassionate hand. I wished to make a ray of sunshine fall on it; and this has been held to be unhealthy, immoral, and monstrous.

I do not set up as a doctor; I have not proposed a remedy; but I have said simply to society:

"This is what you make the poor, breathe their stench, put your finger in their sores, look at their shame and their vice, and strike your breast to think that all this comes about through your fault."

And society has shut its eyes in order not to see, held its nose in order not to smell, and instead of striking its breast has struck on mine.

In a word, I wished to make the Beggars sing, and respectable folk have just brutally closed my mouth with the eternal war cry of the fortunate: "The beggars have no right to speak. Silence the poor!"

"Silence the poor!" was a prudent maxim and the law of obscenity has often been used to enforce it.

In 1881 a huge codification of the law on the liberty of the press was enacted, repealing previous legislation and covering every medium of publication. Article 28 imposed severe penalties for the offense of *l'outrage aux bonnes moeurs*. This law concerning obscene publication was strengthened by amendments in 1882, 1898, and 1908. The process was urged on by Senator Réné Bérenger, whose attitude in these matters earned him the sobriquet of Bérenger-la-Pudeur. He was born in 1830, and his crusading zeal only increased with age.

One of the first victims of the laws of 1881 and 1882 was Louis Desprez in respect of a naturalistic novel of peasant life entitled *Autour d'un Clocher*, written in collaboration with Henri Fèvre, a minor. Published in Belgium at the same time as Huysman's *A Rebours* (1884) and other sensational books, this first essay of young blood was well on the way to passing unnoticed when it was seized in the bookshops by the French authorities. Fèvre escaped prosecution because of his youth. Desprez, before the Cour d'Assises de la Seine, asserted the independence of art in an unqualified form and claimed that the only jury competent to try his work was one drawn from the masters of contemporary French literature: Victor Hugo,

Edmond de Goncourt, Zola, Alphonse Daudet, etc. A jury of small tradesmen found him guilty, and he was sentenced to a month's imprisonment and a fine of one thousand francs. This was in effect a death sentence. Desprez suffered from hip disease which became complicated by tuberculosis. In vain Zola, Clemenceau, Daudet, Goncourt, and others pleaded for a mitigation of the rigors of his prison. He died shortly after his release. The authorities were probably no more moved by this early death of a brilliant young writer than their English compeers cared about the similar end of honest old Vizetelly; but posterity will endorse the tersely expressed verdict of Zola: "Those who assassinated this child are villains."

Seven days after the trial of Desprez, Paul Bonnetain was indicted in respect of *Charlot s'amuse* (a novel dealing with masturbation), published the previous year, but the jury acquitted him.

The publisher of both the two last-mentioned books was the redoubtable Henri Kistemaeckers, of Brussels, the publisher of Maupassant, Huysmans, and other naturalist authors. Eighteen times prosecuted before Belgian juries, he was acquitted every time; prosecuted five times before magistrates without juries, he was thrice acquitted. Finally he took umbrage at a sharp sentence meted out after conviction in respect of advertisements in his journal *La Flirt* and fled to France. The French authorities honorably refused to extradite him.

During the eighties and nineties there were other prosecutions of contemporary novels, but they became less frequent and less important. It was with periodicals that the law of obscenity chiefly concerned itself during this period. A long struggle was maintained against the *Courier Français*, a periodical revived by Jules Roques. Some of the prosecutions were not unconnected with a body founded to combat street prostitution. Roques had given this body his ironical support, pretending to believe that it was protesting against the number of people found dead from hunger and cold in the streets during the terrible winter 1889-90. In 1896 a conviction was obtained, on the complaint of the indefatigable Senator Béranger, in respect of a poem by Hugues Delorme entitled "Les Aisselles."

After World War I a periodical called *Le Grand Guignol* made some violent attacks on Poincaré and Barthou. The editor was arrested in February 1922 on a number of criminal charges, all of which were dropped except that of *outrage aux bonnes moeurs*. Conviction on this charge produced a fine of one thousand francs and six months' imprisonment. In 1923 the editor of *Le Cupidon* was fined for quoting a page of Pietro Aretino and for publishing a short story called "Le Robinet." The same year in the same court a woman was fined for quoting a passage from a novel (not prosecuted) when reviewing it. In 1926 a publisher was imprisoned for issuing a brochure containing articles and drawings from *Le Cupidon*.

The present French law relating to literary obscenity is embodied in the Décret-Loi of July 29, 1939, articles 119–128. It is an offense to make, possess, transport, distribute, sell, import, or export for commercial purposes any writing or pictures *contraires aux bonnes moeurs* or to advertise any such articles. Literary or other merit is no defense but it may be taken into consideration in imposing the penalty. Any obscene articles which are the subject of a prosecution may be seized by the Customs, and the postal authorities may refuse to accept them for transmission.

There are, however, safeguards as follows:

(a) Prosecutions must be instituted within three years of the commission of the offense.

(b) Instead of ordering destruction, a court may donate obscene matter to one of the state museums.

(c) Prosecutions in respect of books can only be brought following a decision of a special commission which advises the Minister of Justice. This commission, called the Commission Consultative de la Famille et de la Natalité Française, was formed by a decree of January 25, 1940.

Outrage aux bonnes moeurs was never defined in any statute and similarly it is nowhere laid down what is contrary to good morals. The question of definition presented no trouble to the redoubtable Bérenger. He confidently asserted:

We consider that it embarrasses us to ask for definitions. The Abbé Sertillanges has excellently said: everything is obscene which troubles the flesh. I would add that everything is immoral which can corrupt a child.

The courts, however, have looked for guidance to those learned writers on jurisprudence who carry so much more weight in French than in English law. Both the courts and the jurists have stressed the essentially mercenary and gross nature of obscenity and have tended to exempt works of art and literature even when they are unsuitable for minors. The courts must give reasons for finding a work obscene and convictions can be quashed if they do not.

Under a law of September 25, 1946, a court decision that a book is obscene may be reviewed after twenty years. The processes can be initiated by the author, publisher, any of their relations, or the Société des Gens de Lettres de France. Under this law the condemnation of Baudelaire's *Les Fleurs du mal* was annulled by the Court of Cassation on May 31, 1949.

In 1947 comics and other literature distributed to French youth gave considerable cause for alarm. As a result, special legislation was passed. A commission was set up to supervise children's literature. Matter favorable to gangsterism, lying, theft, idleness, cowardice, hatred, debauchery, and ethnic prejudice is forbidden, and also the sale of any specific publication designated by the Ministry of the Interior as dangerous to youth. Publishers of periodicals intended for youth must be registered and if they are found guilty of any offense against the code they may be suspended from publishing either temporarily or permanently.

The traditional attitude of the French to what they call *la pudibonderie anglaise* has been one of mild and amused contempt. Books banned in England have, as we have seen, frequently been published in France and interference by the French authorities has been rare. An attack on Frank Harris was exceptional. When he was living in Nice his house was raided in an unsuccessful attempt to find copies of his *My Life and Loves* which were hidden there; and in 1926, after the second volume had been printed in France, Harris was arraigned before a local court. The prosecution was, however, dropped in deference to public protests by men of letters including Henri Barbusse and Romain Rolland.[2] The book was cleared of obscenity by a French court in 1928 and the French translation has never been molested.

In spite of this tolerance, however, in 1946 a sensational literary *cause célèbre* involved an American author—Henry Miller. He, his publishers, and translators into French were prosecuted at the instance of Daniel Parker who, despite his English-sounding name, was a Frenchman and the spiritual heir of Bérenger-la-Pudeur. He acted as president of the Cartel d'Actions Sociales et Morales—a sort of French anti-vice society. The entire French literary press and a crowd of men of letters rallied to Miller's aid, and a committee of defense was formed. Parker cut a sorry figure under the biting satire of his foes and eventually broke down and wept in a broadcast item. In the end the proceedings were quashed by the official device of an *amnistie*. The case so increased the sales of Miller's books that he became a franc millionaire.

Miller's publishers, the Obelisk and Olympia Presses, nevertheless continued to attract the attention of the authorities. In 1950 *Sexus* (the first book of Miller's *The Rosy Crucifixion*) was banned; and later an incident occurred which confirmed suspicions that the French Government were becoming susceptible to representations by the British authorities. On December 10, 1956, the police raided the premises of the Olympia Press and prohibited the sale and circulation of no less than twenty-five of its titles. In the ensuing agitation the victims of the raid managed to produce a letter dated September 3, 1953, sent from the English Home Office to the French police in accordance with an International Convention for the Suppression of Obscene Publications accusing the Press of sending by post "books of a highly obscene character."

The victims of the raid received no support from the Syndicat National des Editeurs, but the possibility that the raid was a result (however belated) of British interference caused a literary scandal. Eventually a compromise was come to whereby although the books were not to be exhibited or advertised they could be sold on demand either on the premises or by mail.[3]

The works of the Marquis de Sade, however deplorable morally and as literature, are of considerable historical and philosophical interest. They have been read and discussed by many writers of eminence and they have had no small influence on the development of literature. Mario Praz, the celebrated Italian critic, gives very serious attention to Sade in his study of nineteenth-century romantic literature.[4]

A complete edition of the works of Sade, planned to consist of twenty-six volumes at about 1,000 francs each, was started by Jean-Jacques Pauvert in 1947. In 1954 and 1955, when most of the volumes had been published, the venture attracted the attention of the Commission Consultative, and prosecution followed. Four titles were the subject of the charge: *La Philosophie dans le boudoir, La Nouvelle Justine, Juliette,* and *Les 120 journées de Sodome.* The case was tried before the 17th Chambre Correctionelle de Paris, where André Breton and Jean Cocteau appeared as witnesses for the defense. In the result the publishers were fined and the books ordered to be destroyed. The court rejected a plea that the publication was intended to circulate among a small circle of intellectuals only, on the ground that the books had been advertised in a nonscientific journal side by side with admittedly erotic works.

On appeal the sentence in so far as it concerned *Juliette* was quashed because the Consultative Commission was not fully attended when it initiated the prosecution of that item. Fines in respect of the other titles were suspended but the destruction orders were confirmed. The appeal court ruled that the law allowed full liberty of discussion of all philosophical views and only the manner of expression was condemned. It is worthy of note that the printer in establishing his bona fides was discharged from the case.

Many other countries uninfluenced by English law as well as France have laws against literary obscenity.

Belgium and Switzerland have literary obscenity laws which are rather similar to the French.

Italian law allows the magistrates to sequestrate obscene books. The law seems to be sensibly administered, to judge by the attitude of the court to a prosecution instigated by the British authorities of an English translation of an Italian historical work entitled *Gian Gastone: Last of the Medici,* which was the second volume of the Lungarno Series issued by Giuseppe Orioli, the first publisher of D. H. Lawrence's *Lady Chatterley's Lover.* The magistrate dismissed the case on the ground that the Italian original freely circulated in his country and he did not see why an English translation should not do the same. If the British authorities objected to the book they could stop its circulation in their own country.

In Germany after World War I the laws of the Weimar Republic allowed a great deal of sexual freedom. Magnus Hirschfield, who was already world-famous as the publisher of a great and scholarly work on homosexuality, published a moral history of the war and the years following. This work employed a more popular style and was profusely illustrated. The author had many imitators. All sorts of voluminous sexual studies with colored plates appeared of varying degrees of probity. Some descended from the popular to the vulgar, while others made little pretense of being other than pornographic. Recently, the Hamburg prosecutor decided not to proceed on a pornography charge in respect of *Lady Chatterley's Lover* filed by the Catholic Association for the Prevention of Public Immorality.[5]

Nudist magazines illustrated with integral photographs of unclothed figures have been cleared of obscenity charges by legal decisions in Denmark, Norway, Sweden, and Switzerland.

Volume I of Henry Miller's *Sexus* was put on the Norwegian market in 1956 and stocked by some of the most reputable bookshops in the country. After eight months the book was ordered to be confiscated and on June 17, 1958, the Oslo Town Court found two booksellers guilty of having "offered for sale, exhibited, or in other ways endeavoured to disseminate obscene writing." On April 30, 1959, the Supreme Court of Norway rejected an appeal.

Since all publishing and printing in the Soviet Union is controlled by public bodies, there is no call for such laws and very little pornography appears to circulate. Other European countries have statutory provisions regarding obscene literature which, on the face of them, are intended to apply only to pornography.

The postwar Japanese criminal code contains provisions regarding literary obscenity which suggest American inspiration.

Obscenity and Freedom

S O FAR THIS BOOK has traced the development of the conception of literary obscenity in those countries which have been conspicuous for the tradition of freedom of thought and liberty of literary expression, and has given some attention to those parts of the world notably affected by that tradition. We have seen how laws originally intended to suppress gross pornography, and still ostensibly having that purpose, have in fact become a limitation, so far as sexual subjects are concerned, on that freedom of intellectual speculation and literary creation which the liberal tradition takes for granted. The narrative has in the main been allowed to speak for itself, but the time has come to assess the extent of the problem involved and to consider what measures are necessary in order to restrain the operation of laws regarding obscene publication to their original and ostensible purpose.

The importance of this matter can hardly be overestimated. If man does not destroy civilization by suicidal war, his most pressing problems will be related to population and breeding. Hitherto these subjects have been left to the mercy of historical and geographical accident and the hazards of war. In future they will be within human control and the possibilities are almost limitless. Furthermore, it is becoming increasingly impossible to control sexual conduct by coercion and ignorance even to the extent that this has been done in the past. Men and women will be more and more free in their sexual conduct, and a rational, informed, and responsible attitude to sex on the part of individuals will be of paramount importance. The choice between celibacy and monogamous marriage, which has been the theory although not the practice of our civilization will, there is little doubt, have to be abandoned in favor of the recognition of a variety of sexual patterns suitable to different types of persons. According to the liberal tradition, these stupendous problems can be solved only in the light of free and educated discussion and experiment. The abuse of the obscenity laws to limit this necessary inquiry is a most serious matter, and the question of preventing the abuse an important one, not only for the old civilizations but for the new emerging communities of Africa and Asia.

There are, of course, large areas of the world dominated by Marxian Communism or politically authoritarian churches where the premises on which the above arguments are based are not acceptable, and where the problem we are considering is not recognized. The climate of intellectual opinion has, however, become less favorable than it was to the liberal tradition even in its home countries—Great Britain, France, and the United States. Before World War II at least lip service was paid to liberal ideas in intellectually reputable quarters other than those dominated by, or influenced by, the Roman Catholic Church, which was generally antiliberal, and old-fashioned Protestant bodies who excepted sexual thought and conduct from the freedom they allowed, as did many Rationalists of the old school. Now there is a by no means negligible body of opinion and practice that is ready to abandon liberal ideas for reasons of political expediency, and sexual ideas and conduct are most vulnerable to this influence.

For the purpose of this book a brief examination of the new illiberalism as expounded by one of its most brilliant and lucid advocates will suffice. In his Maccabean Lecture in Jurisprudence[1] given in 1959, Sir Patrick Devlin, a High Court judge, dealt with the relation of English law to morals. Sir Patrick's thesis may be roughly summarized as follows.

As a matter of historical fact, Christian ideas have been built into our society. Although freedom of religious belief is now allowed, this freedom does not extend to morals. Society has a right to pass moral judgments and in our society its judgments are based on Christianity. Furthermore, it has the right to enforce these judgments because where no common morality is observed society disintegrates. There is no valid distinction between private and public morality and there are no theoretical limits to the power of the State to legislate against immorality. In practice this power is limited because the reasonable (not the rational) man, the man in the street and the man in the jury, is prepared to tolerate a degree of departure from moral standards. The extent of toleration varies from generation to generation but moral standards do not. It is the business of the Church to teach the reasonable man correct moral standards, otherwise the efforts of the law to enforce Christian morals will fail.

Mr. Justice Devlin in this lecture does not refer to "obscene" publications but he quotes with apparent approval a dictum of Mr. Justice Phillimore in 1908:[2] "A man is free to think, to speak and to teach what he pleases as to religious matters, but not as to morals." It is difficult, however, to see how Sir Patrick could do other than approve the operation of the obscenity laws, the more particularly when they affect serious literature, because the avowed intention of writers like Havelock Ellis and D. H. Lawrence was to change the moral standards of the community, and to some extent they have succeeded in doing so.

I have taken Sir Patrick Devlin's lecture to illustrate the fact that the use of the obscenity laws to interfere with serious literature is not always motivated by ignorant fanaticism or misplaced moral zeal. The case for the limitation of intellectual speculation and artistic expression can be supported by informed and rational arguments in terms compatible with current modes of thought. For those who are not convinced by such arguments and who believe that truth and right conduct must be followed in the light of knowledge and freedom, it is of paramount importance to understand the issues involved in the conception of literary obscenity.

Readers of my previous work on the obscenity laws may have noticed that in this book I have placed less stress on the ridiculous positions often assumed by those who administer, invoke, or advocate them. Almost since their inception scorn has been poured on these laws and they have been the butt of wit far brighter than anything I can emulate. If ridicule could have killed them they would have been dead long ago. No doubt this form of attack has been effective in promoting the progress toward liberalism in America, but I believe that it is no longer likely to be a very valuable weapon. In England, at any rate, the censor-morons have had their backs to the wall since the *Lady Chatterley's Lover* case, and a counterattack may well develop. The present situation the world over demands a serious crusade wherever the philosophic ground for freedom of thought and artistic liberty have any chance of obtaining a hearing.

There is little doubt that public opinion in civilized countries supports the existence of laws against pornography and that it would not tolerate their complete abolition. Furthermore, the commercial pornographer is not a character to command sympathy even if he is occasionally unfairly treated and, where he cynically battens on the young, he is properly the object of detestation.

Whether the public attitude to pornography is altogether sound and whether it is likely to continue unchanged are matters which will be considered in the final chapter of this book. Whatever the future may hold, it is clear that the only justification for obscenity laws, within the framework of the liberal tradition, is the contention that certain writing with a sexual content so inflames passion and overthrows reason that it destroys the very conditions necessary for the operation of right judgment in opinion and conduct.

Once the necessity for obscenity laws is conceded it is very difficult to protect serious literature from their operation. The whole conception of obscenity is largely subjective and any law intended to suppress or curb it is bound to be to some extent arbitrary and vague.

The best that has been evolved so far is the position developed by the American courts—especially the exemption from the taint of obscenity of "ideas having the slightest redeeming social importance." The present American legal doctrines on obscenity could with advantage be built into statute law on both sides of the Atlantic.

Even if this were done, further safeguards would be necessary before the minimum requirements for the protection of serious literature would be met.

It must be recognized that however well laws against pornography may be framed, they will always be open to abuse by reactionary authoritarianism, fanatical puritanism, official stupidity, and the sensationalism of the press. It is a delusion to think that even if the law is harsh and arbitrary the authorities can be relied upon to operate it in an intelligent and gentlemanly way. The attacks on the work of Zola, Havelock Ellis, James Joyce, D. H. Lawrence, and other eminent authors belie this notion. Ministers and officials in England today can be as silly as "Jix" and Sir Archibald Bodkin, while the press hysteria about *Lolita* was almost as acute as it was about *The Well of Loneliness* and *To Beg I am Ashamed.*

There is no reason to suppose that the appointment of censorship boards consisting of literary and other experts would improve this situation. If the decisions of such boards cannot be challenged in the courts the rule of law is abrogated, and where they are purely advisory their influence can be very illiberal. Even eminent men of letters can be reactionary. T. S. Eliot, for instance, has said that the Roman and Communist idea of an index of prohibited books seems to him perfectly sound in principle.[3]

In considering this matter it must not be forgotten that the prosecutions and threats of prosecution are by no means the whole story. The indirect effects of fear of the law or deference to the conception of literary obscenity play an important part in curbing intellectual progress and artistic creation. There are the books that are never written and books that are written quite differently from what the author really desires. Then there is the expurgation and bowdlerization of authors' manuscripts by publishers, often, as we have seen in the case of D. H. Lawrence's work, without any indication of what has been done.

One of the results of driving work by authors like James Joyce, D. H. Lawrence, and Henry Miller underground is that it debilitates criticism. No one with pretensions to speak with authority about books—unless he be a James Douglas or John Gordon—likes to be severe on any point concerning a book which is not available to speak for itself, nor does he care to be other than kind to a fellow man of letters who is subject to legal or newspaper attack. In these circumstances authors are deprived of salutary correction by their peers which they are as inclined to respect as much as they resent interference from lawyers, officials, clergymen, newspaper editors, and puritans. There is such a thing as "decent reticence" (a phrase used as the title of *The Times* leader on the *Lady Chatterley's*

Lover case), but its nature and bounds should be dictated by artistic integrity and not by irrelevant moralistic considerations.

Perhaps the most remarkable example of the way in which scholarship can be affected by the notion of obscenity is the treatment of Pepys's diary. The longhand transcription of Pepys's shorthand, kept in the Pepysian Library at Cambridge, has never been published in its entirety. In the fullest edition, certain passages are represented by dots because, the editor tells us in his preface, they "cannot possibly be printed." For instance, when Mrs. Pepys surprised the diarist with Deb the maid, we are not allowed to read that he was embracing the girl "con my hand sub su coats."[4] It is perhaps fortunate that Boswell's journals came into the possession of an American university, who are publishing them in their entirety.

It is now proposed to formulate certain provisions which must be embodied in any law directed against pornography if the somewhat hypothetical evils it is designed to combat are not to be outweighed by the threat to serious literature inherent in all such censorship. In attempting this task, no regard will be paid to the related problems of censorship of the theater, cinema, radio, and television—not because these media are unimportant or that freedom by expression in them is not essential to the intellectual and artistic health of the community, but because though similar the problems involved are substantially different. For one thing, these media are much more likely to arouse public passion than is the case with reading matter. Furthermore, the audiences which they reach are much more indiscriminate. Above all, it is the written word that is the vital operative factor in the process of intellectual progress and artistic development. If this essential avenue is free, questions of freedom and liberty in other media of expression can be discussed in the light of informed reason: if the book is in chains, a shadow is thrown over all other public communication. And since the graphic arts are so closely bound up with book production, it is almost inevitable that they should be covered by the same obscenity law.

Any penalization of literary obscenity should be strictly confined to the criminal law and not allowed to intrude into civil litigation as it did in the case of Elinor Glyn's *Three Weeks*. There is no reason why literary pirates and tricky insurance companies should profit by moralistic pleas.

If the criminal law is to interfere with the writing of books, it is fundamental that the offense penalized on the ground of obscenity should be the publication of matter in circumstances alleged to be harmful to the community. At present there is a very general confusion between an "obscene book" and "obscene publication." The conception of a book being obscene *in esse* is basically false because it is almost impossible to imagine a book that at some time or place could not be of legitimate interest to someone. The offense must therefore be the publication of sexual literature in circumstances likely to overthrow intellectual judgment and by inflaming passion to limit the range of moral choice which should be the pride of the human condition. This would not impose any restriction on freedom to advocate opinions and conduct which are generally disapproved of in any given time and place nor on the liberty of the writer and thinker to endeavor to change the moral standards of the community. It would only be an effort on the part of the law (perhaps unnecessary) to attempt to insure that individual actions and community judgments were calmly and responsibly made.

If obscene publication is allowed to be a crime, it is essential for the protection of personal privacy and individual liberty that the publication involved should be what is normally understood by that word—namely, distribution or exhibition for money or gratuitously to the public at large or to a section of the public. This would rule out the Montalk case and also the showing of obscene post cards which so much concerned the police before the committee on the Obscene Publications Bill at Westminster. Where the sending of indecent letters to individuals and the private exhibition of pornographic pictures is the proper concern of the law, it should be dealt with under the laws against seduction, corruption of minors, and the like. There are, of course, borderline cases where it is difficult to distinguish between what is private and what is public, but the courts are quite used to going into the niceties of this distinction in other matters. We are only concerned with the broad principle that the crime should be in the nature of public nuisance and not of injury to individuals.

A conviction for publishing a book under one set of conditions would not mean that it could not be lawfully published under other conditions, and the rehabilitation by time of books that have been condemned by the courts should be recognized as it is under French law. Prosecutions should be barred if not brought within a year or two of publication, and the institution of legal proceedings in respect of books that have been in general circulation for years (such as the Blackpool case in 1950) should be impossible.

If the offense of obscene publication were of the nature specified above, it follows that the circumstances of publication would be as important a contributing factor as the character of the book. Restrictive conditions of publication would in many cases confer immunity on a work which might otherwise fall foul of the law, and it would be immaterial that single copies might, and probably would, fall into the hands of persons belonging to sections of the public for whom they were not intended. Publication can be generally restricted by price and methods of advertising and marketing; or it can be limited to members of specified professions or societies. Such limitation is repugnant to democratic sentiment, but it may be unavoidable in communities in which large numbers are both literate and semi-educated. It should not, however, be an offense for an individual to obtain any book that appeals to his curiosity or fancy, and the legal fiction that the buyer of an "obscene" book aids and abets the publication thereof should be abandoned.

Not only should any obscene publication crime be public in its nature and dependent on the type of public likely to be affected, but the public at large have an interest of a special character in any prosecution arising from it. If it is sought to suppress a book it is not only the authorities, on one side, and those charged with the publication, on the other, who are the interested parties. Authors should not suffer because pusillanimous publishers or booksellers will not defend themselves in court, as was the case with Havelock Ellis and D. H. Lawrence. Reputable publishers should not be put to loss because provincial bookshops deem it prudent to keep in with the police, as is often the case. In a prosecution for obscene publication, all interested parties should have the right to give evidence on the issue of obscenity. Furthermore, the court should be required to satisfy itself that a conviction is in the public interest, quite apart from any plea that may or may not be made by the defendants. This duty would be similar to that imposed on the divorce courts by English law, and it would protect the reading public from being improperly deprived of works which it has a moral right to be able to read.

The issue of obscenity is essentially one suitable to be referred to a jury. Although juries are quite capable of bringing in wrongheaded verdicts, they are generally more sensitive to changes of opinion and taste than judges and magistrates who, with some notable exceptions, are apt to represent the less defensible aspect of yesterday's morals and fashions. Trial by jury has been considered by the best authorities to be a bulwark of British liberty, and on no occasion is that bulwark more necessary than when it is sought to stifle any expression of thought or artistic impulse.

All prosecutions for obscene publication should therefore be tried by jury and it should not be open to the defense to consent to dispense with the jury nor to submit to summary jurisdiction. The matter which is the subject of the prosecution should be put to the jury as a whole and the judge in his summing-up should give an impartial survey of the evidence. It is no more justifiable for a judge to harangue the jury about the "filthy" and "disgusting" nature of a book than it would be for a judge to say that an accused person was obviously guilty of murder. Trials such as that of Montalk are a travesty of justice, and any expression of his own opinion by the judge on the question put to the jury should be ground for setting aside the conviction on appeal.

If the conception of obscenity *in esse* is abandoned, the destruction of "obscene" articles cannot be defended in strict logic; but it may be necessary to give the courts powers of confiscation in order to check trade in pornography. Orders made under such powers should be entirely ancillary to sentences for the offense of obscene publication and only allowed in connection with a conviction. All interested parties should be entitled to be heard and the public interest taken into consideration by the court. No material should ever be destroyed until it has been ascertained whether it is not of interest to some library, gallery, or museum.

If the law against pornography is to be effective it is probably necessary to give the police powers of search and seizure before trial. Such powers, however, should never be exercisable except under court orders applicable to specific premises. Such orders should only be allowed by law after sworn evidence that commercial transactions of a public nature are carried on from the premises concerned. The sale or exchange of single copies of books by libraries, scholars, bibliophiles, and secondhand booksellers should be excluded. We have seen that under the Obscene Publications Act, 1959, private libraries may be in danger of police raids and noticed the damage that can ensue from such raids even when innocence is finally established.

As a rule, laws against obscenity in literature are fortified by provisions relating to the transmission by mail and the import of obscene matter. The posting or import of such matter may be an offense and the postal and Customs authorities may be given special powers of detention and seizure. The Post Office is often given power to open packets in the search for obscene matter, and the normal powers of the Customs to search imported merchandise and baggage are used for the same purpose.

There seems to be no good reason why the posting of packages which are not objectionable on the outside or the import of goods should be made criminal on the ground of alleged "obscenity," because if an antisocial act has been committed it will be part and parcel of the publication of obscene matter. The opening of sealed postal packets (except for grave reasons, of which suspected obscenity is not one) is quite unjustifiable, and the opening of second-class mail is only justified for the purpose of seeing that the contents qualify for reduced rates. Any matter detained or seized by either the postal or the Customs authorities should be required to be brought before a court of law, who would have to decide whether the detention or seizure was necessary to prosecute or prevent an instance of obscene public publication. Interference with private correspondence and personal property found in passengers' baggage should, of course, be out of the question.

No country whose traditions are liberal should subscribe to international postal or Customs conventions insofar as they assist other countries to operate illiberal obscenity laws.

However carefully drawn up on the lines indicated above a law of obscene publication might be, it would be necessary to provide specific protection for certain classes of books. Literary classics and current foreign literature should be exempt from the operation of the law unless they are published with adventitious appeals to salacity in the way of meritricious illustrations and the like. Special provisions are desirable in regard to works of sex education, nudist publications, and children's books when published by sincere and responsible people. Public and scholarly libraries, authors, printers, and secondhand booksellers also require special protection. Comments on each of these categories will be made in the paragraphs which follow.

The great literary classics of the world should be freely available for all, and where they are in ancient or foreign languages and unexpurgated and unbowdlerized, translations should be allowed. Whether for fear of the law or for reasons of commercial prudery, no such English translations of Greek and Roman works are generally available. The great Loeb series leaves certain Latin passages in the original and translates certain Greek passages into Latin, while the Penguin translations resort to polite evasions of the direct classical sexual diction. I have never seen the insult, recorded by Tacitus, which one of the maids of Nero's wife made to her tormentor (*castiora esse muliebria Octaviae quam os tuus*) plainly translated. When Thomas Denman made effective use of this quotation in defense of Queen Caroline, the law reports translated *muliebria* into Greek. Integral translations of Martial, Juvenal, Petronius, Aristophanes, and the Greek Anthology are either nonexistent or hard to come by and liable to be attacked by censormorons. All this creates a false and sentimentalized view of the classical world of the sort fostered by the late Professor Gilbert Murray.

The position is much the same in respect of the classics of European and Oriental literature. In most translations of Boccaccio's *Decameron* one or two tales draw unnecessary attention to themselves by appearing in the original Italian.

Translations of literary classics into French are generally more reliable than English translations, but expurgation and bowdlerization is not unknown.

Besides the acknowledged classics of literature, there are certain books originally written as pornography in the past which have become of legitimate historical and literary interest to scholars, men of letters, and serious readers generally. No student of eighteenth-century literature need blush to exchange the time of day with the gay and moralizing Fanny Hill; and it is ridiculous that reams should be written by distinguished authors about Sade when no one is supposed to have looked at his erotic books. I say "looked at" because only the research student or the aspiring Ph.D. would want to pursue *Justine* and *Juliette* to the bitter end; nevertheless, a nodding acquaintance with these ladies would discredit the more fatuous adulation paid to "the divine Marquis" by some of his admirers. Then there are pornographic books of legitimate literary interest because of their distinguished authorship: one need only mention Musset's *Gamiani* and the poems written by Verlaine under the pseudonym of Pablo de Herlagnez, of which one of the judges in Montalk's case appeared to be ignorant. The necessity of making pornographic material available to scholars and men of letters must be made plain even to the most strait-laced by G. Wilson Knight's *Lord Byron's Marriage*. By means of a learned analysis of the admittedly pornographic *Don Leon*, falsely attributed to Byron, the author throws a flood of light on the mystery of the poet's life and work. Books of this character would circulate as freely as the situation demands if the law with regard to restricted publication were reasonably elastic and interference with scholarly libraries and occasional transactions by secondhand booksellers and individuals were impossible.

Current foreign books which are reputably published and acknowledged by literary critics should be specifically protected from the operation of any law of obscene publication, whether in the original language or in translation. There is no case for saying that a Britisher or American may not read a book that is part of the current literature of France or Germany. The interference of the British Customs with the importation of the novels of Jean Genet is, for instance, completely unjustifiable.

Under English law it does not appear to be permissible even to tender evidence regarding a book's status and availability abroad. If the jury in the Penguin Books case knew anything about the freeing from obscenity of *Lady Chatterley's Lover* in America, they did not learn it from the evidence given in court.

Books of sex education written and published under responsible auspices also call for specific protection. It is thought by many people concerned with education and social well-being that such books ought to be much more explicit than they are and the illustrations to them far less diagrammatic. This question is essentially one for educationalists and not for the clumsy adjudication of the law. The prosecution of sincere books like Edward Charles's *Sexual Impulse* and Eustace Chesser's *Love Without Fear* should be quite impossible.

It should also be specifically enacted that the publication of photographs and other pictures of the naked human body is not in itself an offense. This would mean that sincere artists could throw away their fig leaves and wisps of drapery and that nudist magazines containing integral photographs of genuine nudists' activities need fear nothing from the law. Where these magazines are embellished by "art" supplements and posed close-ups the specific exemption need not apply and such protection could stand or fall by the general law of obscene publication.

Children's books lie on the margin of the concern of this work which is the protection of serious adult literature from censorship and persecution by obscurantists and puritans. There is no objection in principle to legislation against irresponsible and avaricious manufacturers of horror comics, though parental, pedagogic, and religious authority may be a better protection for the childish mind than the law. The problem is also wider than that presented by the horror comics themselves. Detailed descriptions of crime in the disreputable Sunday press, waxwork chambers of horrors, and even some of Grimms' fairy tales are very terrifying to some children, while lurid descriptions of hell fire are worst of all.

A note of warning must, however, be sounded. Specific legislation on children's literature might be used to restrain beneficial developments in books for children, in deference to fictitious notions about the "purity" of the child's mind. Children have a certain interest in excretion and sex and there is no reason why school books should not take these subjects in their stride. Anatomy primers and elementary manuals of hygiene need not avoid the sexual functions. Again, children brought up on farms know that animals have a sex life and sometimes witness its manifestations. They are probably all the better for it. Why then should the fairy tale and the animal story be studiously bowdlerized for children? Most English versions of the medieval Reynard the Fox stories are so treated. New educational theories and modern psychology may effect a great change in reputable children's books, but it should be made under responsible and qualified guidance.

Care should also be taken both by legislatures and the courts to see that laws enacted with the ostensible purpose of protecting juveniles do not in fact restrict the range of adult reading.

Learned and scholarly libraries and also ordinary public libraries such as those run by the local authorities in Britain should be entirely outside the scope of any law of obscene publication both as regards the procuring of books and the extent to which books are lent or otherwise made available to readers. The learned and scholarly libraries can be trusted to transact their affairs in the highest interests of science, literature, and art; and public nuisance is not likely to arise from their activities. Public libraries are responsible to elected bodies who are very sensitive to public opinion, and are more likely to err on the side of prudish censorship than to cause public harm by injudicious publication. The two categories of library are, however, faced with different problems which deserve some comment.

The British Museum Library may be taken as a type of the great scholarly libraries of the world. Like most of such institutions—including the Vatican Library—it possesses a large number of books which for various reasons are unsuitable to be issued without discrimination or special precautions.

Numerous items in the Catalogue of Printed Books have a press mark which indicates that before the book is issued the Superintendent of the Reading Room will interview the reader and satisfy himself that he is a suitable person to have the book. This category covers books dealing with sexual matters, many of them in general circulation, books with illustrations which are considered offensive even though they might be overlooked by other readers, and rare and valuable books. Frequently the books have to be read in the North Library under conditions permitting of special supervision.

Next there is a great store of books not in the general catalogue kept in what is known as the "Private Case." Here are all the great pornographic classics such as the works of Sade, Rétif de la Bretonne, and Aretino. Here, of course, dwells the irrepressible Fanny Hill together with other heroes and heroines whose adventures the courts have found "obscene." The category includes an extensive collection of erotica bequeathed to the Museum by Henry Spencer Ashbee, who compiled one of the standard bibliographies of such books under the pseudonym of Pisanus Fraxi. He also gave the Museum a magnificent collection of early editions of Cervantes. "Private Case" books can be seen only by those who know of their existence and can persuade the Keeper of the Printed Books that they are engaged on serious research. A bibliography of erotica compiled by Rolf S. Reade[5] included the British Museum Private Case as well as the Enfer de la Bibliothèque Nationale and other similar collections.

Finally there is a category of uncatalogued books in the Museum whose very existence is not supposed to be known. It consists mainly of defamatory libels and books giving away Masonic, official, and other "secrets." The collection includes the life of Charles Bradlaugh by Charles R. Mackay.

At the London Library certain books are kept "in the Librarian's room" and a personal interview is necessary before they are issued to members. This is a lending library and responsibility for the care and further "publication" of the book rests with the member once the Librarian has satisfied himself that the member concerned is a suitable and reliable borrower.

No exception can be taken to precautions of the kind instanced above. Apart from moral and social considerations libraries are bound to exercise caution over the issue or circulation of controversial items because there are people who believe themselves to be under a moral or religious obligation to steal, mutilate, or deface books expressing opinions of which they disapprove or conveying information which they find inconvenient, while even mildly erotic illustrations may attract the attentions of the sexual maniac. Although the wisdom of trying to protect fools from books is open to dispute, the necessity of protecting books from fools is not. Then, where the book is valuable the plain thief must be taken into consideration, and he may be a most distinguished figure in the learned world as witness the depredations at the British Museum of the late and unlamented Thomas James Wise.[6]

The omission of books from the catalogue of a library is, however, a very different matter from taking precautions over issue. At the British Museum the practice causes unnecessary frustration and waste of time and patience although *bona fide* scholars who visit the Museum personally and know of the existence of uncatalogued books can always rely on the liberal good sense and courteous assistance of the officials. The catalogue is, however, printed and sold to subscribers at home and abroad, and the omissions seriously impair the utility and usefulness of a monumental work of reference. All books consigned to the purgatorical "Private Case" or damned to the secret inferno should now be admitted to the paradise of the general catalogue where their sinful nature could be indicated by some sign equivalent to the admonitory Φ of the Bodleian or the scarcely less witty ꙮ of the Boston Athenaeum.

There is also ground for uneasiness as to whether a library could be called to account with regard to books not catalogued on the ground of "obscenity" in view of the legal doctrine that there can be no right of property in obscene matter. The Archbishop of Canterbury and the Bishop of London are *ex officio* trustees of the British Museum. Dr. Geoffrey Fisher, the late Archbishop, once lectured an agnostic scientist (who was subsequently dismissed[7] from the Museum's service) on the exercise of Christian virtues in the discharge of his official duties. Is it fantastic to envisage some Savonarola of the future, risen to the episcopate, inaugurating a great burning of the books?

It is the duty of an ordinary library to use its financial resources to make available to adult borrowers a fair and representative cross-section of the reputable literature generally available to the reading public. No ideological or censorial considerations should influence their necessarily selective purchases, and the representations of religious pressure groups and locally prominent obscurantists should be ignored. The practice of withdrawing books from the open shelves is objectionable because it distorts the view of the literary situation which the library's selection gives to the visitor: it should only be resorted to where political pressure makes it the only alternative to not acquiring a book at all.

Some public libraries, particularly in big provincial cities, have reference departments which vie with the great learned libraries and are used by scholars and students. Care and discretion are, of course, called for regarding the conditions of issue, but it is preposterous that the law should enable government officials to interfere with their choice of acquisitions as was done at Birmingham over Genet.

If this outline of an optimum law is accepted so far, it follows that responsibility must rest primarily on the publisher for the matter and the manner of his publications. He is in a far better position than the author to judge the climate of public taste and legal opinion, and an author who chooses a reputable and well-established publisher should not be liable to prosecution for the alleged obscenity of his work. Similarly printers and booksellers should be protected so far as they deal with reputable publishers in the ordinary way of trade. That the law should require printers to act as censors is fair neither to them nor to the public. The fact that in their evidence before the Select Committee in 1957 the British Federation of Master Printers said that they did not wish to be relieved of this responsibility was probably due to commercial vanity. As to booksellers, they cannot be expected to read all they sell nor are they necessarily qualified to assess the legal propriety of a book, and they should be penalized only if they conduct their business in a way calculated to make a salacious appeal. The principle that obscene publication is in its nature a public offense should protect a secondhand bookseller who sells single copies of obscene books acquired in the normal course of his trade, but the protection should be specifically enacted.

I am well aware that the suggestions contained in this chapter for the form of a law of obscene publication will satisfy no one, but come under fire from both sides in the conflict between liberal and authoritarian ideas. On the one side it will be condemned as a series of weak-kneed concessions to ignorance and reaction and a bolstering-up of a medieval conception which is slowly dying in the light of progress. The other side will regard it as a reckless sacrifice of public morality and social stability for the dubious advantages of intellectual speculation, education, and freedom of artistic creation.

I can only say that the proposals are an honest and realistic effort to meet a concrete situation. Such a thing as pornography does exist. This phenomenon is widely considered to be an actual and potential cause of evil and misery and it excites passionate desires to suppress it which find expression in the criminal, and sometimes the civil, laws of nearly all civilizations. These laws are of their nature arbitrary and, as has been demonstrated by the historical chapters of this book, dangerous to serious scientific, educational, and artistic literature. These laws are often ignorantly and fanatically administered by puritans, and, what is more, cleverly abused and exploited by the exponents of religious and secular authoritarian ideas. What is required from those who have the ideals of freedom and liberty at heart is a constructive approach from which the spirit of compromise is not entirely absent.

The position is as set out above in those parts of Europe where the tradition of intellectual freedom has grown up and dominated the policy of nations and also in those parts of the new world where that tradition has been carried. As literacy spreads in the developing countries of Asia and Africa, who are somewhat prone to imitate the defects as well as the merits of Western civilization, similar situations are likely to spring up. My suggestions are offered with humility but at the same time some confidence to the legislators, judges, officials, and the common people of both old and new states.

My own contribution to a solution of the problem has been a negative one in the sense that I have been solely concerned with such safeguards and limitations as any law of literary obscenity must embody if serious literature is to have a modicum of protection, and I have sought to relate these precautions to the general shape of the obscenity laws as they exist today. The more positive side of the problem—how to make the law an effective weapon against pornography, to the extent to which that is possible, is the business of others. One thing is certain, no laws which antagonize literary, artistic, and intellectual opinion (as the obscenity laws of Britain, America, and France do) will be very successful in achieving their object.

The solution of the more positive aspect of the problem must depend on the nature and importance of the evil to be combated —subjects about which, as the final chapter of this book will demonstrate, there is little evidence of clear thinking.

Pornography

THIS BOOK HAS BEEN CONCERNED with the protection of freedom of thought and liberty of artistic creation from the abuse of laws originally and ostensibly designed to suppress the publication of pornography. We have seen that the Supreme Court of the United States has ruled that obscenity law must not restrict the constitutional right of American citizens to advocate ideas however controversial and distasteful to prevailing opinion, although the uniform implementation of this judgment in the various states and throughout the lower courts is sometimes found wanting. In England we have seen the passing of an Act of Parliament intended to protect literature from obscenity prosecutions. This Act, however, did not protect the publishers of *Lady Chatterley's Lover* from an unsuccessful prosecution, and the prosecuting counsel in the case included the unorthodox morality of the novel in his advocacy. It is also not certain that the Act has entirely freed literature from the old trammels of the common law. We have seen that even recently France has been by no means blameless of interfering with literature on the ground of obscenity. I have argued that the question of the character and administration of literary obscenity laws is of urgent importance in all parts of the world where the freedom of the press is relied upon as a means of promoting human welfare.

In maintaining this thesis I have somewhat uncritically accepted the existence of pornography as a generally recognized social menace and followed the normal vague and varying use of the word. Before concluding my book it is necessary, in order to complete the picture presented to the reader and to prevent misunderstandings that might weaken my case, to look more precisely at the meaning of this word and more closely at the reality behind it.

There is a large volume of writing devoted to sexual subject matter which makes no pretense to be a contribution to literature and which claims no scientific or artistic merit. Its publication meets no intellectual or social interest except perhaps that of the psychiatrist. If by some chance it escapes oblivion it can do no more than satisfy some historical curiosity regarding the manners of the time or the private character of a great name. The titles of pornographic books frequently advertise the nature of their contents: e.g., *Lustful Stories*; *The New Ladies' Tickler*, or the adventures of Lady Lovesport; *The Autobiography of a Flea*; and *Flossie*, a Venus of fifteen (falsely attributed to Swinburne). The distinguishing feature of this type of publication is that its sole aim is entertainment by sexual stimulation. Its authors are either strangers to artistic integrity and moral responsibility or have taken temporary leave of those controlling influences.

The bulk of pornography is badly written, tedious, and boring; but by no means all. Men of the literary standing of Goethe and Maupassant have lent their pens to its production, and Alfred de Musset wrote *Gamiani* to demonstrate that the French language was capable of being used to produce a book of the utmost license without employing a coarse word or inelegant expression. Indeed a great deal of pornography is quite readable taken in small doses, although the difficulties of the pornographer's task—the repeated presentation of sexual incidents which must rise to a crescendo of excitement—are all too apparent. The impossibility of avoiding monotony was once for all expressed, as we have seen, by John Cleland through the mouth of his Fanny Hill. Again, much pornography is badly printed and shabbily produced, but not all of it. Some pornographic books display great typographic and pictorial artistry on good paper in excellent binding. In fact, pornography is produced with a very wide range of literary skill and standard of book production.

Pornography is in fact no more than a species of the much larger genus of subliterature which aims solely at entertainment divorced from the higher aims of literature and indifferent to moral and social responsibility. The line between this subliterature and true literature is not sharply discernible and the better sort of pornography is often classed as literature and the worst literature, if it has a sexual content, is often condemned as pornography. Furthermore, the terms "pornography" and "pornographic" are often applied to genuine literary and scientific works by people who disapprove of their content or style. If in literary style and standards of production pornography plumbs depths unknown to other kinds of subliterature, that is a result of legal suppression and social disapproval, which, although restricting the extent of a moral phenomenon, always make what is left worse than it otherwise would have been. This was so in the case of prohibition in America and more generally in regard to prostitution.

In a recent study[1] Drs. Eberhard and Phyllis Kronhausen have attempted a more exact definition of pornography than can result from following the common usage of the word as above. They distinguish between "erotic realism" and "hard core obscenity" and stigmatize only the latter with the pejorative designation "pornography." The essence of erotic realism, they say, is the truthful description of the basic realities of life as the author experiences it. So far as sexual stimulation is concerned, such descriptions (by reason of revulsion, absence of appreciation of humor, or other responses on the part of the reader) may have a decidedly anti-erotic effect. On the other hand, it is perfectly proper for the reader to respond erotically to such writing.

Erotic realism, by the authors' classification, embraces the erotic classics of the Oriental and classical worlds, the erotic writing of Poggio, Aretino, Brantôme, Rabelais, Casanova, Pepys, Zola, and Henry Miller. They specifically include Mark Twain's *Conversation at the Social Fireside as it was at ye time of the Tudors temp. circ. 1601*, a scandalous satire on Elizabethan morals and manners, of which the author said, "If there is a decent word in it, it is because I overlooked it." Frank Harris's *My Life and Loves* and Vladimir Nabokov's *Lolita* are also included, while D. H. Lawrence's *Lady Chatterley's Lover* and Edmund Wilson's *Hecate County* are instanced as outstanding examples of erotic realism that has been mistaken for pornography. In the Kronhausens' view erotic realism reflects a basically healthy and therapeutic attitude to life, and its effects on the average person are generally beneficial.

From an examination of numerous examples of "hard core obscenity" or pornography the Kronhausens conclude that this class of writing can be distinguished by a typical general structure or make-up. A book which is designed to act as a sexual stimulant must present to the reader's mind a succession of erotic scenes which rise in a crescendo of intensity until they culminate in an orgiastic climax. Besides conformity to this general structure pornographic books may be recognized by the recurrence of unrealistic situations which provide fantastic wish fulfillments for their readers. Among the typical criteria are: easy seduction, sadistic defloration, incest, permissive parent figures, profanation of the sacred, indiscriminate use of "four-letter" words, supersexed males, nymphomaniacs, homosexuality, and flagellation. The perils of profligacy such as unwanted pregnancy and venereal disease are not mentioned or are lightly brushed aside. The Kronhausens insist on the paucity of evidence regarding the emotional and social effects of pornography, and venture the opinion, based on psychiatric clinical experience, that instead of being the cause of delinquent conduct it may more often than not act as a safety valve for antisocial tendencies.

The Kronhausens' mention of flagellation as one of the typical subjects of pornography prompts some comment on writing intended to meet the tastes of flagellomaniacs. Flagellomania is a subspecies of sadism—the association of the sexual impulse with cruelty, and those subject to the deviation take pleasure in whipping or being whipped, watching whippings or imagining them. Its roots almost always spring from infantile or adolescent experiences of the chastisement either of the persons themselves or of others. Swinburne, for instance, sustained a mental fixation as the result of his experience of birching at Eton. To this abnormality he gave crude rein in the brothels of Euston Road and in his contributions to *The Whippingham Papers*. It finds refined and sublimated expression from time to time in his poetry.

Flagellomania is peculiarly *le vice anglais*. The English have been very loath to give up judicial flogging and they lag behind most of the civilized world in their attitude to the beating of children in the school and in the home. A considerable volume of subliterature is produced, mainly on the Continent, to pander to this taste. The books follow a fairly uniform pattern. When we read that Miss Whipsome is to be the new governess at the old rectory we can guess what is afoot.

A definition of pornography in the sense of reprehensible sexual writing that all right-minded people are supposed to want suppressed by law has become almost classic. The phrase, used by Judge Woolsey in his celebrated *Ulysses* judgment, is "dirt for dirt's sake," and it appears to be a very satisfactory description in the eyes of most writers and speakers on the subject of pornography. But if we ask ourselves what is this dirt for whose very sake it is blameworthy to write, what is the answer? Do we mean "sex for sex sake"? If so, why not?—unless we believe that sex is dirt. It may be urged that the pornographer seeks to denigrate and debase sex. But this is by no means true as a general rule. Insofar as his generally modest literary talents permit, the pornographer very often is only concerned to depict normal sexuality as gay, pleasant, enjoyable, and infinitely attractive. When this end is pursued with literary skill (often accompanied with artistic illustration) the book is allowed by clement judges to be "erotic" rather than "pornographic." Henry Miller's erotic work may be taken as an example of ebullient reveling in sexuality and carnality in a spirit that ranges from the comic to the reverent. Miller's work is, of course, literature but are books written in the same spirit, even if lacking in literary skill and a sense of responsibility, necessarily evil?

Our society allows any amount of sexual stimulation at all times by poster, newspaper, cinema, theater, and women's dress in public; but it frowns on sexual satisfaction and aids thereto. In the society of the future (if indeed men are advancing to a better world) I believe that this emphasis will be reversed. Life will be less sex-obsessed but, at proper times and seasons, physical love will be restored to its ancient dignity, variety, and gaiety. Both modesty and the art of love will come into their own again. In that society the erotic book, we may expect, will play a part. And a pornographic book is really nothing more than a badly written erotic book.

But what are we to think of books written with the intention of stimulating not normal sexual passion but abnormalities and deviations, or which seek to degrade and blacken the sexual function? In Verlaine's *Hombres* and Genet's *Journal du Voleur*, for instance, male homosexuality takes the place of normal passion while Sade not only associates sex with cruelty but degrades it in every possible way. There are plenty of trashy books which present perverse and degrading attitudes to sex without the genius of the writers mentioned. Are these books a menace to society? On our present knowledge the question must be admitted to be an open one.

It may well be that the reading of such books, instead of increasing the type of conduct with which they deal, acts as a catharsis for the impulses concerned and substitutes imaginative fantasy for real deeds. Many persons of twisted sexual impulses shrink from putting their ideas into practice and enjoy them only in imagination. All sadists are not cruel—and conversely much cruelty is not sadistic.

The question of the effects of erotic and pornographic books which appeal to abnormal impulses is part of the general problem of the relation between reading and conduct on which some comment should be made.

It is frequently asserted by judges, magistrates, and other high-sounding authorities that pornographic books are the cause of sexual crime and antisocial conduct. There is evidence that pornography is sometimes associated with crime and depravity, but there is little evidence that this association is a causal relationship. When books are blamed for evil consequences and antisocial conduct, the fault is generally with the reader rather than with the book. Gilles de Rais, the companion in arms of Joan of Arc, who after her death was executed for a series of sadistic child murders, certainly attributed his corruption to the reading of Suetonius as a youth; but it is only necessary to observe that multitudes of men must have read Suetonius without any ill-effects whatever, and that it would be absurd to condemn a book because it was proved to have had an undesirable effect on an unbalanced person.

The police say that nudist magazines are often used for the purpose of masturbation: but is there any evidence that the masturba-

tion would not have taken place without the magazine? We have
seen that the English police were anxious to maintain the legal
fiction that the showing of a picture by one person to another constitutes "publication" because obscene post cards played a part
in some cases of the homosexual seduction of youths. But is there
any evidence that such post cards actually further the objects of
the seducer? A Parisian woman in the latter part of the nineteenth
century procured the blinding of her lover to make him dependent
on her. Among the books of devotion in her *prie-dieu* the police
found a "slim volume of lewd verse"[2] whose secret author and cir-
culator was Ernest Pinard, the Imperial Advocate who had thun-
dered against the scandal of *Madame Bovary* and the immorality
of *Les Fleurs du mal*. Who shall sort this tangle of hypocrisy, re-
ligiosity, jealousy, and cold-blooded villainy into a chain of cause
and effect?

It would be, of course, a poor service to the cause of intellectual
and artistic freedom, which it is the purpose of this book to further,
to assert that literature has no effect on conduct and morals. Indeed, one of the potential values of literature is that it does exercise
a great influence; and the importance of freedom is that it allows
the good to be distinguished from the bad. Admittedly great literature may have regrettable results on conduct where its unfortunate
tendencies are not corrected by knowledge and an enlightened
moral sense. In 1954[3] a cadet of the French military college at
Saint-Cyr bullied his mistress into killing her little daughter—
either as an *acte gratuit* or as a ritual murder, probably the former. The young man's reading consisted largely of André Gide,
Nietzsche, d'Annunzio, and Jean-Paul Sartre, and these authors
may have had a bad effect on his mind. But none of their works
can be stigmatized as pornography and, whatever their intentions
in writing, erotic stimulation was not among them. Their books
are great literature. Is the world to be denied them because they
may unbalance the immature mind or the personality with a pro-
pensity for evil? Certainly not; but something like this argument
is sometimes put forward. One of the silliest contributions to the
Lolita controversy came from Philip Toynbee who argued[4] that
the book should be suppressed if it could be shown that a single
little girl was likely to be seduced as a result of its publication. This

kind of criterion would ultimately rob the world of its literature because almost every great book, including the Bible, must have been the cause of crime or misdoing at some time or other. Certainly in the past people have found encouragement in the Bible for witch burning and slave trading.

When considering the extent to which readers are likely to be susceptible to the normal or abnormal stimulus given by pornography account should be taken of the extent to which they may be immunized by media of communication other than printing, for though obscenity laws may make pornographic books expensive and difficult to obtain, acquaintance with pornographic material and attitudes is by no means restricted.

In many languages there is a volume of traditional oral obscenity. In English this consists of a vast corpus of "smutty" stories, "dirty" jokes, limericks, comic ballads, and parodies of serious poems, some knowledge of which is by no means confined to the male sex. Limericks are very numerous and sometimes reach a high degree of perfection. A number of the more common were recorded by Norman Douglas and privately published with his semi-serious introduction and notes in 1928. In 1954 a collection of over 1,700 (including variations and translations) was published in Paris. During the world wars obscene stories and verses were carried all over the globe by the English-speaking forces and many of them have an international appeal. For instance the erotic pun on which the limerick recording the devotion of a young plumber of Leigh to his job is based can be rendered in French, German, and Arabic. This limerick has been done into Latin:

> Prope mare erat tubulator
> Qui virginem ingrediebatur.
> Desine ingressus
> Audivi progressus:
> Est mihi inquit tubulator.

That knowledge of the most bizarre sexual activity is not confined to any one class of English society is shown by the wide range of subject matter covered by contemporary cloacal *graffiti*. There is in private possession a collection of some five thousand transcriptions made by the late Dr. Pelham H. Box. The authors are for the most part semi-educated; but it is safe to say that there is scarcely a form of sexual activity, normal or deviated, solitary, dual or concerted, known to either the modern or the ancient world, that is not represented.

The survey conducted in this chapter suggests that there is a roughly discernible class of worthless and pernicious writing which can usefully be designated by the term "pornography." The lines of distinction are not, however, clear cut between this class and harmless, even beneficial, eroticism, or between it and true literature. Further, very little is known about the real nature and extent of the harm done by pornography as we have attempted to define it. Insofar as it does harm it is probably not the sexual stimulation involved that is harmful but its association with irresponsible, depraved, vicious, and antisocial ideas. Such ideas, however, can be, and often are, advocated without any obscenity, and no one in the liberal tradition suggests that they can be combated by legal suppression. The case for laws against pornography is, therefore, much weaker than is generally supposed and they should not be enacted or enforced, even when every protection is provided for real literature, without caution and continual investigation, lest more harm than good result.

Real freedom of thought and artistic creation requires the complete abolition of all literary obscenity laws but this is an ideal unattainable anywhere in the foreseeable future. The motivation of sex censorship goes very deep into human psychology, having its roots in man's ambivalent attitude to sex. Biologically eroticism is a temporary phenomenon: what lures us at night repels us at morning. Consequently we are all tempted to be both readers of erotic books and censors of sexual literature. Moral integrity and clear thinking should enable modern communities to resolve the tensions created by these opposing attitudes without hurt to the spread of truth, the increase of beauty, and the furtherance of the good life.

APPENDIX

OFFICIAL CENSORSHIP in the United States is exercised on both city and state levels, in addition to the laws of the Federal government which act principally through the Post Office and the Customs Department. Within this legal framework the definition of obscenity has been allowed to change as the prevailing social climate toward obscenity has changed with time.

The following court opinions are important for their clarification of our modern legal definition of obscenity. They appear here in their entirety, with the exception of footnotes and citations which have been omitted. Grateful appreciation is given to Arthur A. Charpentier, Librarian of The Association of the Bar of the City of New York, for his assistance in the preparation of this appendix.

United States District Court
S.D. New York
December 6, 1933

WOOLSEY, District Judge.

The motion for a decree dismissing the libel herein is granted, and, consequently, of course, the Government's motion for a decree of forfeiture and destruction is denied.

Accordingly a decree dismissing the libel without costs may be entered herein.

I. The practice followed in this case is in accordance with the suggestion made by me in the case of *United States v. One Book Entitled "Contraception,"* and is as follows:

After issue was joined by the filing of the claimant's answer to the libel for forfeiture against "Ulysses," a stipulation was made between the United States Attorney's office and the attorneys for the claimant providing:

1. That the book "Ulysses" should be deemed to have been annexed to and to have become part of the libel just as if it had been incorporated in its entirety therein.

2. That the parties waived their right to a trial by jury.

3. That each party agreed to move for decree in its favor.

4. That on such cross motions the Court might decide all the questions of law and fact involved and render a general finding thereon.

5. That on the decision of such motions the decree of the Court might be entered as if it were a decree after trial.

It seems to me that a procedure of this kind is highly appropriate in libels for the confiscation of books such as this. It is an especially advantageous procedure in the instant case because on account of the length of "Ulysses" and the difficulty of reading it, a jury trial would have been an extremely unsatisfactory, if not an almost impossible, method of dealing with it.

II. I have read "Ulysses" once in its entirety and I have read those passages of which the Government particularly complains several times. In fact, for many weeks, my spare time has been devoted to the consideration of the decision which my duty would require me to make in this matter.

"Ulysses" is not an easy book to read or to understand. But there has been much written about it, and in order properly to approach the consideration of it it is advisable to read a number of other books which have now become its satellites. The study of "Ulysses" is, therefore, a heavy task.

III. The reputation of "Ulysses" in the literary world, however, warranted my taking such time as was necessary to enable me to satisfy myself as to the intent with which the book was written, for, of course, in any case where a book is claimed to be obscene it must first be determined whether the intent with which it was written was what is called, according to the usual phrase, pornographic— that is, written for the purpose of exploiting obscenity.

If the conclusion is that the book is pornographic that is the end of the inquiry and forfeiture must follow.

But in "Ulysses," in spite of its unusual frankness, I do not detect anywhere the leer of the sensualist. I hold, therefore, that it is not pornographic.

IV. In writing "Ulysses," Joyce sought to make a serious experiment in a new, if not wholly novel, literary genre. He takes persons of the lower middle class living in Dublin in 1904 and seeks not only to describe what they did on a certain day early in June of that year as they went about the City bent on their usual occupations, but also to tell what many of them thought about the while.

Joyce has attempted—it seems to me, with astonishing success —to show how the screen of consciousness with its ever-shifting kaleidoscopic impressions carries, as it were on a plastic palimpsest, not only what is in the focus of each man's observation of the actual things about him, but also in a penumbral zone residua of past impressions, some recent and some drawn up by association from the domain of the subconscious. He shows how each of these impressions affects the life and behavior of the character which he is describing.

What he seeks to get is not unlike the result of a double or, if that is possible, a multiple exposure on a cinema film which would give a clear foreground with a background visible but somewhat blurred and out of focus in varying degrees.

To convey by words an effect which obviously lends itself more appropriately to a graphic technique, accounts, it seems to me, for much of the obscurity which meets a reader of "Ulysses." And it also explains another aspect of the book, which I have further to consider, namely, Joyce's sincerity and his honest effort to show exactly how the minds of his characters operate.

If Joyce did not attempt to be honest in developing the technique which he has adopted in "Ulysses" the result would be psychologically misleading and thus unfaithful to his chosen technique. Such an attitude would be artistically inexcusable.

It is because Joyce has been loyal to his technique and has not funked its necessary implications, but has honestly attempted to tell fully what his characters think about, that he has been the subject of so many attacks and that his purpose has been so often misunderstood and misrepresented. For his attempt sincerely and honestly to realize his objective has required him incidentally to use certain words which are generally considered dirty words and has led at times to what many think is a too poignant preoccupation with sex in the thoughts of his characters.

The words which are criticized as dirty are old Saxon words known to almost all men and, I venture, to many women, and are such words as would be naturally and habitually used, I believe, by the types of folk whose life, physical and mental, Joyce is seeking to describe. In respect of the recurrent emergence of the theme of sex in the minds of his characters, it must always be remembered that his locale was Celtic and his season Spring.

Whether or not one enjoys such a technique as Joyce uses is a matter of taste on which disagreement or argument is futile, but to subject that technique to the standards of some other technique seems to me to be little short of absurd.

Accordingly, I hold that "Ulysses" is a sincere and honest book and I think that the criticisms of it are entirely disposed of by its rationale.

V. Furthermore, "Ulysses" is an amazing *tour de force* when one considers the success which has been in the main achieved with such a difficult objective as Joyce set for himself. As I have

stated, "Ulysses" is not an easy book to read. It is brilliant and
dull, intelligible and obscure by turns. In many places it seems to
me to be disgusting, but although it contains, as I have mentioned
above, many words usually considered dirty, I have not found anything that I consider to be dirt for dirt's sake. Each word of the
book contributes like a bit of mosaic to the detail of the picture
which Joyce is seeking to construct for his readers.

If one does not wish to associate with such folk as Joyce describes,
that is one's own choice. In order to avoid indirect contact with
them one may not wish to read "Ulysses"; that is quite understandable. But when such a real artist in words, as Joyce undoubtedly
is, seeks to draw a true picture of the lower middle class in a European city, ought it to be impossible for the American public legally
to see that picture?

To answer this question it is not sufficient merely to find, as I
have found above, that Joyce did not write "Ulysses" with what is
commonly called pornographic intent, I must endeavor to apply a
more objective standard to his book in order to determine its effect
in the result, irrespective of the intent with which it was written.

VI. The statute under which the libel is filed only denounces,
in so far as we are here concerned, the importation into the United
States from any foreign country of "any obscene book." Section
305 of the Tariff Act of 1930, Title 19 United States Code, Section
1305. It does not marshal against books the spectrum of condemnatory adjectives found, commonly, in laws dealing with matters of
this kind. I am, therefore, only required to determine whether
"Ulysses" is obscene within the legal definition of that word.

The meaning of the word "obscene" as legally defined by the
Courts is: tending to stir the sex impulses or to lead to sexually
impure and lustful thoughts. . . .

Whether a particular book would tend to excite such impulses
and thoughts must be tested by the Court's opinion as to its effect
on a person with average sex instincts—what the French would call
l'homme moyen sensuel—who plays, in this branch of legal inquiry, the same role of hypothetical reagent as does the "reasonable man" in the law of torts and "the man learned in the art" on
questions of invention in patent law.

The risk involved in the use of such a reagent arises from the inherent tendency of the trier of facts, however fair he may intend to be, to make his reagent too much subservient to his own idiosyncrasies. Here, I have attempted to avoid this, if possible, and to make my reagent herein more objective than he might otherwise be, by adopting the following course:

After I had made my decision in regard to the aspect of "Ulysses," now under consideration, I checked my impressions with two friends of mine who in my opinion answered to the above stated requirement for my reagent.

These literary assessors—as I might properly describe them—were called on separately, and neither knew that I was consulting the other. They are men whose opinion on literature and on life I value most highly. They had both read "Ulysses," and, of course, were wholly unconnected with this cause.

Without letting either of my assessors know what my decision was, I gave to each of them the legal definition of obscene and asked each whether in his opinion "Ulysses" was obscene within that definition.

I was interested to find that they both agreed with my opinion: that reading "Ulysses" in its entirety, as a book must be read on such a test as this, did not tend to excite sexual impulses or lustful thoughts but that its net effect on them was only that of a somewhat tragic and very powerful commentary on the inner lives of men and women.

It is only with the normal person that the law is concerned. Such a test as I have described, therefore, is the only proper test of obscenity in the case of a book like "Ulysses" which is a sincere and serious attempt to devise a new literary method for the observation and description of mankind.

I am quite aware that owing to some of its scenes "Ulysses" is a rather strong draught to ask some sensitive, though normal, persons to take. But my considered opinion, after long reflection, is that whilst in many places the effect of "Ulysses" on the reader undoubtedly is somewhat emetic, nowhere does it tend to be an aphrodisiac.

"Ulysses" may, therefore, be admitted into the United States.

ROTH

V.

UNITED STATES

Certiorari to the United States Court of Appeals for
the Second Circuit.

No. 582. Argued April 22, 1957.—Decided June 24, 1957.

(Together with No. 61, *Alberts* v. *California,* appeal from the Superior
Court of California, Los Angeles County, Appellate Department,
argued and decided on the same dates.)

MR. JUSTICE BRENNAN delivered the opinion of the Court.

The constitutionality of a criminal obscenity statute is the question in each of these cases. In *Roth,* the primary constitutional
question is whether the federal obscenity statute violates the provision of the First Amendment that "Congress shall make no law . . .
abridging the freedom of speech, or of the press . . . ." In *Alberts,*
the primary constitutional question is whether the obscenity provisions of the California Penal Code invade the freedoms of speech
and press as they may be incorporated in the liberty protected from
state action by the Due Process Clause of the Fourteenth Amendment.

Other constitutional questions are: whether these statutes violate
due process, because too vague to support conviction for crime;
whether power to punish speech and press offensive to decency and
morality is in the States alone, so that the federal obscenity statute
violates the Ninth and Tenth Amendments (raised in *Roth*); and
whether Congress, by enacting the federal obscenity statute, under
the power delegated by Art. I, § 8, cl. 7, to establish post offices and
post roads, pre-empted the regulation of the subject matter (raised
in *Alberts*).

Roth conducted a business in New York in the publication and
sale of books, photographs and magazines. He used circulars and
advertising matter to solicit sales. He was convicted by a jury in the
District Court for the Southern District of New York upon 4
counts of a 26-count indictment charging him with mailing obscene
circulars and advertising, and an obscene book, in violation of the

federal obscenity statute. His conviction was affirmed by the Court of Appeals for the Second Circuit. We granted certiorari.

Alberts conducted a mail-order business from Los Angeles. He was convicted by the Judge of the Municipal Court of the Beverly Hills Judicial District (having waived a jury trial) under a misdemeanor complaint which charged him with lewdly keeping for sale obscene and indecent books, and with writing, composing and publishing an obscene advertisement of them, in violation of the California Penal Code. The conviction was affirmed by the Appellate Department of the Superior Court of the State of California in and for the County of Los Angeles. We noted probable jurisdiction.

The dispositive question is whether obscenity is utterance within the area of protected speech and press. Although this is the first time the question has been squarely presented to this Court, either under the First Amendment or under the Fourteenth Amendment, expressions found in numerous opinions indicate that this Court has always assumed that obscenity is not protected by the freedoms of speech and press. . . .

The guaranties of freedom of expression in effect in 10 of the 14 States which by 1792 had ratified the Constitution, gave no absolute protection for every utterance. Thirteen of the 14 States provided for the prosecution of libel, and all of those States made either blasphemy or profanity, or both, statutory crimes. As early as 1712, Massachusetts made it criminal to publish "any filthy, obscene, or profane song, pamphlet, libel or mock sermon" in imitation or mimicking of religious services. . . . Thus, profanity and obscenity were related offenses.

In light of this history, it is apparent that the unconditional phrasing of the First Amendment was not intended to protect every utterance. This phrasing did not prevent this Court from concluding that libelous utterances are not within the area of constitutionally protected speech. . . . At the time of the adoption of the First Amendment, obscenity law was not as fully developed as libel law, but there is sufficiently contemporaneous evidence to show that obscenity, too, was outside the protection intended for speech and press.

The protection given speech and press was fashioned to assure

unfettered interchange of ideas for the bringing about of political
and social changes desired by the people. This objective was made
explicit as early as 1774 in a letter of the Continental Congress to
the inhabitants of Quebec:

"The last right we shall mention, regards the freedom of the
press. The importance of this consists, besides the advancement of
truth, science, morality, and arts in general, in its diffusion of liberal sentiments on the administration of Government, its ready
communication of thoughts between subjects, and its consequen-
tial promotion of union among them, whereby oppressive officers
are shamed or intimidated, into more honourable and just modes
of conducting affairs." . . .

All ideas having even the slightest redeeming social importance
—unorthodox ideas, controversial ideas, even ideas hateful to the
prevailing climate of opinion—have the full protection of the guaranties, unless excludable because they encroach upon the limited
area of more important interests. But implicit in the history of the
First Amendment is the rejection of obscenity as utterly without redeeming social importance. This rejection for that reason is mir-
rored in the universal judgment that obscenity should be
restrained, reflected in the international agreement of over 50 nations, in the obscenity laws of all of the 48 States, and in the 20
obscenity laws enacted by Congress from 1842 to 1956. This is the
same judgment expressed by this Court in *Chaplinsky* v. *New
Hampshire* . . . :

". . . There are certain well-defined and narrowly limited classes
of speech, the prevention and punishment of which have never
been thought to raise any Constitutional problem. *These include
the lewd and obscene . . . . It has been well observed that such utterances are no essential part of any exposition of ideas, and are of
such slight social value as a step to truth that any benefit that may
be derived from them is clearly outweighed by the social interest in
order and morality. . . .*" (Emphasis added.)

We hold that obscenity is not within the area of constitutionally
protected speech or press.

It is strenuously urged that these obscenity statutes offend the constitutional guaranties because they punish incitation to impure sexual *thoughts*, not shown to be related to any overt antisocial conduct which is or may be incited in the persons stimulated to such *thoughts*. In *Roth*, the trial judge instructed the jury: "The words 'obscene, lewd and lascivious' as used in the law, signify that form of immorality which has relation to sexual impurity and has a tendency to excite lustful *thoughts*." (Emphasis added.) In *Alberts*, the trial judge applied the test laid down in *People* v. *Wepplo* . . . namely, whether the material has "a substantial tendency to deprave or corrupt its readers by inciting lascivious *thoughts* or arousing lustful desires." (Emphasis added.) It is insisted that the constitutional guaranties are violated because convictions may be had without proof either that obscene material will perceptibly create a clear and present danger of antisocial conduct, or will probably induce its recipients to such conduct. But, in light of our holding that obscenity is not protected speech, the complete answer to this argument is in the holding of this Court in *Beauharnais* v. *Illinois* . . . :

"Libelous utterances not being within the area of constitutionally protected speech, it is unnecessary, either for us or for the State courts, to consider the issues behind the phrase 'clear and present danger.' Certainly no one would contend that obscene speech, for example, may be punished only upon a showing of such circumstances. Libel, as we have seen, is in the same class."

However, sex and obscenity are not synonymous. Obscene material is material which deals with sex in a manner appealing to prurient interest. The portrayal of sex, *e. g.*, in art, literature and scientific works, is not itself sufficient reason to deny material the constitutional protection of freedom of speech and press. Sex, a great and mysterious motive force in human life, has indisputably been a subject of absorbing interest to mankind through the ages; it is one of the vital problems of human interest and public concern. As to all such problems, this Court said in *Thornhill* v. *Alabama* . . . :

"The freedom of speech and of the press guaranteed by the Constitution embraces at the least the liberty to discuss publicly and truthfully *all matters of public concern* without previous restraint or fear of subsequent punishment. The exigencies of the colonial period and the efforts to secure freedom from oppressive administration developed a broadened conception of these liberties as adequate to supply the public need for *information and education with respect to the significant issues of the times.* . . . Freedom of discussion, if it would fulfill its historic function in this nation, must embrace *all issues about which information is needed or appropriate to enable the members of society to cope with the exigencies of their period.*" (Emphasis added.)

The fundamental freedoms of speech and press have contributed greatly to the development and well-being of our free society and are indispensable to its continued growth. Ceaseless vigilance is the watchword to prevent their erosion by Congress or by the States. The door barring federal and state intrusion into this area cannot be left ajar; it must be kept tightly closed and opened only the slightest crack necessary to prevent encroachment upon more important interests. It is therefore vital that the standards for judging obscenity safeguard the protection of freedom of speech and press for material which does not treat sex in a manner appealing to prurient interest.

The early leading standard of obscenity allowed material to be judged merely by the effect of an isolated excerpt upon particularly susceptible persons. . . . Some American courts adopted this standard but later decisions have rejected it and substituted this test: whether to the average person, applying contemporary community standards, the dominant theme of the material taken as a whole appeals to prurient interest. The *Hicklin* test, judging obscenity by the effect of isolated passages upon the most susceptible persons, might well encompass material legitimately treating with sex, and so it must be rejected as unconstitutionally restrictive of the freedoms of speech and press. On the other hand, the substituted standard provides safeguards adequate to withstand the charge of constitutional infirmity.

Both trial courts below sufficiently followed the proper standard. Both courts used the proper definition of obscenity. In addition, in the *Alberts* case, in ruling on a motion to dismiss, the trial judge indicated that, as the trier of facts, he was judging each item as a whole as it would affect the normal person, and in *Roth*, the trial judge instructed the jury as follows:

". . . The test is not whether it would arouse sexual desires or sexual impure thoughts in those comprising a particular segment of the community, the young, the immature or the highly prudish or would leave another segment, the scientific or highly educated or the so-called worldly-wise and sophisticated indifferent and unmoved. . . .

"The test in each case is the effect of the book, picture or publication considered as a whole, not upon any particular class, but upon all those whom it is likely to reach. In other words, you determine its impact upon the average person in the community. The books, pictures and circulars must be judged as a whole, in their entire context, and you are not to consider detached or separate portions in reaching a conclusion. You judge the circulars, pictures and publications which have been put in evidence by present-day standards of the community. You may ask yourselves does it offend the common conscience of the community by present-day standards.

. . . . .

"In this case, ladies and gentlemen of the jury, you and you alone are the exclusive judges of what the common conscience of the community is, and in determining that conscience you are to consider the community as a whole, young and old, educated and uneducated, the religious and the irreligious—men, women and children."

It is argued that the statutes do not provide reasonably ascertainable standards of guilt and therefore violate the constitutional requirements of due process. . . . The federal obscenity statute makes punishable the mailing of material that is "obscene, lewd, lascivious, or filthy . . . or other publication of an indecent character." The California statute makes punishable, *inter alia*, the keeping for sale or advertising material that is "obscene or indecent." The thrust of the argument is that these words are not sufficiently precise because they do not mean the same thing to all people, all the time, everywhere.

Many decisions have recognized that these terms of obscenity statutes are not precise. This Court, however, has consistently held that lack of precision is not itself offensive to the requirements of due process. ". . . [T]he Constitution does not require impossible standards"; all that is required is that the language "conveys sufficiently definite warning as to the proscribed conduct when measured by common understanding and practices. . . ." These words, applied according to the proper standard for judging obscenity, already discussed, give adequate warning of the conduct proscribed and mark ". . . boundaries sufficiently distinct for judges and juries fairly to administer the law . . . . That there may be marginal cases in which it is difficult to determine the side of the line on which a particular fact situation falls is no sufficient reason to hold the language too ambiguous to define a criminal offense. . . ."

In summary, then, we hold that these statutes, applied according to the proper standard for judging obscenity, do not offend constitutional safeguards against convictions based upon protected material, or fail to give men in acting adequate notice of what is prohibited.

Roth's argument that the federal obscenity statute unconstitutionally encroaches upon the powers reserved by the Ninth and Tenth Amendments to the States and to the people to punish speech and press where offensive to decency and morality is hinged upon his contention that obscenity is expression not excepted from the sweep of the provision of the First Amendment that "*Congress* shall make *no law* . . . abridging the freedom of speech, or of the press . . . ." (Emphasis added.) That argument falls in light of our holding that obscenity is not expression protected by the First Amendment. We therefore hold that the federal obscenity statute punishing the use of the mails for obscene material is a proper exercise of the postal power delegated to Congress by Art. I, § 8, cl. 7. In *United Public Workers* v. *Mitchell* . . . this Court said:

"... The powers granted by the Constitution to the Federal Government are subtracted from the totality of sovereignty originally in the states and the people. Therefore, when objection is made that the exercise of a federal power infringes upon rights reserved by the Ninth and Tenth Amendments, the inquiry must be directed toward the granted power under which the action of the Union was taken. If granted power is found, necessarily the objection of invasion of those rights, reserved by the Ninth and Tenth Amendments, must fail. . . ."

Alberts argues that because his was a mail-order business, the California statute is repugnant to Art. I, § 8, cl. 7, under which the Congress allegedly pre-empted the regulatory field by enacting the federal obscenity statute punishing the mailing or advertising by mail of obscene material. The federal statute deals only with actual mailing; it does not eliminate the power of the state to punish "keeping for sale" or "advertising" obscene material. The state statute in no way imposes a burden or interferes with the federal postal functions. ". . . The decided cases which indicate the limits of state regulatory power in relation to the federal mail service involve situations where state regulation involved a direct, physical interference with federal activities under the postal power or some direct, immediate burden on the performance of the postal functions. . . ."

The judgments are

Affirmed.

GROVE PRESS, INC.
and Readers' Subscription, Inc., Plaintiffs,

v.

ROBERT K. CHRISTENBERRY,
individually and as Postmaster of the City of New York,
Defendant.

United States District Court
S. D. New York.
July 21, 1959.

FREDERICK VAN PELT BRYAN, District Judge.

These two actions against the Postmaster of New York, now consolidated, arise out of the denial of the United States mails to the recently published Grove Press unexpurgated edition of "Lady Chatterley's Lover" by D. H. Lawrence.

Plaintiffs seek to restrain the Postmaster from enforcing a decision of the Post Office Department that the unexpurgated "Lady Chatterley's Lover," and circulars announcing its availability, are non-mailable under the statute barring obscene matter from the mails. . . . They also seek a declaratory judgment to the effect (1) that the novel is not "obscene, lewd, lascivious, indecent or filthy" in content or character, and is not non-mailable under the statute or, in the alternative, (2) that if the novel be held to fall within the purview of the statute, the statute is to that extent invalid and violates plaintiffs' rights in contravention of the First and Fifth Amendments.

Grove Press, Inc., one of the plaintiffs, is the publisher of the book. Readers' Subscription, Inc., the other plaintiff, is a book club which has rights to distribute it.

[1] Defendant has moved and plaintiffs have cross-moved for summary judgment, pursuant to Rule 56, F.R.Civ.P., 28 U.S.C. There are no disputed issues of fact. The cases are before me for final determination on the pleadings, the decision of the Postmaster General, the record before him and supplemental affidavits.

On April 30, 1959 the New York Postmaster withheld from dispatch some 20,000 copies of circulars deposited for mailing by Readers' Subscription, which announced the availability of the new Grove edition of Lady Chatterley. At about the same time he also detained a number of copies of the book which had been deposited for mailing by Grove Press.

[2]   On May 8, 1959 letters of complaint issued by the General Counsel of the Post Office Department were served on Grove and Readers' Subscription alleging that there was probable cause to believe that these mailings violated 18 U.S.C. § 1461, and advising them of a departmental hearing. The respondents filed answers denying these allegations and a hearing was held before the Judicial Officer of the Post Office Department on May 14, 1959.

The General Counsel, as complainant, introduced the Grove edition and the circulars which had been detained and rested.

The respondents offered (1) testimony as to their reputation and standing in the book publishing and distribution fields and their purpose in publishing and distributing the novel; (2) reviews of the book in leading newspapers and literary periodicals throughout the country; (3) copies of editorials and comments in leading newspapers concerning publication of the book and its anticipated impact; (4) news articles dealing with the banning of the book by the Post Office; and (5) expert testimony by two leading literary critics, Malcolm Cowley and Alfred Kazin, as to the literary stature of the work and its author; contemporary acceptance of literature dealing with sex and sex relations and their own opinions as to the effect of the book on its readers. The editorials and comments and the news articles were excluded.

The Judicial Officer before whom the hearing was held did not decide the issues. On May 28 he issued an order referring the proceedings to the Postmaster General "for final departmental decision."

On June 11, 1959 the Postmaster General rendered a departmental decision finding that the Grove edition "is obscene and nonmailable pursuant to 18 U.S.Code § 1461," and that the Readers' Subscription circulars "give information where obscene material, namely, the book in issue in this case, may be obtained and are nonmailable. . . ."

This litigation, which had been commenced prior to the decision, was then brought on for hearing.

I

The basic question here is whether the unexpurgated "Lady Chatterley's Lover" is obscene within the meaning of 18 U.S.C. § 1461, and is thus excluded from the protections afforded freedom of speech and the press by the First Amendment.

However, the defendant takes the position that this question is not before me for decision. He urges that the determination by the Postmaster General that this novel is obscene and non-mailable is conclusive upon the court unless it is found to be unsupported by substantial evidence and is clearly wrong. He argues, therefore, that I may not determine the issue of obscenity *de novo*.

Thus, an initial question is raised as to the scope of the court's power of review. In the light of the issues presented, the basis of the Postmaster General's decision, and the record before him, this question is not of substance.

(1) Prior to Roth v. United States, . . . the Supreme Court had "always assumed that obscenity is not protected by the freedoms of speech and press." However, until then the constitutional question had not been directly passed upon by the court. In Roth the question was squarely posed.

The court held, in accord with its long-standing assumption, that "obscenity is not within the area of constitutionally protected speech or press."

The court was faced with a dilemma. On the one hand it was required to eschew any impingement upon the cherished freedoms of speech and the press guaranteed by the Constitution and so essential to a free society. On the other hand it was faced with the recognized social evil presented by the purveyance of pornography.

The opinion of Mr. Justice Brennan for the majority makes it plain that the area which can be excluded from constitutional protection without impinging upon the free speech and free press guarantees is narrowly limited. He says . . . :

"All ideas having even the slightest redeeming social importance —unorthodox ideas, controversial ideas, even ideas hateful to the prevailing climate of opinion—have the full protection of the guarantees, unless excludable because they encroach upon the limited area of more important interests."

He gives stern warning that no publication advancing such ideas can be suppressed under the guise of regulation of public morals or censorship of public reading matter. As he says . . . :

"The fundamental freedoms of speech and press have contributed greatly to the development and well-being of our free society and are indispensable to its continued growth. Ceaseless vigilance is the watchword to prevent their erosion by Congress or by the States. The door barring federal and state intrusion into this area cannot be left ajar; it must be kept tightly closed and opened only the slightest crack necessary to prevent encroachment upon more important interests."

It was against the background of these constitutional requirements that the Court laid down general standards for judging obscenity, recognizing that it was "vital that [such] standards . . . safeguard the protection of freedom of speech and press for material which does not treat sex" in an obscene manner. The standards were "whether to the average person, applying contemporary community standards, the dominant theme of the material taken as a whole appeals to prurient interest."

The Court did not attempt to apply these standards to a specific set of facts. It merely circumscribed and limited the excluded area in general terms.

Plainly application of these standards to specific material may involve no little difficulty as the court was well aware. Cases involving "hard core" pornography, or what Judge Woolsey referred to as "dirt for dirt's sake," purveyed furtively by dealers in smut, are relatively simple. But works of literary merit present quite a different problem, and one which the majority in Roth did not reach as such.

Chief Justice Warren, concurring in the result, said of this problem . . . :

". . . The history of the application of laws designed to suppress the obscene demonstrates convincingly that the power of government can be invoked under them against great art or literature, scientific treatises, or works exciting social controversy. Mistakes of the past prove that there is a strong countervailing interest to be considered in the freedoms guaranteed by the First and Fourteenth Amendments."

And Mr. Justice Harlan, dissenting, also deeply concerned, had this to say . . . :

". . . The suppression of a particular writing or other tangible form of expression is . . . an *individual* matter, and in the nature of things every such suppression raises an individual constitutional problem, in which a reviewing court must determine for *itself* whether the attacked expression is suppressible within constitutional standards. Since those standards do not readily lend themselves to generalized definitions, the constitutional problem in the last analysis becomes one of particularized judgments which appellate courts must make for themselves.

"I do not think that reviewing courts can escape this responsibility by saying that the trier of the facts, be it a jury or a judge, has labeled the questioned matter as 'obscene,' for, if 'obscenity' is to be suppressed, the question whether a particular work is of that character involves not really an issue of fact but a question of constitutional *judgment* of the most sensitive and delicate kind."

Mr. Justice Frankfurter, concurring in Kingsley International Pictures Corp. v. Regents, . . . expressed a similar view. He pointed out that in determining whether particular works are entitled to the constitutional protections of freedom of expression "We cannot escape such instance-by-instance, case-by-case . . . [constitutional adjudication] in all the variety of situations that come before this Court." And Mr. Justice Harlan, in the same case, also concurring in the result, speaks of "the necessity for individualized adjudication. In the very nature of things the problems in this area are ones of individual cases. . . ."

These views are not inconsistent with the decisions of the majority determining both Roth and Kingsley upon broader constitutional grounds.

It would seem that the Court itself made such "individualized" or "case by case" adjudications as to the obscenity of specific material in at least two cases following Roth. In One, Inc. v. Olesen . . .

and Sunshine Book Co. v. Summerfield . . . the courts below had
found in no uncertain terms that the material was obscene within
the meaning of Section 1461. In each case the Supreme Court in a
one sentence per curiam opinion granted certiorari and reversed on
the authority of Roth.

One, Inc. v. Olesen, and Sunshine Book Co. v. Summerfield, involved determination by the Post Office barring material from the
mails on the ground that it was obscene. In both the District Court
had found that the publication was obscene and that the determination of the Post Office should be upheld. In both the Court of
Appeals had affirmed the findings of the District Court.

Yet in each the Supreme Court, without discussion, summarily
reversed on the authority of Roth. As Judge Desmond of the New
York Court of Appeals said of these cases—"Presumably, the court
having looked at those books simply held them not to be obscene."

[3] It is no less the duty of this court in the case at bar to scru-
tinize the book with great care and to determine for itself whether
it is within the constitutional protections afforded by the First
Amendment, or whether it may be excluded from those protections
because it is obscene under the Roth tests.

(2) Such review is quite consistent with the Administrative Procedure Act, assuming that the act is applicable here.

This is not a case where the agency determination under review
is dependent on "a fair estimate of the worth of the testimony of
witnesses or its informed judgment on matters within its special
competence or both." . . .

There were no disputed facts before the Postmaster General. The
facts as to the mailings and the detainer were stipulated and the
only issue before him was whether "Lady Chatterley's Lover" was
obscene.

The complainant relied on the text of the novel and nothing more
to establish obscenity. Respondents' evidence was wholly uncontra-
dicted, and, except for the opinions of the critics Cowley and Kazin
as to the effect of the book upon its readers, it scarcely could have
been. The complainant conceded that the book had literary merit.
The views of the critics as to the place of the novel and its author
in twentieth century English literature have not been questioned.

As the Postmaster General said, he attempted to apply to the book "the tests which, it is my understanding, the courts have established for determining questions of obscenity." Thus, all he did was to apply the statute, as he interpreted it in the light of the decisions, to the book. His interpretation and application of the statute involved questions of law, not questions of fact.

The Postmaster General has no special competence or technical knowledge on this subject which qualifies him to render an informed judgment entitled to special weight in the courts. There is no parallel here to determinations of such agencies as the Interstate Commerce Commission, the Securities and Exchange Commission, the National Labor Relations Board, the Federal Communications Commission, the Federal Power Commission, or many others on highly technical and complicated subject matter upon which they have specialized knowledge and are particularly qualified to speak.

No doubt the Postmaster General has similar qualifications on many questions involving the administration of the Post Office Department, the handling of the mails, postal rates and other matters. . . . But he has no special competence to determine what constitutes obscenity within the meaning of Section 1461, or that "contemporary community standards are not such that this book should be allowed to be transmitted in the mails" or that the literary merit of the book is outweighed by its pornographic features, as he found. Such questions involve interpretation of a statute, which also imposes criminal penalties, and its application to the allegedly offending material. The determination of such questions is peculiarly for the courts, particularly in the light of the constitutional questions implicit in each case.

It has been suggested that the court cannot interfere with the order of the Postmaster General unless it finds that he abused his discretion. But it does not appear that the Postmaster General has been vested with "discretion" finally to determine whether a book is obscene within the meaning of the statute.

It is unnecessary to pass on the questions posed by the plaintiffs as to whether the Postmaster General has any power to impose prior restraints upon the mailing of matter allegedly obscene and whether the enforcement of the statute is limited to criminal proceedings, though it seems to me that these questions are not free from doubt.

[4] Assuming power in the Postmaster General to withhold obscene matter from dispatch in the mails temporarily, a grant of discretion to make a final determination as to whether a book is obscene and should be denied to the public should certainly not be inferred in the absence of a clear and direct mandate. As the Supreme Court pointed out under comparable circumstances in Hannegan v. Esquire, Inc., ... to vest such power in the Postmaster General would, in effect, give him the power of censorship and that "is so abhorrent to our traditions that a purpose to grant it should not be easily inferred."

[5] No such grant of power to the Postmaster General has been called to my attention and I have found none. Whatever administrative functions the Postmaster General has go no further than closing the mails to material which is obscene within the meaning of the statute. This is not an area in which the Postmaster General has any "discretion" which is entitled to be given special weight by the courts.

The Administrative Procedure Act makes the reviewing court responsible for determining all relevant questions of law, for interpreting and applying all constitutional and statutory provisions and for setting aside agency action not in accordance with law. ... The question presented here falls within this framework.

Thus, the question presented for decision is whether "Lady Chatterley's Lover" is obscene within the meaning of the statute and thus excludable from constitutional protections. I will now consider that question.

II

This unexpurgated edition of "Lady Chatterley's Lover" has never before been published either in the United States or England, though comparatively small editions were published by Lawrence himself in Italy and authorized for publication in France, and a number of pirated copies found their way to this country.

Grove Press is a reputable publisher with a good list which includes a number of distinguished writers and serious works. Before publishing this edition Grove consulted recognized literary critics and authorities on English literature as to the advisability of publication. All were of the view that the work was of major literary importance and should be made available to the American public.

No one is naive enough to think that Grove Press did not expect to profit from the book. Nevertheless the format and composition of the volume, the advertising and promotional material and the whole approach to publication, treat the book as a serious work of literature. The book is distributed through leading bookstores throughout the country. There has been no attempt by the publisher to appeal to prurience or the prurient minded.

The Grove edition has a preface by Archibald MacLeish, former Librarian of Congress, Pulitzer Prize winner, and one of this country's most distinguished poets and literary figures, giving his appraisal of the novel. There follows an introduction by Mark Schorer, Professor of English Literature at the University of California, a leading scholar of D. H. Lawrence and his work. The introduction is a critique of the novel against the background of Lawrence's life, work and philosophy. At the end of the novel there is a bibliographical note as to the circumstances under which it was written and first published. Thus, the novel is placed in a setting which emphasizes its literary qualities and its place as a significant work of a major English novelist.

Readers' Subscription has handled the book in the same vein. The relatively small number of Readers' Subscription subscribers is composed largely of people in academic, literary and scholarly fields. Its list of books includes works of high literary merit, including books by and about D. H. Lawrence.

There is nothing of "the leer of the sensualist" in the promotion or methods of distribution of this book. There is no suggestion of any attempt to pander to the lewd and lascivious minded for profit. The facts are all to the contrary.

Publication met with unanimous critical approval. The book was favorably received by the literary critics of such diverse publications as the New York Times, the Chicago Tribune, the San Francisco Call Bulletin, the New York Post, the New York Herald Tribune, Harpers and Time, to mention only some. The critics were not agreed upon their appraisal. Critical comment ranged from acclaim on the one hand to more restrained views that this was not the best of Lawrence's writing, and was dated and in parts "wooden." But as MacLeish says in the preface,

". . . in spite of these reservations no responsible critic would deny the book a place as one of the most important works of fiction of the century, and no reader of any kind could undertake to express an opinion about the literature of the time or about the spiritual history that literature expresses without making his peace in one way or another with D. H. Lawrence and with this work."

Publication of the Grove edition was a major literary event. It was greeted by editorials in leading newspapers throughout the country unanimously approving the publication and viewing with alarm possible attempts to ban the book.

It was against this background that the New York Postmaster impounded the book and the Postmaster General barred it. The decision of the Postmaster General, in a brief of four pages, relied on three cases, Roth v. United States, supra; United States v. One Book Called "Ulysses," . . . and Besig v. United States. . . . While he quotes from Roth the Postmaster General relies principally on Besig, which was not reviewed by the Supreme Court. It may be noted that the Ninth Circuit relied heavily on Besig in One Book, Inc. v. Olesen, supra, which was summarily reversed by the Supreme Court on the authority of Roth.

He refers to the book as "currently withheld from the mails in the United States and barred from the mails by several other major nations." His only discussion of its content is as follows:

"The contemporary community standards are not such that this book should be allowed to be transmitted in the mails.

"The book is replete with descriptions in minute detail of sexual acts engaged in or discussed by the book's principal characters. These descriptions utilize filthy, offensive and degrading words and terms. Any literary merit the book may have is far outweighed by the pornographic and smutty passages and words, so that the book, taken as a whole, is an obscene and filthy work.

"I therefore see no need to modify or reverse the prior rulings of this Department and the Department of the Treasury with respect to this edition of this book."

This seems to be the first time since the notable opinions of Judge Woolsey and Judge Augustus Hand in United States v. One Book Called "Ulysses," supra, in 1934 that a book of comparable literary stature has come before the federal courts charged with violating the federal obscenity statutes. That case held that James Joyce's "Ulysses" which had been seized by the Customs under Section 305 of the Tariff Act of 1930, 19 U.S.C.A. § 1305, was not obscene within the meaning of that statute. It thoroughly discussed the standards to be applied in determining this question.

[6] The essence of the Ulysses holdings is that a work of literary merit is not obscene under federal law merely because it contains passages and language dealing with sex in a most candid and realistic fashion and uses many four-letter Anglo-Saxon words. Where a book is written with honesty and seriousness of purpose, and the portions which might be considered obscene are relevant to the theme, it is not condemned by the statute even though "it justly may offend many." "Ulysses" contains numerous passages dealing very frankly with sex and the sex act and is free in its use of four-letter Anglo-Saxon words. Yet both Judge Woolsey in the District Court, and Judge Hand in the Court of Appeals, found that it was a sincere and honest book which was not in any sense "dirt for dirt's sake." They both concluded that "Ulysses" was a work of high literary merit, written by a gifted and serious writer, which did not have the dominant effect of promoting lust or prurience and therefore did not fall within the interdiction of the statute.

Roth v. United States, supra, decided by the Supreme Court in 1957, twenty-three years later, unlike the Ulysses case, did not deal with the application of the obscenity statutes to specific material. It laid down general tests circumscribing the area in which matter is excludable from constitutional protections because it is obscene, so as to avoid impingement on First Amendment guarantees.

The court distilled from the prior cases (including the Ulysses case, which it cited with approval) the standards to be applied— "whether to the average person, applying contemporary community standards, the dominant theme of the material taken as a whole appeals to prurient interest."

The court saw no significant difference between this expression of the standards and those in the American Law Institute Model Penal Code to the effect that

". . . A thing is obscene if, considered as a whole, its predominant appeal is to prurient interest, i.e., a shameful or morbid interest in nudity, sex, or excretion, and if it goes substantially beyond customary limits of candor in description or representation of such matters. . . ."

These standards are not materially different from those applied in Ulysses to the literary work considered there. Since the Roth case dealt with these standards for judging obscenity in general terms and the Ulysses case dealt with application of such standards to a work of recognized literary stature, the two should be read together.

A number of factors are involved in the application of these tests.

As Mr. Justice Brennan pointed out in Roth, sex and obscenity are by no means synonymous and "[t]he portrayal of sex, e. g., in art, literature and scientific works, is not in itself sufficient reason to deny material the constitutional protection of freedom of speech and press." As he said, sex has been "a subject of absorbing interest to mankind through the ages; it is one of the vital problems of human interest and public concern." The subject may be discussed publicly and truthfully without previous restraint or fear of subsequent punishment as long as it does not fall within the narrowly circumscribed interdicted area.

[7] Both cases held that, to be obscene, the dominant effect of the book must be an appeal to prurient interest—that is to say, shameful or morbid interest in sex. Such a theme must so predominate as to submerge any ideas of "redeeming social importance" which the publication contains.

[8] It is not the effect upon the irresponsible, the immature or the sensually minded which is controlling. The material must be judged in terms of its effect on those it is likely to reach who are conceived of as the average man of normal sensual impulses, or, as Judge Woolsey says, "what the French would call l'homme moyen sensuel." . . .

[9, 10] The material must also exceed the limits of tolerance imposed by current standards of the community with respect to freedom of expression in matters concerning sex and sex relations. Moreover, a book is not to be judged by excerpts or individual passages but must be judged as a whole.

All of these factors must be present before a book can be held obscene and thus outside constitutional protections.

Judged by these standards, "Lady Chatterley's Lover" is not obscene. The decision of the Postmaster General that it is obscene and therefore non-mailable is contrary to law and clearly erroneous. This is emphasized when the book is considered against its background and in the light of its stature as a significant work of a distinguished English novelist.

D. H. Lawrence is one of the most important novelists writing in the English language in this century. Whether he is, as some authorities say, the greatest English novelist since Joseph Conrad, or one of a number of major figures, makes little difference. He was a writer of great gifts and of undoubted artistic integrity.

The text of this edition of "Lady Chatterley's Lover" was written by Lawrence toward the close of his life and was his third version of the novel, originally called "Tenderness."

The book is almost as much a polemic as a novel.

In it Lawrence was expressing his deep and bitter dissatisfaction with what he believed were the stultifying effects of advancing industrialization and his own somewhat obscure philosophic remedy of a return to "naturalness." He attacks what he considered to be the evil effects of industrialization upon the wholesome and natural life of all classes in England. In his view this was having disastrous consequences on English society and on the English countryside. It had resulted in devitalization of the upper classes of society and debasement of the lower classes. One result, as he saw it, was the corrosion of both the emotional and physical sides of man as expressed in his sexual relationships which had become increasingly artificial and unwholesome.

The novel develops the contrasts and conflicts in characters under these influences.

The plot is relatively simple.

Constance Chatterley is married to a baronet, returned from the first world war paralyzed from the waist down. She is physically frustrated and dissatisfied with the artificiality and sterility of her life and of the society in which she moves. Her husband, immersed in himself, seeks compensation for his own frustrations in the writing of superficial and brittle fiction and in the exploitation of his coal mining properties, a symbol of the creeping industrial blight. Failing to find satisfaction in an affair with a man in her husband's circle, Constance Chatterley finds herself increasingly restless and unhappy. Her husband half-heartedly urges her to have a child by another man whom he will treat as his heir. Repelled by the suggestion that she casually beget a child, she is drawn to Mellors, the gamekeeper, sprung from the working class who, having achieved a measure of spiritual and intellectual independence, is a prototype of Lawrence's natural man. They establish a deeply passionate and tender relationship which is described at length and in detail. At the conclusion she is pregnant and plans to obtain a divorce and marry the gamekeeper.

This plot serves as a vehicle through which Lawrence develops his basic theme of contrast between his own philosophy and the sterile and debased society which he attacks. Most of the characters are prototypes. The plot and theme are meticulously worked out with honesty and sincerity.

The book is replete with fine writing and with descriptive passages of rare beauty. There is no doubt of its literary merit.

It contains a number of passages describing sexual intercourse in great detail with complete candor and realism. Four-letter Anglo-Saxon words are used with some frequency.

These passages and this language understandably will shock the sensitive minded. Be that as it may, these passages are relevant to the plot and to the development of the characters and of their lives as Lawrence unfolds them. The language which shocks, except in a rare instance or two, is not inconsistent with character, situation or theme.

Even if it be assumed that these passages and this language taken in isolation tend to arouse shameful, morbid and lustful sexual desires in the average reader, they are an integral, and to the author a necessary part of the development of theme, plot and character. The dominant theme, purpose and effect of the book as a whole is not an appeal to prurience or the prurient minded. The book is not "dirt for dirt's sake." Nor do these passages and this language submerge the dominant theme so as to make the book obscene even if they could be considered and found to be obscene in isolation.

What the Postmaster General seems to have done is precisely what the Supreme Court in Roth and the courts in the Ulysses case said ought not to be done. He has lifted from the novel individual passages and language, found them to be obscene in isolation and therefore condemned the book as a whole. He has disregarded the dominant theme and effect of the book and has read these passages and this language as if they were separable and could be taken out of context. Thus he has "weighed" the isolated passages which he considered obscene against the remainder of the book and concluded that the work as a whole must be condemned.

[11] Writing about sex is not in itself pornographic, as the Postmaster General recognized. Nor does the fact that sex is a major theme of a book condemn the book as obscene. Neither does the use of "four letter" words, despite the offense they may give. "Ulysses" was found not to be obscene despite long passages containing similar descriptions and language. As Judge Woolsey said there . . .:

"The words which are criticized as dirty are old Saxon words known to almost all men and, I venture, to many women, and are such words as would be naturally and habitually used, I believe, by the types of folk whose life, physical and mental, Joyce is seeking to describe."

Such words "are, almost without exception of honest Anglo-Saxon ancestry and were not invented for purely scatological effect."

[12] The tests of obscenity are not whether the book or passages from it are in bad taste or shock or offend the sensibilities of an individual, or even of a substantial segment of the community. Nor are we concerned with whether the community would approve of Constance Chatterley's morals. The statute does not purport to regulate the morals portrayed or the ideas expressed in a novel, whether or not they are contrary to the accepted moral code, nor could it constitutionally do so. . . .

Plainly "Lady Chatterley's Lover" is offensive to the Postmaster General, and I respect his personal views. As a matter of personal opinion I disagree with him for I do not personally find the book offensive.

But the personal views of neither of us are controlling here. The standards for determining what constitutes obscenity under this statute have been laid down. These standards must be objectively applied regardless of personal predilections.

There has been much discussion of the intent and purpose of Lawrence in writing Lady Chatterley. It is suggested that the intent and purpose of the author has no relevance to the question as to whether his work is obscene and must be disregarded.

[13] No doubt an author may write a clearly obscene book in the mistaken belief that he is serving a high moral purpose. The fact that this is the author's purpose does not redeem the book from obscenity.

But the sincerity and honesty of purpose of an author as expressed in the manner in which a book is written and in which his theme and ideas are developed has a great deal to do with whether it is of literary and intellectual merit. Here, as in the Ulysses case, there is no question about Lawrence's honesty and sincerity of purpose, artistic integrity and lack of intention to appeal to prurient interest.

Thus, this is an honest and sincere novel of literary merit and its dominant theme and effect, taken as a whole, is not an appeal to the prurient interest of the average reader.

This would seem to end the matter. However, the Postmaster General's finding that the book is non-mailable because it offends contemporary community standards bears some discussion.

I am unable to ascertain upon what the Postmaster General based this conclusion. The record before him indicates general acceptance of the book throughout the country and nothing was shown to the contrary. The critics were unanimous. Editorial comment by leading journals of opinion welcomed the publication and decried any attempts to ban it.

[14] It is true that the editorial comment was excluded by the Judicial Officer at the hearing. But it seems to me that this was

error. These expressions were relevant and material on the question of whether the book exceeded the limits of freedom of expression in matters involving sex and sex relations tolerated by the community at large in these times.

The contemporary standards of the community and the limits of its tolerance cannot be measured or ascertained accurately. There is no poll available to determine such questions. Surely expressions by leading newspapers, with circulations of millions, are some evidence at least as to what the limits of tolerance by present day community standards are, if we must embark upon a journey of exploration into such uncharted territory.

Quite apart from this, the broadening of freedom of expression and of the frankness with which sex and sex relations are dealt with at the present time require no discussion. In one best selling novel after another frank descriptions of the sex act and "four-letter" words appear with frequency. These trends appear in all media of public expression, in the kind of language used and the subjects discussed in polite society, in pictures, advertisements and dress, and in other ways familiar to all. Much of what is now accepted would have shocked the community to the core a generation ago. Today such things are generally tolerated whether we approve or not.

[15, 16] I hold that, at this stage in the development of our society, this major English novel, does not exceed the outer limits of the tolerance which the community as a whole gives to writing about sex and sex relations.

One final word about the constitutional problem implicit here.

It is essential to the maintenance of a free society that the severest restrictions be placed upon restraints which may tend to prevent the dissemination of ideas. It matters not whether such ideas be expressed in political pamphlets or works of political, economic or social theory or criticism, or through artistic media. All such expressions must be freely available.

A work of literature published and distributed through normal channels by a reputable publisher stands on quite a different footing from hard core pornography furtively sold for the purpose of profiting by the titillation of the dirty minded. The courts have been deeply and properly concerned about the use of obscenity statutes to suppress great works of art or literature. As Judge Augustus Hand said in Ulysses . . .:

". . . The foolish judgments of Lord Eldon about one hundred years ago, proscribing the works of Byron and Southey, and the finding by the jury under a charge by Lord Denman that the publication of Shelley's 'Queen Mab' was an indictable offense are a warning to all who have to determine the limits of the field within which authors may exercise themselves."

To exclude this book from the mails on the grounds of obscenity would fashion a rule which could be applied to a substantial portion of the classics of our literature. Such a rule would be inimical to a free society. To interpret the obscenity statute so as to bar "Lady Chatterley's Lover" from the mails would render the statute unconstitutional in its application, in violation of the guarantees of freedom of speech and the press contained in the First Amendment.

It may be, as the plaintiffs urge, that if a work is found to be of literary stature, and not "hard core" pornography, it is *a fortiori* within the protections of the First Amendment. But I do not reach that question here. For I find that "Lady Chatterley's Lover" is not obscene within the meaning of 18 U.S.C. § 1461, and is entitled to the protections guaranteed to freedoms of speech and press by the First Amendment. I therefore hold that the order of the Postmaster General is illegal and void and violates plaintiffs' rights in contravention of the Constitution.

Defendant's motion for summary judgment is denied. Plaintiffs' cross-motions for summary judgment are granted. An order will issue permanently restraining the defendant from denying the mails to this book or to the circulars announcing its availability.

Settle order on notice.

NOTES

CHAPTER I: *The Control of Books*

1. Typis Polyglottis Vaticanis, 1948.
2. *Voltaire* by Alfred Noyes, 3rd edition (London, 1939); and see "Voltaire" in A *Pacifist in Trouble* by William Ralph Inge (London, 1939).
3. *The Times*, Feb. 12, 1959.
4. See *The Vicissitudes of Shelley's Queen Mab* by H. B. Forman (London, 1887).
5. *Daily Telegraph*, Jan. 10, 1940.
6. *Athenae Oxonienses* (1813–20), IV, p. 731. Dr. Johnson repeats the substance of this account in his life of the Earl of Dorset, and Pepys relates the incident in his diary for July 1, 1663.
7. 1 Sid. 168 (1663).
8. R. v. *Read* (1708), 11 Mod. Rep. 142.

CHAPTER II: *Edmund Curll*

1. R. v. *Curll* (1737), 2 Stra. 788.

CHAPTER III: *From George III to Victoria*

1. "The Evolution of Literary Decency," *Blackwood's*, March 1900.
2. Lockhart's *Life* (1839), VI, p. 406.
3. R. v. *Creevey* (1813), 1 M. & S 273; R. v. *Mary Carlile* (1819), B. & Ald. 167; *Steele* v. *Brannan* (1872), L.B. 7 C.P. 261. The Judicial

Proceedings Act, 1926, aimed at sensational newspaper reporting, enacted specific restrictions.

4. *Edinburgh Review*, January 1809.

CHAPTER IV: *Campbell and Cockburn*

1. *Memoirs*, English translation (London, 1899), Ch. VIII.
2. *Ladies Fair and Frail* by Horace Bleackley (London, 1909), reference Fanny Murray.
3. Translator's preface to Kock's *The Modern Cymon*.
4. *"Obscene" Literature and Constitutional Law* (New York, 1911), p. 83.
5. *The Times*, April 20, 1933.
6. *Swinburne* by Georges Lafourcade (London, 1932), pp. 132-42.
7. L.R. 3 Q.B. 360 (1868). Reprinted Letchworth, *Dent*, 1937.
8. For the relation of the case to the birth control movement see *Contraception* by Marie Stopes (Bibliography *infra*).
9. *Life of Charles Bradlaugh, M.P.*, by Charles R. Mackay (London, 1888). A suppressed copy in the British Museum is annotated in manuscript by a W. H. Johnson, who claims to be the author.
10. I am indebted to Vernon Symonds for details about Carrington.
11. *My Days and Dreams* by Edward Carpenter (London, 1916), Ch. XI.

CHAPTER V: *Havelock Ellis*

1. *A Pacifist in Trouble* by William Ralph Inge (London, 1939)— "Havelock Ellis."
2. *The Poison of Prudery* (London, 1929), p. 165.
3. *Havelock Ellis* by Isaac Goldberg (New York and London, 1926).

CHAPTER VI: *The New Century in England*

1. *The Truth about Publishing* by Sir Stanley Unwin, 7th edition (London, 1960), p. 315.

CHAPTER VII: *D. H. Lawrence, James Joyce, and Others*

1. Introduction to Edward D. McDonald's bibliography (Bibliography *infra*).
2. *The Times, Daily News*, and *Daily Express*, Nov. 15, 1915.

3. *The Intelligent Heart* by Harry T. Moore (New York and London, 1955), p. 202.
4. Introduction to Edward D. McDonald's bibliography (Bibliography *infra.*).
5. Passages previously omitted: Chapters VIII, He wanted to wallow . . . with her flesh; XI, "Let me come—let me come"; XII, Ursula lay still . . . about her mistress; XV, But the air was cold . . . always laughing . . . She let him take her . . . house felt to her.
6. See Bibliography *infra.*
7. The titles are given under *Pansies* in the Bibliography *infra.*
8. See Bibliography *infra.*
9. *James Joyce* by Richard Ellmann (New York and Oxford University Press, 1959), p. 521.
10. *Time and Tide*, June 1, 1935.
11. *John O'London's*, March 17, 1960.
12. His *The Truth about a Publisher* (London, 1960), p. 171.
13. *Keeping it Dark or the Censor's Handbook* by Bernard Causton and G. Gordon Young (London, 1930).
14. A *Lawyer's Notebook* anonymous [E. S. P. Haynes] (London, 1932), p. 116.
15. *Quarterly Review*, October 1922.
16. *Retrospect of an Unimportant Life by* Herbert Hensley Henson, Vol. II (Oxford University Press, 1944), pp. 229 and 230.
17. *The First Three Years* by Eric Partridge (London, 1930).

CHAPTER VIII: *Potocki of Montalk*

1. *Here lies John Penis* by the Count Geoffrey Potocki de Montalk (Paris, n.d.) (British Museum Suppressed Books).
2. *Verlaine, poète saturnien* by Marcel Coulon (Paris, 1929). Translated by Edgell Rickwood (London, 1932).
3. R. v. *De Montalk* (1932), 23 Cr. App. Rep. 182.

CHAPTER IX: *The Nineteen Thirties in England*

1. *The Times*, Dec. 4 and 6, 1934.
2. *The Times*, March 13, 1935.
3. *Daily Telegraph*, October 11, 1934.
4. *My Father's Son* by Richard Lumford [*pseudo.* of Richard Rumbold] (London, 1949), Ch. XVII.
5. *Lord Byron's Marriage* (London, 1957).

6. *Daily Herald*, Jan. 24, 1935.
7. See Chapter IV, *supra.*
8. *The Author*, March 1935.
9. Included in *Abinger Harvest* (London, 1936).
10. *The Times*, Oct. 3, 17, and 24, 1935. *Plan* for December 1935 and January 1936.
11. House of Lords, Feb. 13, 1934.
12. Letter to *The Times*, Jan. 5, 1935.
13. *Star*, March 29, 1934.
14. *New Statesman*, April 2, 1938.
15. *New Statesman* and *Time and Tide*, April 16, 1938.

CHAPTER X: *England in Wartime and After*

1. A fuller report is given in my contribution to *Sex, Society and the Individual* (Bibliography *infra*).
2. *Western Morning News*, May 5 and 21, 1942 (Plymouth).
3. *The Guardian*, Aug. 13, 1942 (Bodmin).
4. *Western Morning News*, Oct. 30, 1942.
5. *The British Medical Journal*, July 14 and 21, 1934.
6. See Economy Educator Services in Bibliography *infra*.
7. *Journal of Sex Education*, Oct.-Nov. 1950 and Feb.-Nov. 1951 (London). *New Statesman*, Nov. 18, 1950.
8. *Evening Chronicle*, Sept. 28, 1950 (Newcastle).
9. *News of the World*, May 20, 1951. W. H. Smith's Trade Circular, May 26, 1951.
10. *Plan*, November 1952 (London).
11. *Daily Express* and the *News Chronicle*, Aug. 2, 1946.
12. *The Times*, Feb. 1, 4, and 7, 1957.
13. *Sunday Express*, Nov. 1, 1959.
14. October 1958.
15. *The Times*, June 18, 1954.
16. *John O'London's*, May 5, 1960.
17. Accessories and Abettors Act, 1861, section 8; and Magistrates' Courts Act, 1952, section 35.
18. *News of the World*, Aug. 21, 1955.

CHAPTER XI: *The Obscene Publications Act, 1959*

1. *The Times*, Oct. 7, 1953.
2. *The Times*, March 20, 1954.

3. *The Times,* July 30, 1954.
4. *The Times,* March 16, 1954.
5. *Galletly* v. *Laird* and *M'Gown* v. *Robertson* S.C. (J.) 16.
6. *The Times,* Aug. 12, Sept. 5 and 19, 1953.
7. *The Times,* May 19 and 21, 1954.
8. *The Times,* July 27 and Sept. 18, 1954.
9. *The Times,* Nov. 30 and Dec. 1, 1954.
10. *The Times,* Dec. 3, 1954.
11. *The Times,* June 30 and July 3, 1954.
12. *New Statesman,* Nov. 6, 1954.
13. Oct. 27, 1954.
14. The text is printed as Appendix II to his *Obscenity and the Law* (London, 1956).
15. *The Times,* Dec. 3, 1958.
16. Magistrates' Courts Act, 1952, section 25.
17. H.C. 122, 57-58 Q. 927. The Act was elucidated as regards publication to individuals, and republication, by the Court of Criminal Appeal in R. v. *Barker* (*The Times,* Feb. 20, 1962).
18. H.C. 122, 57-58, pp. 56-57.
19. H.C. 123-1, 57-58, p. 9.
20. H.C. 122, 57-58 Q. 424-34.

CHAPTER XII: *Censorship in America*

1. *Walt Whitman* by John Addington Symonds (1893), p. xxxi.
2. Repeated *"Obscene" Literature and the Constitutional Law* (1911), p. 103.
3. *Halsey* v. *New York Society* (1922), 234 N.Y.1, 136 N.E. 219.
4. *Frank Harris* by Vincent Brome (London, 1959), p. 197.
5. *People of State of N.Y.* v. *Viking Press Inc.* (1933), 147 Misc. (N.Y.) 813, 264 N.Y. Supp. (534).
6. *U.S.* v. *Dennett* (1930), 39 F. (2d) 564, 76 A.L.R. 1092 (C.C.A. 2d 1930).
7. *U.S.* v. *One Obscene Book Entitled "Married Love,"* 48 F. (2d) 821 (S.D. N.Y. 1931).

CHAPTER XIII: *Toward Freedom in America*

1. *Shakespeare and Company* by Sylvia Beach (London, 1960), p. 96.
2. *James Joyce* by Richard Ellmann (New York and Oxford University Press, 1959), p. 521.

3. *Time Magazine*, Dec. 18, 1933.
4. *U.S.* v. *One Book Entitled "Ulysses,"* 72 F. (2d) 705 (C.C.A. 2d, 1934), affirming 5 F. Supp. 182 (S.D. N.Y., 1933).
5. Ch. XXXV "Planned Parenthood" in *The Best is Yet* by Morris L. Ernst (Penguin, 1947).
6. *Maurice Parmelee, Claimant, Appellant* v. *United States of America* (No. 7332).
7. *The Smut Peddlers* by James Jackson Kilpatrick (London, 1961), pp. 136-41.
8. *The Bertrand Russell Case*, edited by Horace M. Kallen and John Dewey (New York, 1941).
9. *Daily Express* and *News Chronicle*, Aug. 2, 1946.
10. *Besig* v. *U.S.*, 208 F. 2d 142 (9th Cir., 1953).
11. *Doubleday and Co.* v. *New York*, 335 U.S. 48 (1948).
12. *Commonwealth* v. *Gordon*, 66 Pa. D. and C. 101 (1949).
13. *Cw.* v. *Feigenbaum*, 166 Pa. Super 120; 70 A. (2d) 389 (1950).
14. The Roth case and its consequences are dealt with in *The Smut Peddlers* by James Jackson Kilpatrick (London, 1961).
15. *Censorship Bulletin*, Vol. II, No. 4 (New York, 1958).

CHAPTER XIV: *Lady Chatterley's Lover*

1. *The Intelligent Heart*. The Story of D. H. Lawrence by Harry T. Moore (London, 1955), p. 383.
2. Extended as *A Propos of Lady Chatterley's Lover* (London, 1930), which is reprinted in *Sex Literature and Censorship* (see Bibliography *infra* under D. H. Lawrence).
3. United States District Court. Southern District of New York. Civil 147-87. *Grove Press Inc.* and *Readers' Subscription Inc.* against *Robert K. Christenberry*, individually and as Postmaster of the City of New York. *New York Times*, June 12 and July 22, 1959, and see Bibliography *infra* under D. H. Lawrence.
4. *New York Times*, March 26, 1960.
5. *New York Times*, June 3, 1960.
6. Aug. 9, 1959.
7. *Sunday Times*, June 11, 1961.
8. *The Times*, Oct. 7, 1953.
9. *John O'London's*, May 5, 1960.
10. *The Times*, Aug. 15, 1960.
11. *The Times*, Aug. 18, 1960.
12. *The Times*, Aug. 20, 1960.

13. *The Times*, Sept. 9, 1960.
14. *The Times*, Sept. 17, 1960.
15. *The Times*, Oct. 21, 1960.
16. *Evening News*, Oct. 20, 1960.
17. *The Times*, Oct. 21, 1960.
18. *The Times*, Oct. 28 and 29, Nov. 1-3, 1960. The covert commendations of anal intercourse in the book were not explained by either side (see "Lawrence, Joyce and Powys" by G. Wilson Knight in *Essays in Criticism* for October 1961 and *R. v. Penguin Books Ltd.* by John Sparrow in *Encounter* for February 1962).
19. *The Times*, Nov. 3, 1960.
20. *Daily Mail*, Nov. 7 and 10, 1960.
21. *News of the World*, Nov. 6, 1960.
22. Nov. 13 and 18, 1960, respectively.
23. *The Times*, Nov. 14, 1960.
24. *Daily Telegraph*, Nov. 30, 1960.
25. *The Times*, Feb. 3, 1961.
26. *Daily Mirror*, Nov. 3, 1960.
27. Nov. 4, 1960.
28. Nov. 6, 1960.
29. Nov. 13, 1960.
30. *Observer*, Feb. 19, 1961.
31. *The Times*, Nov. 9, 1960.
32. *The Times*, Nov. 11, 1960.
33. *The Times*, Nov. 9, 1960.
34. *The Times*, Nov. 25, 1960.
35. *The Times*, Dec. 15, 1960, and House of Lords Official Report, Dec. 14, 1960.
36. *Scotsman*, Nov. 17, 1960.
37. *The Times*, Nov. 23, 1960.
38. *The Times*, Feb. 4, 1961.
39. *The Times*, Nov. 25, 1960.

CHAPTER XV: *The Ladies' Directory*

1. Described in "Now the Call Girls have a Trade Paper" in *Men Only* for July 1960 (London).
2. *News Chronicle*, Sept. 17 and 22, 1960. *The Times*, Sept. 22, 1960.
3. *The Times*, Dec. 13-15 and 22, 1960.
4. *The Times*, March 15, 1961.
5. *The Times*, May 5, 1961.

6. London, 1960.
7. *Observer*, May 7, 1961, and *The Times* correspondence, May 11, 1961.
8. *Observer*, June 26, 1961.
9. R. v. *Clayton and Halsey* (*The Times*, May 30, July 24, Aug. 1, and Sept. 7, 1962).

CHAPTER XVI: *Scotland, Ireland, and the British Commonwealth Overseas*

1. *News of the World*, Dec. 13, 1959.
2. Edinburgh, M. MacDonald, 1959. See *Plan* for December 1958 and March 1959.
3. St. John-Stevas, *op. cit.*, p. 186. Ch. VIII gives a detailed account of the Eire censorship.
4. Appendix III of St. John-Stevas, *op. cit.*, gives a detailed digest of the comparative law on obscene publications for all British Commonwealth, and many foreign, countries. See also "Book Censorship in the Commonwealth," *The Author*, autumn 1960.
5. *New Statesman*, Aug. 20, 1960. The ban was lifted by the Supreme Court of Canada (*The Times*, March 16, 1962).
6. *The Times*, May 11, 1961.
7. *The Times*, Dec. 14, 1959, and March 30, 1960.
8. *The Times*, July 22 and 26, Sept. 21, 1960.
9. *Evening Standard*, March 22, 1956. *News of the World*, March 25, 1956.
10. *The Times*, June 9, 1960.
11. *The Times*, July 6, 1960.
12. *The Times*, June 12, 1961.
13. *The Times*, Dec. 16, 1960.
14. *The Times*, Dec. 19, 1960.
15. *The Times*, Dec. 28, 1960.

CHAPTER XVII: *French and Other Laws*

1. *The Times*, Sept. 28, 1960.
2. *Frank Harris* by Vincent Brome (London, 1959), pp. 197-99.
3. *The Times*, Jan. 29, 1957. Official molestation continued and the press sued the Ministry of the Interior for damages (*Observer*, March 18, 1962).

4. *The Romantic Agony*, see Bibliography *infra*.
5. *Daily Telegraph*, March 9, 1961.

CHAPTER XVIII: *Obscenity and Freedom*

1. *The Enforcement of Morals* by the Hon. Sir Patrick Devlin (London, 1959). A Third Programme broadcast reply by Prof. H. L. A. Hart appeared in *The Listener* of July 7, 1959 and an article by Richard Wollheim in *Encounter* for November 1959. A favorable *Times* leader of March 19, 1959 was followed by letters to the editor, one of which (March 24, 1959) drew attention to the support Sir Patrick's views would have given witch-hunting. Sir Patrick developed his argument before the Holdsworth Club at Birmingham and Prof. Hart severely criticizes his thesis in *The Oxford Lawyer* (*The Times*, March 18, 1961).
2. R. v. *Boulter*, 72 J.P. 188.
3. *The Use of Poetry and the Use of Criticism* (London, 1933).
4. *Samuel Pepys*: The Man in the Making by Arthur Bryant (Cambridge University Press, 1943), p. 366.
5. See Bibliography *infra*.
6. "Thomas J. Wise in Perspective" by John Carter in *Thomas J. Wise*: Centenary Studies, edited by William B. Todd (University of Texas, and Edinburgh, 1959).
7. *The Times*, Dec. 14, 1960, and Feb. 4, 1961.

CHAPTER XIX: *Pornography*

1. See Bibliography *infra*.
2. *Flaubert*, a biography by Philip Spencer (London, 1952), p. 152.
3. *Crime of Passion* by Derick Goodman (London, 1958), p. 198.
4. *Observer*, Feb. 8, 1959.

BIBLIOGRAPHY

Relative to the Conception of
Literary Obscenity

I. *General*   V. *France*
II. *Special Aspects*   VI. *Other Countries*
III. *England*   VII. *Individuals*
IV. *The United States*   VIII. *Bibliographies*

I. GENERAL

Sex Expression in Literature by Victor Francis Calverton, with an introduction by Harry Elmer Barnes (New York, 1926).

To the Pure: A Study of Obscenity and the Censor by Morris L. Ernst and William Seagle (New York, 1928; London, 1929).

Sex in Civilization, edited by V. F. Calverton and S. D. Schmalhausen, with an introduction by Havelock Ellis (New York and London, 1929).

Mrs. Grundy: A History of Four Centuries of Morals Intended to Illuminate Present Problems in Great Britain and the United States by Leo Markun (New York and London, 1930).

Cato or the Future of Censorship by William Seagle. Today and Tomorrow Series (London and New York, 1930).

"The Revaluation of Obscenity" in *More Essays of Love and Virtue* by Havelock Ellis (London and New York, 1931).

Social Control of Sex Expression by Geoffrey May (London, 1930; New York, 1931).

Sex in the Arts: A Symposium, edited by John Francis MacDermott and Kendall B. Taft (New York and London, 1932).
Particularly "Sex and Censorship" by Morris L. Ernst.

The Fear of Books by Holbrook Jackson (London and New York, 1932).

Art and Morality by Oliver de Selincourt (London, 1935).

Encyclopaedia Sexualis, edited by Victor Robinson (New York, 1936).
Articles on censorship and obscenity and excellent biographies.

Les Crises de la morale et de la moralité dans l'histoire de le civilisation et de la littérature des pays anglo-saxons by Paul Yvon (Paris, 1937).

Love and Death: A Study in Censorship by G. Legman (*Breaking Point,* New York, 1949).

The Banned Books of England (London and New York, 1937) and *Above all Liberties* (London and New York, 1942) by Alec Craig.

"Recent Developments in the Law of Obscene Libel" by Alec Craig in *Sex, Society and the Individual*, ed. A. P. Pillay and Albert Ellis (Bombay, 1953).

Continues the narrative of *Above all Liberties*.

Law and Contemporary Problems, Vol. XX, No. 4, "Obscenity and the Arts" (School of Law, Duke University, autumn 1955).

A symposium on the anthropological, aesthetic, moral, and legal (American and English) aspects of obscenity.

Obscenity and the Law by Norman St. John-Stevas, with an introduction by Sir Alan P. Herbert (London and New York, 1956).

Occasioned by the Obscene Publications Bill, 1959, and includes a digest of the obscenity laws of most countries.

Pornography and the Law: The Psychology of Erotic Realism and Pornography by Eberhard and Phyllis Kronhausen (New York, 1959).

Includes studies of erotic and pornographic books.

The Smut Peddlers by James Jackson Kilpatrick (New York, 1960; London, 1961).

Primarily concerned with the suppression of commercial pornography but embraces the whole problem of censorship on the ground of obscenity in the U.S.A.

"Censorship of Sexual Literature" by Alec Craig in *The Encyclopedia of Sexual Behaviour*, edited by A. Ellis and A. Abarbanel. 2 vols. (New York, 1961).

Symposium on Pornography and Obscenity by C. B. Cox ("The Teaching of Literature"), Norman St. John-Stevas ("The English Censorship Laws"), Donald Davie ("Literature and Morality"), Martin Jarrett-Kerr ("A Christian View"), and C. S. Lewis ("Four-Letter Words"); *Critical Quarterly*, summer 1961.

To Deprave and Corrupt: Original studies in the nature and definition of "obscenity" edited by John Chandos (London and New York, 1962).

Contributors: William B. Lockhart, Robert C. McClure, Lord Birkett, Norman St. John-Stevas, Ernest Van Den Haag, Maurice Girodias, Walter Allen, and Claire and W.M.S. Russell.

II. SPECIAL ASPECTS

The Literary Policy of the Church of Rome by Joseph Mendham, 2nd edition (London, 1830).

Les mauvais livres, les mauvais journaux et les romans, 4th edition

(Brussels, Société pour la Propagation des Bon Livres, 1843).
Contains comments from the moralistic point of view on writers like Byron, Dumas, and Gautier.

Contraception: its Theory, History and Practice by Marie Carmichael Stopes (London, 1923), 7th edition (London, 1949), American ed. (New York, 1931).
Covers attempts to suppress contraceptive literature.

Medical History of Contraception by N. E. Himes (Baltimore and London, 1936).
Covers attempts to suppress contraceptive literature.

La Carne, la Morte e il Diavolo nella Letteratura Romantica by Mario Praz (Milan, 1930). Translated by Angus Davidson under the title *The Romantic Agony* (London and New York, 1933), 2nd edition (London and New York, 1951).
Covers the work of Sade and similar literature.

Seduction of the Innocent by Fredric Wertham (New York and Toronto, 1953).
A study of horror comics.

An Unhurried View of Erotica by Ralph Ginzburg, with an introduction by Dr. Theodor Reik and preface by George Jean Nathan (New York, 1958; London, 1959).

Sex, Vice and Business by Monroe Fry (New York, 1959).
Covers pornography sales organization.

Does Pornography Matter? edited by C. H. Rolph (London, 1961).
Contributors: The Rt. Hon. Lord Birkett, PC, Sir Herbert Read, Geoffrey Gorer, Rev. Dr. Donald Soper, Dr. Robert Gosling, Dom Denys Rutledge, and the editor.

The Erotic in Literature: A historical survey of pornography as delightful as it is indiscreet by David Loth (New York, 1961; London, 1962).

III. ENGLAND

"Comic Dramatists of the Restoration" (1841) in Lord Macaulay's *Critical and Historical Essays.*

Books Condemned to be Burnt by James Anson Farrar (London, 1892).

The Hicklin Case from the Law Reports (Court of Queen's Bench), Vol. III, 1867-68 (London, 1937).
Includes the celebrated Cockburn definition of obscenity.

Report and minutes of evidence of the Joint Select Committee on Lotteries and Indecent Advertisements, 1908 (H.C. 275).
Covers "indecent literature" and recommends changes in the law relating thereto.

The Decline of Liberty in England by E. S. P. Haynes (London, 1916). Chapter V deals specifically with obscene libel. This book and the author's *The Case for Liberty* (London, 1919) and *The Enemies of Liberty* (London, 1923) make a philosophical defense of liberty, supported by references to contemporary events. His anonymous *A Lawyer's Notebook* (London, 1932), *More from a Lawyer's Notebook* (London, 1933), and *The Lawyer's Last Notebook* (London, 1934) constitute a miscellany of information, some of which concerns literary censorship.

Books and Persons by Arnold Bennett (London and New York, 1917). A collection of contributions to *The New Age*, four of them dealing with the censorship.

On British Freedom by Clive Bell (London, 1923).

The Poison of Prudery: An Historical Survey by Walter M. Gallichan (London and Boston, 1929).

Do we Need a Censor? by Lord Brentford (London, 1929). The author was Sir William Joynson-Hicks before being raised to the peerage.

Sexual Reform Congress, London, September 8-14, 1929, edited by Norman Haire (London, 1930). This report contains valuable papers on censorship in which the law of obscene libel is specifically dealt with by H. F. Rubinstein, Laurence Housman, Marie C. Stopes, George Ives, Bertrand Russell, Desmond MacCarthy, F. P. Streeton, and Hertha Riese. The substance of Desmond MacCarthy's paper also appeared under the title "Obscenity and the Law" in *Life and Letters*, May 1929.

Dirty Hands, or the True-Born Censor by R. P. Blackmur (Cambridge, Minority Pamphlet No. 5, 1930).

Keeping it Dark, or the Censor's Handbook, by Bernard Causton and G. Gordon Young, with a foreword by Rebecca West (London, 1930). Deals with literary, dramatic, and film censorship.

Balls and Another Book for Suppression by Richard Aldington. Blue Moon Booklet No. 7 (L. Lahr, 68 Red Lion Street, London, 1930). Light satires against censorship.

The Law and Obscenity by Frederick Hallis (London, 1932).

Banned in England: An Examination of the Law Relating to Obscene Publications by Gilbert Armitage (London, 1932).

The Cloven Hoof: A Study of Contemporary London Vices by Taylor Croft (London, 1932). Contains a chapter "Pornography and Obscene Displays."

Abinger Harvest by E. M. Forster (London, 1936).
    Includes "Liberty in England," a paper read at the International Congress of Authors in 1935.
Obscene Literature in Law and Practice by Sir Edward Tindal Atkinson, Director of Public Prosecutions (London, 1937).
"Into Whose Hands?": An Examination of Obscene Libel in its Legal, Sociological and Literary Aspects by George Ryley Scott (London, 1945).
The Reform of the Law, edited by Glanville Williams (London, 1951).
    A section is devoted to obscene libel.
Reports and minutes of evidence of Select Committees of the House of Commons on obscene publications (H.C. 245, 56-67; 122, 123, and 123-1, 57-58). *Memoranda of evidence submitted to the Select Committees of the House of Commons on Obscene Publications by the Progressive League, Alec Craig, the Society of Labour Lawyers* (London, Progressive League, 1958).
The Enforcement of Morals by The Hon. Sir Patrick Devlin. Maccabaean Lecture in Jurisprudence of the British Academy, 1959 (London and New York, 1959).
    The thesis of this lecture is relevant to the English obscenity law although literary obscenity is not explicitly dealt with.
A Question of Obscenity by Kenneth Allsop.
A Question of Obscenity by Robert Pitman.
    Two essays taking opposite sides in the censorship debate, bound together (Northwood, Middlesex, Scorpion Press, 1960).
Censors: The Rede Lecture 1961 by Lord Radcliffe (London, 1961; New York, 1962).
    Covers the Obscene Publications Act, 1959, and the *Lady Chatterley's Lover* verdict.
"The Censor as Aedile" in *The Times Literary Supplement*, Aug. 4, 1961.
    Covers the relationship between "conspiracy to corrupt public morals" and obscene publication.
Erotic Literature in England by C. R. Dawes (MS in British Museum).

IV. THE UNITED STATES

"Obscene" Literature and Constitutional Law: A Forensic Defense of Freedom of the Press by Theodore Schroeder (New York, privately printed for forensic uses, 1911).
    A collection and revision of the author's writings on the thesis that the American obscenity laws are unconstitutional.

Books and Battles: American literature 1920-1930 by Irene and Allen Cleaton (Boston, 1937).

Covers censorship, etc.

The Laughing Horse, February 1930 (University of California).

This number is devoted to censorship.

A *Challenge to Sex Censors* by Theodore Schroeder (New York, privately printed to promote the aims of the Free Speech League, 1938).

Freedom of Expression in Literature, reprinted from the Annals of the American Academy of Political and Social Science, Philadelphia, November 1938.

The Censor Marches On: Recent Milestones in the Administration of the Obscenity Law in the United States by Morris L. Ernst and Alexander Lindley (New York, 1940).

Appendix A reprints opinions delivered in leading American cases.

The Little Magazine: A History and Bibliography by Frederick J. Hoffman, Charles Allen, and Carolyn F. Ulrich (Princeton University, 1946), 2nd edition (Princeton University, 1947).

Covers obscenity proceedings against American magazines.

Commonwealth versus Gordon et al. An opinion filed March 18, 1949, by the Honorable Curtis Bok. Reprinted from Pennsylvania District and County Reports (Philadelphia, 1950).

Report of Pornographic Materials by the Gathings Committee, 1952 (Washington, Government Printing Office, 1958).

The Right to Read: The Battle against the Censorship by Paul Blanshard (Boston, 1955).

Covers politics, religion, sex (chapters 6 and 7), and comics (chapter 9).

Law and Contemporary Problems, autumn 1955 (Duke University).

This number devoted to "Obscenity and the Arts."

Censorship Bulletin by the American Book Publishers' Council, New York, quarterly, December 1955.

Comstockery in America by Robert W. Haney (Boston, 1960).

V. FRANCE

Les Procès littéraires au XIX siècle by Alexandre Zévaès [*pseudo.* of Gustave Alexandre Bourson], 2nd edition (Paris, 1924).

The Background of Modern French Literature by C. H. C. Wright (Boston, 1926).

L'Outrage aux moeurs by Lionel D'Autrac, 5th edition (Paris, 1929).

The Erotic History of France by Henry L. Marchand (New York, 1933).

"Les Livres contraires aux bonnes moeurs" by Maurice Garçon (*Mercure de France*, Aug. 15, 1931).

VI. OTHER COUNTRIES

Mrs. Grundy in Scotland by Willa Muir (London, 1936).

The Bell, September 1941 (Dublin) and subsequent numbers contain a discussion on Eire censorship.

"Obscene Books and the Law in Belgium" by Marc Lanval in the *International Journal of Sexology*, August 1952 (Bombay).

Censorship and Press Control in South Africa by Alex. Hepple (published by the author, P.O. Box 2864, Johannesburg, 1960).

VII. INDIVIDUALS

CHARLES BAUDELAIRE

Baudelaire by Enid Starkie (London, 1957; Norfolk, Conn., 1958).
   Contains an account of *Les Fleurs du Mal* prosecution. A report of the trial is given at p. 330 of the Conard edition of *Les Fleurs du Mal*.

ANNIE BESANT

Autobiography by Annie Besant (London, 1893).

The First Five Lives of Annie Besant by Arthur E. Nethercot (Chicago, 1960; London, 1961).
   The above two books contain accounts of the *Fruits of Philosophy* prosecution.

CHARLES BRADLAUGH

The Queen v. *Charles Bradlaugh and Annie Besant* (London, A. and H. B. Bonner and R. Forder, n.d.).
   A verbatim report of the trial (pp. 2-324) and the appeal (pp. 325-55).

Charles Bradlaugh by Hypatia Bradlaugh Bonner, 2 vols. (London, 1894).
   This biography by Bradlaugh's daughter contains a very full account of the *Fruits of Philosophy* prosecution.

SIR RICHARD BURTON

The Arabian Knight: A Study of Sir Richard Burton by Seton Dearden (London, 1936), revised edition (London, 1953).

JAMES BRANCH CABELL

Jurgen and the Censor (New York, privately printed, 1920).

ERSKINE CALDWELL

God's Little Acre by Erskine Caldwell (New York) [1933].
   The appendix to this edition gives an account of the prosecution of the book, including the Magistrate's decision.

"My Twenty-five Years of Censorship" by Erskine Caldwell. *Esquire*, October 1938 (Chicago).

EDWARD CARPENTER

My Days and Dreams by Edward Carpenter (London, 1916), 3rd edition (London, 1921).

　　Covers the difficulties put in the author's path by literary prudery.

CHARLES CARRINGTON

Joint Select Committee on Lotteries and Indecent Advertisements, 1908 (see Part III *supra*).

EDWARD CHARLES

The Sexual Impulse case.

The Banned Books of England by Alec Craig (London and New York, 1937), Ch. II.

EUSTACE CHESSER

"Recent Developments in the Law of Obscene Libel" by Alec Craig in *Sex, Society and the Individual*, edited by A. P. Pillay and Albert Ellis (Bombay, 1953).

　　Contains a report of the *Love Without Fear* case.

ANTHONY COMSTOCK

Anthony Comstock: Roundsman of the Lord by Heywood Broun and Margaret Leech (New York, 1927; London, 1928).

EDMUND CURLL

The Unspeakable Curll, Bookseller; to which is added a full list of his books by Ralph Straus (London, 1927).

MARY WARE DENNETT

Who's Obscene? by Mary Ware Dennett (New York, 1930).

　　A study of *The Sex Side of Life* conviction and similar cases.

The Censor Marches On by Morris L. Ernst and Alexander Lindey (New York, 1940).

　　Appendix A includes the opinion of the appeal court in *The Sex Side of Life case*.

J. P. DONLEAVY

Correspondence in *The Spectator*, November 4, 11, and 25; December 2 and 20, 1960.

LAWRENCE DURRELL

"Books that Shocked"—21: *The Black Book* by Adrian Stockton. *Books and Bookmen*, June 1961 (London).

ECONOMY EDUCATOR SERVICES

Cornwall Autumn Assizes No. 469, October 29, 1942. *Rex* v. *The Economy Educator Services Ltd.*, and others.

Court of Criminal Appeal, January 13, 1943. *Rex* v. *Ralph Hellyer Clemoes*.

Publishers' Circular, Nov. 21, 1942.

HAVELOCK ELLIS

A *Note on the Bedborough Trial* by Havelock Ellis (London, privately printed, 1898; New York, privately reprinted, 1925).

Studies in the Psychology of Sex by Havelock Ellis, 4 vols. (New York, 1936).
  The forewords and the postscript refer to the Bedborough case.

At Scotland Yard by John Sweeney (London, 1904), 2nd edition (London, 1905).

"Havelock Ellis" in *A Pacifist in Trouble* by William Ralph Inge (London, 1939).

My Life by Havelock Ellis (Boston, 1939; London, 1940).

Biographies by Isaac Goldberg, Houston Peterson, and Arthur Calder-Marshall pay adequate attention to the Bedborough case.

MORRIS L. ERNST

The Best is Yet . . . by Morris L. Ernst (New York, 1945; Penguin Books, 1947).
  Autobiographical reminiscences, including his fight with the censorship.

JAMES T. FARRELL

Magistrate's decision in *The World I Never Made* case, 1937 (British Museum Printed Books).

"The Author as Plaintiff, etc." in *Reflections at Fifty* by James T. Farrell (New York, 1954). Published in England under the title *Reflections at Fifty and Other Essays* (London, 1956).
  Testimony in the Studs Lonigan trilogy case (1948).

Commonwealth versus Gordon et al. (Philadelphia, 1950).
  The Honorable Curtis Bok's opinion covered the Studs Lonigan trilogy and *The World I Never Made*.

GUSTAVE FLAUBERT

Flaubert, a biography, by Philip Spencer (London, 1952; New York, 1953).
  Contains an account of the *Madame Bovary* prosecution. A report of the trial is given at Tom. I, p. 649, of the *Pléiade* edition of the *Oeuvres*.

MAURICE GIRODIAS

" 'I am a Pornographer' " by Kenneth Allsop. *Spectator*, Oct. 21, 1960, and subsequent correspondence.

ELINOR GLYN

Elinor Glyn: A biography by Anthony Glyn (London and New York, 1955).
  Covers the legal history of *Three Weeks*.

RADCLYFFE HALL

The Life and Death of Radclyffe Hall by Una, Lady Troubridge (London, 1961).

"Books that Shocked," No. 1: *The Well of Loneliness* by Desmond Elliott. *Books and Bookmen*, April 1959 (London).

The People of the State of New York v. *Donald Friede and Covici Friede*.

    The American *Well of Loneliness* case.

JAMES HANLEY

Police Proceedings regarding *Boy*.

FRANK HARRIS

Frank Harris by Vincent Brome (London, 1959; New York, 1960).

NORAH C. JAMES

The First Three Years by Eric Partridge. An account and bibliography of the Scholaris Press (London, 1930).

    Contains an account of the *Sleeveless Errand* case.

JAMES JOYCE

Ulysses by James Joyce (New York, 1934; London, 1936; reprinted to 1958).

    The appendices to this edition give the legal history of the book, including the decisions in *U.S.* v. *Ulysses* which were separately printed in 1954. The defending brief is a valuable historical and bibliographical document.

My Thirty Years' War: An autobiography by Margaret C. Anderson (New York and London, 1930).

    Contains accounts of the proceedings against *The Little Magazine* in respect of *Ulysses*.

Shakespeare and Company by Sylvia Beach (New York, 1959; London, 1960).

    Includes an account of the early publication of *Ulysses* in book form.

James Joyce by Richard Ellmann (New York and Oxford University Press, 1959).

    The most detailed biography.

JACK KAHANE

Memoirs of a Booklegger by Jack Kahane (London, 1939).

    Covers the history of the Obelisk Press.

STANLEY KAUFFMANN

The Philanderer by Stanley Kauffmann, 2nd edition (London, 1956).

    This and the Penguin edition contain the summing-up of the prosecution.

CHARLES KNOWLTON

Fruits of Philosophy by Charles Knowlton, edited with an introductory note by Norman E. Himes (Mount Vernon, 1937).

D. H. LAWRENCE

Lady Chatterley's Lover, Including My Skirmish with Jolly Roger by D. H. Lawrence (privately printed, 1929).

The Paintings of D. H. Lawrence (London, Mandrake Press, 1929).

Pansies by D. H. Lawrence (privately printed, 1929).

Includes titles excluded from the ordinary trade edition (London, 1929), namely: "The Noble Englishman," "Women Want Fighters for Their Lovers," "Ego-bound Women," "There is No Way out," "My Naughty Book," "The Little Wowser," "The Young and Their Moral Guardians," "What Matters," "What Does She Want?," "Don't Look at Me!," "To Clarinda," "Demon Justice," "Be a Demon," "The Jeune Fille."

Pornography and Obscenity by D. H. Lawrence. *Criterio Miscellany* No. 5 (London, 1929).

Reprinted from *This Quarter*, July-September 1929.

A Propos of Lady Chatterley's Lover, being an essay extended from "My Skirmish with Jolly Roger," by D. H. Lawrence (London, Mandrake Press, 1930).

A Bibliography of the Writings of D. H. Lawrence with a foreword by D. H. Lawrence (Philadelphia, 1925), and *The Writings of D. H. Lawrence 1925-1930*, a bibliographical supplement (Philadelphia, 1931) by Edward D. McDonald.

These bibliographies give particulars of privately printed and expurgated editions.

Phoenix: The posthumous papers . . . of D. H. Lawrence, with an introduction by Edward D. McDonald (London and New York, 1936).

Reprints *Pornography and Obscenity*, the introductions to *Pansies* and *The Paintings*, and the foreword to McDonald's bibliography.

Pornography and so on by D. H. Lawrence (London, 1936).

Reprints *Pornography and Obscenity* and the introduction to *The Paintings*.

The Frieda Lawrence Collection of D. H. Lawrence Manuscripts: A descriptive bibliography by E. W. Tedlock, Jr. (University of New Mexico Press, 1948).

Covers manuscript and published versions of *The White Peacock*, *The Rainbow*, and *Lady Chatterley's Lover*.

Selected Essays by D. H. Lawrence (Penguin Books, 1950).

Includes the introduction to *The Paintings*.

Sex, Literature and Censorship, Essay by D. H. Lawrence, with introductions by Harry T. Moore and H. F. Rubinstein (New York, 1953; London, 1955). New edition with Judge Bryan's decision on *Lady Chatterley's Lover* (New York, 1959).

Reprints *Pornography and Obscenity, A Propos of Lady Chatterley's Lover,* and the introductions to *Pansies* and to *The Paintings.*

Lady Chatterley's Lover by D. H. Lawrence, with an introduction by Mark Schorer [reprinted from the first number of *The Evergreen Review*] and a letter from Archibald MacLeish (New York, Grove Press, 1959).

United States District Court: Southern District of New York. Civil 147-87. *Grove Press Inc. against Robert K. Christenberry.*

The Intelligent Heart by Harry T. Moore (New York and London, 1955); revised edition (Penguin Books, 1960).

The most informative of the biographies about the banning and bowdlerizing of Lawrence's work.

Lady Chatterley's Lover by D. H. Lawrence (Penguin Books, 1960; second edition, with introduction by Richard Hoggart, 1961).

The pagination of both editions is that used for reference at the trial.

The Trial of Lady Chatterley. Regina v. *Penguin Books Limited.* The Transcript of the Trial edited by C. H. Rolph (Penguin Books, 1961).

"The Last Trial of Lady Chatterley" by Sybille Bedford. *Esquire,* April 1961 (Chicago).

On Moral Courage by Compton Mackenzie (London, 1962). Published in the United States under the title *Certain Aspects of Moral Courage* (New York, 1962).

Includes studies of Lawrence in relation to the censorship based on personal acquaintance with him.

HENRY MILLER

My Friend Henry Miller: An intimate biography by Alfred Perlès (London and New York, 1956).

This book and the *Smut Peddlers* by James Jackson Kilpatrick *(supra)* give information about prosecutions involving Miller's books.

"Defense of the Freedom to Read."

A letter from Miller to his Norwegian lawyer in *The Best of Miller* edited by Lawrence Durrell (New York, 1959; London, 1960).

Obscenity and the Law of Reflection by Henry Miller (Yonkers, Oscar Boradinsky, 1945).

Reprinted in *Remember to Remember* (New York, 1947) but not in the London edition.

"Obscenity in Literature" in *New Directions* 16 (Parisppany, N.J., and London, 1957).

VLADIMIR NABOKOV

L'Affaire Lolita: Défense d'Ecrivain (Paris, Olympia Press, 1957). " 'Lolita' in America" by F. W. Dupee, *Encounter*, February 1959 (London).

ALFRED NOYES

Two Worlds for Memory by Alfred Noyes (London and New York, 1953).
An autobiography covering the author's activities in relation to James Joyce and Sir Roger Casement.

GIUSEPPE ORIOLI

Adventures of a Bookseller by G. Orioli (London and New York, 1938). Covers the author's dealings with D. H. Lawrence and the attack on *Gian Gastone*. See also *Pinorman* by Richard Aldington (London, 1954).

MAURICE PARMELEE

Nudism in Modern Life: The New Gymnosophy by Maurice Parmelee, with introduction by Havelock Ellis. Including the decision of the United States Court of Appeals for the District of Columbia regarding the alleged obscenity of nudist illustrations. 5th edition (May's Landing, N.J., 1952).

COUNT POTOCKI OF MONTALK

Whited Sepulchres being an account of my trial and imprisonment for a parody of Verlaine and some other verses by Count Potocki of Montalk (London, *Right Review*, 1936).

BERTRAND RUSSELL

Why I am Not a Christian by Bertrand Russell (London and New York, 1957).
The appendix by Paul Edwards is an account of the College of the City of New York affair based on *The Bertrand Russell Case* edited by Horace M. Kallen and John Dewey (New York, 1941).
Bertrand Russell: The Passionate Sceptic by Alan Wood (London, 1957; New York, 1958).

LE MARQUIS DE SADE

L'Affaire Sade Procès intente aux éditions Jean-Jacques Pauvert (Paris, 1957).

SIR CHARLES SEDLEY

Sir Charles Sedley by V. de Sola de Pinto (London, 1927).

BERNARD SHAW

Bernard Shaw by Frank Harris (London, 1931).

Gives Shaw's attitude to *Lady Chatterley's Lover* and the incident regarding the burning of *My Life and Loves.*

MARIE STOPES

The Censor Marches On by Morris L. Ernst and Alexander Lindey (New York, 1940).

Appendix A includes Judge Woolsey's opinion in the *Married Love* case.

U.S. v. *One Obscene Book Entitled "Married Love,"* 48 F. (2d) 821 (S.D.N.Y. 1931).

SIR STANLEY UNWIN

The Truth about Publishing (London and Boston, 1926) 7th edition (London and New York, 1960), and *The Truth about a Publisher* (London and New York, 1960) by Sir Stanley Unwin.

Cover the problems presented to a publisher by the English obscenity law.

ROLAND DE VILLIERS

Joint Select Committee on Lotteries and Indecent Advertisements, 1908 (see Part III *supra*).

KATHLEEN WINSOR

"Strange Fruit and Forever Amber" by Morris L. Ernst and Alexander Lindey in *The Author,* winter 1946 (London).

"The Forever Amber Trial" by Alexander Lindey in *The Author,* summer 1947 (London).

VIII. BIBLIOGRAPHIES

A *World Bibliography of Bibliographies* by Theodore Besterman, 3 vols., 3rd and final edition (Geneva, 1955-56) under "Condemned Books."

Catalogue des ouvrages condamnés comme contraire à la morale publique et aux bonnes moeurs de 1er Janvier 1814 à 31 Decembre 1873 (Paris, 1873).

Catalogue des ouvrages, écrits, et dessins de toute nature poursuivis, supprimés ou condamnés depuis le 21 Octobre 1814 jusqu'au 31 Juillet 1877. Edition entièrement nouvelle etc. by Fernand Drujon (Paris, 1879).

Index Librorum Prohibitorum, Centuria Librorum Absconditorum and *Catena Librorum Tacendorum* by Pisanus Fraxi [pseudo. of Henry Spencer Ashbee] (London, privately printed, 1877, 1879, 1885). Reprinted London, 1960.

Bibliotheca Arcana seu Catalogus Librorum Penetralium, being brief notices of books that have been secretly printed, prohibited by law, seized, anathematized, burnt or bowdlerized, by Spectacular Morum [pseudo. of Rev. John M. McClellan, who appears to have written Preface. Compiled by Sir William Laird Clowes]. (London, 1885.)

Bibliographie des ouvrages rélatifs à l'amour etc. by M. le Cte D'I [pseudo. of Jules Gay. 3rd edition, 6 vols.]. (Turin, 1871-73), 4th edition, 4 vols. (Parish, 1894-1900).

L'Enfer de la Bibliothèque Nationale etc. by G. Apollinaire, F. Fleuret, and L. Perceau (Paris, 1913, reprinted 1919). British Museum "Private Case" has copy with additions to March 1934.

Bibliographie du roman érotique au XIXe siècle by Louis Perceau. 2 tom. (Paris, 1930.)

Registrum Librorum Eroticorum Vel. (sub hac specie) Dubiorum: Opus Bibliographicum Et Praepicue Bibliothecariis Destinatum compiled by Rolf S. Reade [pseudo. of Alfred Rose] 2 vols. (London, privately printed, 1936).

Index Librorum Prohibitorum (Rome, Typis Polyglottis Vaticanis, 1948).

"The Bibliography of Nudism" by Alec Craig. Offprinted from *Sun and Health* No. 14 (Aarhus, 1954) and published in the United Kingdom by the Progressive League.

"A Propos des livres contraires aux bonnes moeurs" by Daniel Becourt. *Bibliographie de la France*. Journal général et officiel de la librairie. 2e Partie: Chronique, Jan. 13, 1956.

Banned Books: Informal Notes on Some Books banned for Various Reasons at Various Places by Anne Lyon Haight (New York, 1935); 2nd edition (New York and London, 1955); 3rd edition (New York, 1958).

INDEX

Alec Craig was born on St. George's Day in the year of Queen Victoria's Diamond Jubilee in the parish of St. Mary, Islington. He was educated at the London School of Economics. After serving in a line regiment in France during World War I, Mr. Craig was employed in both military and civilian activities in England and the Middle East. He was a founder member of the Progressive League. His volume *The Banned Books of England* was published in 1937 and was a pioneer work in the field of literary censorship. His other books include *Sex and Revolution, Above all Liberties,* and several volumes of verse.

THIS BOOK WAS SET IN

ELECTRA AND BASKERVILLE TYPES,

PRINTED, AND BOUND BY THE HADDON CRAFTSMEN

DESIGN IS BY LARRY KAMP.